Outlook® 2000
fast&easy™

Lisa D. Wagner

W0006984

PRIMA
TECH

A DIVISION OF PRIMA PUBLISHING

A Division of Prima Publishing

Prima Publishing and colophon are registered trademarks of Prima Communications, Inc. PRIMA TECH and Fast & Easy are trademarks of Prima Communications, Inc., Rocklin, California 95677.

Publisher: Stacy L. Hiquet
Associate Publisher: Nancy Stevenson
Managing Editor: Dan J. Foster
Senior Acquisitions Editor: Deborah F. Abshier
Senior Editor: Kelli R. Crump
Project Editor: Kevin Harreld
Copy Editor: Judy Ohm
Technical Reviewer: Jacqueline Harris
Interior Layout: Marian Hartsough
Cover Design: Prima Design Team
Indexer: Emily Glossbrenner

Microsoft, Windows, Windows NT, Outlook, MSN, and FrontPage are trademarks or registered trademarks of Microsoft Corporation.

Important: If you have problems installing or running Outlook 2000, go to Microsoft's Web site at **www.microsoft.com**. Prima Publishing cannot provide software support.

ISBN: 0-7615-1927-0
Library of Congress Catalog Card Number: 98-68393
Printed in the United States of America

99 00 01 02 DD 10 9 8 7 6 5 4 3 2 1

To Lori Swan

who has a whole new outlook of her own

Acknowledgments

Special thanks to all the people at Prima Publishing who make complex projects flow seamlessly: the ever-dedicated project editor and fellow Hoosier Kevin Harreld; publisher Matt Carleson for giving me the nod; and especially to Debbie Abshier, simply the most outstanding author liaison in the business—thanks for the solo flight. To all those folks in the production trenches who go unnamed—my most sincere appreciation for all your blood, sweat, and tears. I know what it takes to do what you do, and you all do phenomenal work. To my comrades of THE EXPERIENCE: thanks for dancing playfully with me. Also thanks to my friends and family for their love and support—and for knowing when to go home and let me work. Jeri, you're my rock. And Lori, my parfait . . . well, you know how I feel.

About the Author

LISA D. WAGNER is the founder of Jasper Ink, an independent writing, consulting, and Web design firm in Indianapolis. Lisa has more than ten years' experience in the computer and publishing industries. She has authored and contributed to several computer books, including *Create FrontPage 2000 Web Pages In a Weekend* and *Microsoft Money 99 Fast & Easy*, and on topics such as Windows 95, Microsoft Office, and computer hardware. A graduate of Butler University, Lisa is also an active singer, actor, and theater producer. She is past president of Women in the Arts, Inc., and an active participant in THE EXPERIENCE (www.theexperience.org), a non-profit organization promoting the celebration of diversity and empowering individuals to change the world heart by heart. Lisa welcomes your questions and comments via e-mail at lisa@jasperink.com and invites you to visit her company's Web site, www.jasperink.com.

Contents at a Glance

Contents

Introduction

This new *Fast & Easy* guide from Prima Publishing will help you unleash the power of Microsoft Outlook 2000. Outlook is a messaging and contact management program that will allow you to do all the things that other Personal Information Management (PIM) programs do, and it will also make it easier than ever to make your information work together. For example, you can make your contact information work seamlessly with your e-mail messages in Outlook.

Outlook 2000 Fast & Easy provides you with all the information you need to begin using the powerful features of Outlook 2000 today. As you read this book, you'll tackle many of the features Outlook has to offer. You'll learn at a record pace with the step-by-step approach, clear language, and illustrations of exactly what you will see on your screen.

Who Should Read This Book?

Outlook 2000 Fast & Easy is ideal as a learning tool or as a step-by-step task reference. The easy-to-follow, highly visual nature of this book makes it the perfect learning tool for a beginning computer user. Veteran computer users who are new to this version of Outlook will also find this book helpful.

Current users of Outlook 2000 can utilize this book when they need occasional reminders about the steps required to perform a particular task. It is designed to cut straight to the chase to provide the information you need without having to sort through pages of dense text.

Added Advice to Make You a Pro

As you use *Outlook 2000 Fast & Easy*, you'll notice that it focuses on the steps necessary for a task and keeps explanations to a minimum. Included in the book are some elements that are designed to provide additional information, without encumbering your progress through the steps:

- **Tips** provide helpful hints and suggestions for working with features in Outlook 2000.

- **Notes** give you information about a feature, or comments about how to use a feature effectively in your day-to-day activities.

As a bonus, two helpful appendixes will give you additional tips on installing Outlook 2000 and working with shortcut keys. Finally, the glossary is designed to take the mystery out of Outlook 2000 by providing definitions of key terms used throughout the book.

Read and enjoy this book! It is certainly the fastest and easiest way to learn Outlook 2000.

PART I

Getting Started with Outlook 2000

1

Welcome to Outlook 2000

Welcome to Outlook, your electronic tool for managing appointments, addresses, e-mail, and notes. When you first begin using Outlook, you may feel a bit intimidated by all of the buttons, icons, and menus that appear on the screen. Don't worry! After just a few lessons, you will understand and be able to use many of the components of Outlook to organize and simplify your busy life. In this chapter, you'll learn how to:

- Start Outlook
- Use Outlook for the first time
- Exit and log off

Starting Outlook

The first time you open Microsoft Outlook, you will need to answer a few simple questions so that Outlook can configure your Internet and mail connections properly.

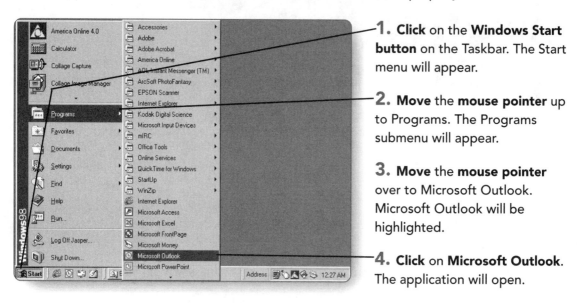

1. **Click** on the **Windows Start button** on the Taskbar. The Start menu will appear.

2. **Move** the **mouse pointer** up to Programs. The Programs submenu will appear.

3. **Move** the **mouse pointer** over to Microsoft Outlook. Microsoft Outlook will be highlighted.

4. **Click** on **Microsoft Outlook**. The application will open.

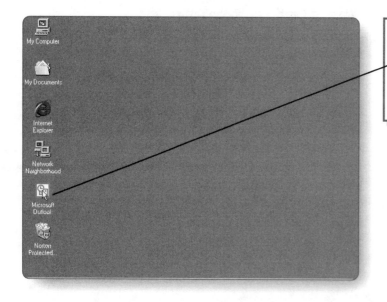

TIP

You also can start Outlook by clicking on its icon on the Windows Taskbar.

Working with the Choose Profile Dialog Box

When you install Outlook in a corporate environment, others may use your computer to check their e-mail. If you don't want their e-mail to be mixed with yours, you can enable a Choose Profile dialog box, which will appear when Outlook starts, and prompt the user to choose a profile. A *profile* stores information specific to your e-mail account, such as your dial-up connection. When logged into a profile, you can access only the e-mail for that profile.

If you are the sole user of the computer, Outlook simply opens without presenting the Choose Profile dialog box.

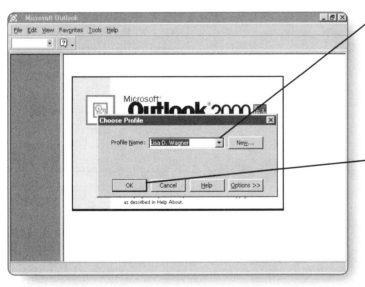

1. **Click** on the **down arrow** to the right of the Profile Name list box. A drop-down list will appear.

2. **Click** on the **profile** you want. It will be selected.

3. **Click** on **OK**. If you have not yet set up your faxing software, the Symantec WinFax Starter Edition Wizard will open next. Otherwise, Outlook will open and display the contents of your Inbox.

Using Outlook for the First Time

The first time that you start Microsoft Outlook, Outlook will ask you a few simple questions to help it determine how to best configure Outlook for your needs.

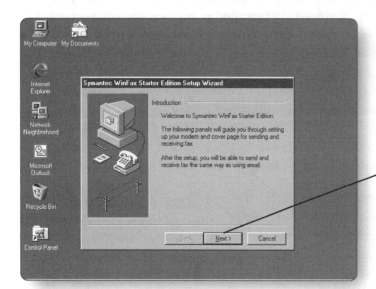

NOTE

If Outlook is already set up on your computer, you may not see these messages.

1. **Click** on **Next** to start the Symantec WinFax Starter Edition Setup Wizard. The User Information page will appear.

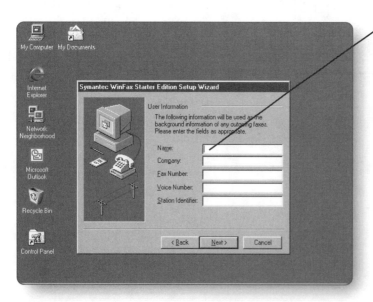

2. **Follow** the **onscreen instructions** to complete the Wizard by providing your fax number and other requested information. Keep clicking on Next to move through the Wizard pages. When complete, the Finish page will appear in the Wizard.

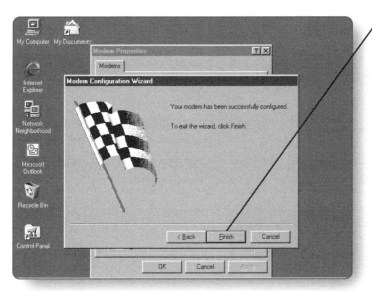

3. Click on **Finish.** The Wizard will close and Outlook will open with a new message box.

TIP

For more information on working with faxes, see Chapter 9, "Sending and Receiving Faxes."

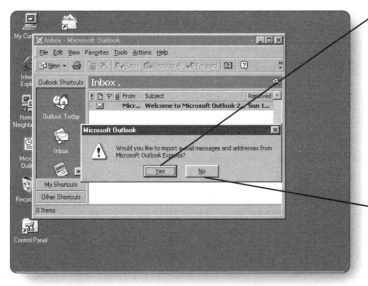

4a. Click on **Yes** if you want to import any existing addresses and messages into Outlook from Outlook Express. The Import Wizard will appear. Complete the wizard and click on Finish. The Import Wizard will close.

OR

4b. Click on **No**. The dialog box will close and another message box will appear.

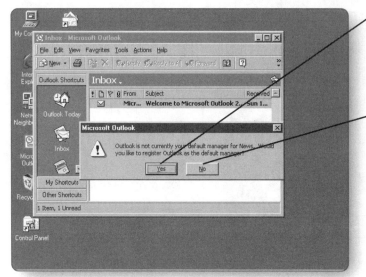

5a. **Click** on **Yes** if you want to make Outlook your default newsgroup reader.

OR

5b. **Click** on **No**. The dialog box will close, and Outlook will open to show your Inbox.

Congratulations! You've just successfully started Outlook. A new message titled "Welcome to Microsoft Outlook 2000" will automatically appear in your Inbox, in addition to any other messages you may have received.

If you are at home, you probably do not have a direct connection to the Internet. In order to send and receive new messages in Outlook, you will need to log on to your dial-up service. A dial-up service provider could be MSN (Microsoft Network), AOL (America Online), or any other local provider. Follow the normal procedure that you use for accessing the Internet through your service provider to get logged on.

Exiting Outlook

When you are ready to exit Outlook, you have two choices.

1. **Click** on **File**. The File menu will appear.

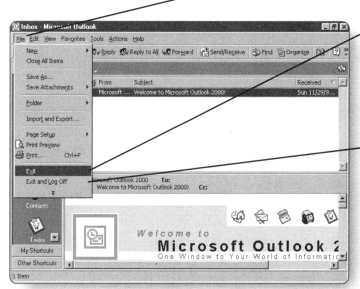

2a. **Click** on **Exit**. You will exit Outlook but remain logged on to your Internet Service Provider.

OR

2b. **Click** on **Exit and Log Off**. You will exit Outlook and log off your Internet Service Provider.

2

Finding Your Way in Outlook

Outlook has many features that are used in other Windows-based applications. If you are familiar with these applications, you may already know how to use these features. What's more, the way you use Outlook may not be the same way someone else uses the program. Fortunately, Outlook has several options for displaying information. In this chapter, you'll learn how to:

- Use toolbars and move with scroll bars
- Select commands from menus
- Explore dialog boxes and understand Outlook icons
- Use the Outlook bar and Outlook Today
- Display the Folder list

Understanding the Outlook Environment

When you first start Outlook, you see the Information viewer. By default, the Information viewer displays the contents of the Inbox. The Inbox stores your incoming e-mail messages.

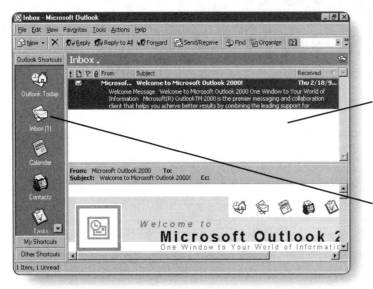

The information displayed in the Information viewer will change depending on which folder is open.

- **Information viewer**. The display area for e-mail messages, calendar items, contacts, tasks, journal items, or notes.

- **Folders**. Folders are displayed as icons on the Outlook bar. The selected folder's contents will be displayed in the Information viewer.

Using Toolbars

Toolbars are located at the top of the Outlook screen and contain buttons; each button represents a commonly used command. You'll find the same commands within Outlook's menus, but the toolbar buttons are easier and faster.

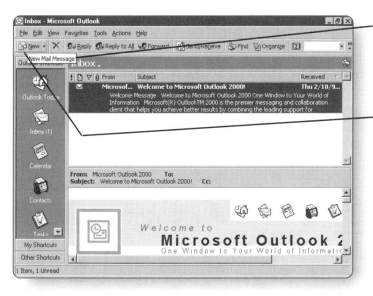

1. Move the **mouse pointer** over any toolbar button. The toolbar button's name will display in a ScreenTip.

2. Click on a **toolbar button**. The command associated with the toolbar button will be executed.

Moving with Scroll Bars

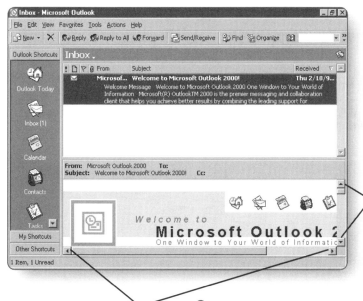

Scroll bars allow you to change the contents of your screen when there is more information than can fit on one screen. The vertical scroll bar appears on the right edge of the screen, and the horizontal scroll bar appears on the bottom of the Inbox window.

1. Click on the **up arrow** or the **down arrow** on the vertical scroll bar to move up or down on the screen.

2. Click on the **left arrow** or the **right arrow** on the horizontal scroll bar to move to the left or right on the screen.

NOTE

If you don't have a horizontal scroll bar, automatic column sizing might be turned on. To turn it off, click on View, Current View, Customize Current View. Click on the Other Settings button, then click in the check box next to Automatic column sizing to remove the check. Click on OK until all open dialog boxes are closed.

Using Menus

If you look above the toolbar, you'll see the menu bar. The words on the menu bar are called *commands*. When you click on a command, a drop-down menu appears that contains several other commands.

1. Click on **File**. The File menu will appear.

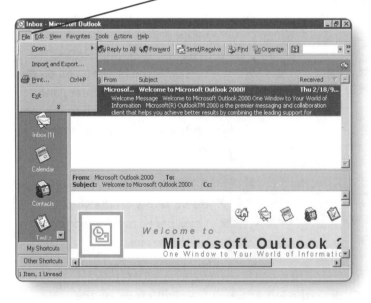

Some things to note on the menu are the following:

- **Common commands.** Your most commonly used items appear first. The others remain hidden and out of the way, giving you easy access to the commands you use most.

● **Expanded menu**. If the menu remains open for a moment, it will expand to show all of the commands available on the menu.

● **Unavailable commands**. The drop-down menu may have some commands that appear light gray, or dimmed. This means that these commands are not available at this time.

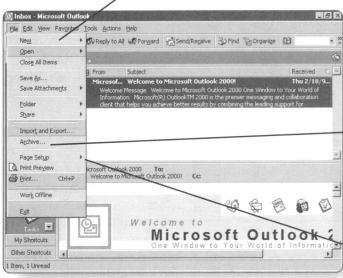

● **Ellipsis**. If a command in the drop-down menu is followed by three periods, called an *ellipsis*, a dialog box will open when you click on the command.

● **Extended menus**. Some of the commands on the drop-down menus have an arrow to the right of the command. This indicates that another menu will appear when you place your mouse over or click on the command.

2. **Click anywhere** in the Information viewer. The menu will close.

3. Click on **another command** in the menu bar. A drop-down menu will appear.

4. Move the **mouse pointer** down to a command that has a right-pointing arrow. The submenu will appear.

5. Click on the **command** you want to perform. The associated action will occur.

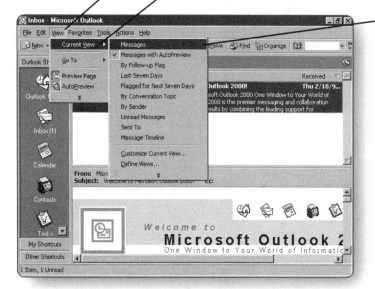

TIP

You can use the keyboard rather than the mouse to select a command. Simply hold down the Alt key on the keyboard and press the letter corresponding to the underlined character in the command. For example, to open the Favorites menu, press and hold down Alt and o on the keyboard.

Exploring Dialog Boxes

Dialog boxes are windows that appear on the screen asking for more information.

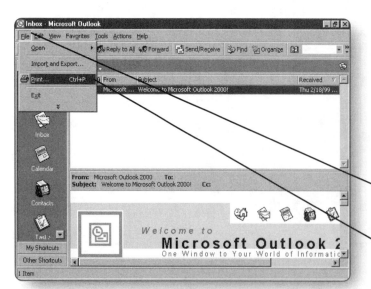

1. Click on **File**. The File menu will appear.

2. Click on **Print**. The Print dialog box will open.

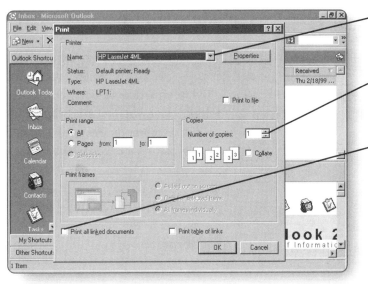

- **Click** on a **down arrow** to make a selection from a drop-down list.

- **Click** on the **up or down arrows** to increase or decrease a number.

- **Click** in a **check box** to turn on or off a feature.

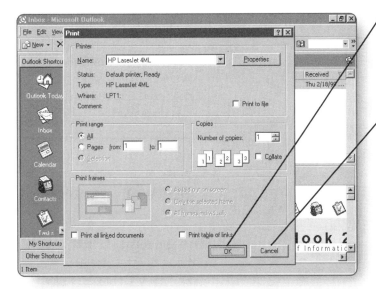

4. **Click** on **OK** to close the dialog box and perform the command.

OR

5. **Click** on **Cancel** to exit the dialog box without performing the command.

TIP

Press the Esc key on the keyboard to cancel a dialog box, or click on the Close button in the upper-right corner of the dialog box.

Using the Outlook Bar

The Outlook bar is the gray column located on the left side of the screen. The Outlook bar contains icons that allow you to change what is displayed in the Information viewer. Each icon represents a shortcut to a folder. When you first start Outlook, the Information viewer displays the contents of the Inbox folder.

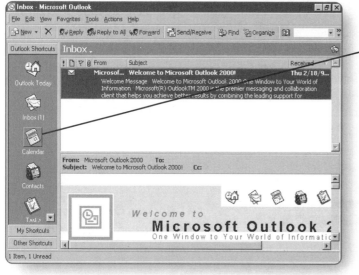

1. Click on **any icon**. The items associated with the icon will appear in the Information viewer.

> **NOTE**
>
> The Outlook bar can be toggled on or off. If you do not see the Outlook bar, click on View, and then click on Outlook bar. A check mark will appear next to the Outlook bar if it is displayed.

2. Click on the **Inbox icon**. E-mail messages will appear again.

There are many icons on the Outlook bar that are not immediately visible. You can click on the scroll bar arrows to see more icons, or switch to a different Outlook group. The default Outlook groups are Outlook Shortcuts, My Shortcuts, and Other Shortcuts.

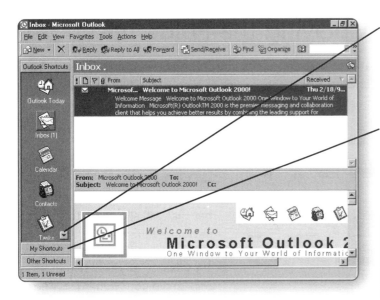

- **Outlook scroll bar arrows**. Click on the up or down arrow at the top or bottom of the Outlook bar to scroll up or down.

- **Outlook bar group buttons**. Click on an Outlook group button to display different icons.

NOTE

An Outlook group is a way to organize folders on the Outlook bar. You can add, delete, or rename the Outlook groups by clicking the right mouse button on the Outlook bar and clicking on one of the options on the shortcut menu.

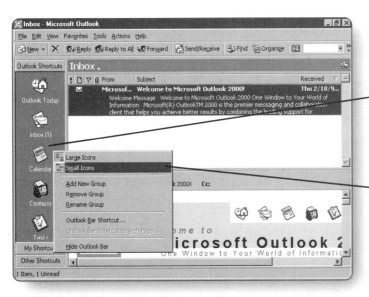

You can make the icons on the Outlook bar larger or smaller, depending on your preference.

3. Click the **right mouse button** in a gray area of the Outlook bar. A shortcut menu will appear.

4. Click on an **icon size** with the left mouse button. The size of the icons will be increased or reduced accordingly.

Displaying the Folder List

The icons that appear on the Outlook bar are also referred to as *folders*. If you choose not to display the Outlook bar, you can use the folder list to navigate in Outlook.

1. Click on **View**. The View menu will appear.

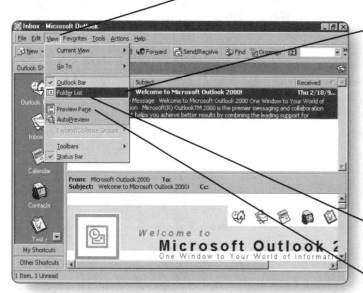

2. Click on **Folder List**. A pane will open next to the Outlook bar that will allow you to navigate your folders.

3. Click on **any folder** that appears in your folder list. The contents of the selected folder will appear in the Information viewer.

4. Click on **View, Folder List**. The folder list will turn off.

5. Click on **View, Preview Pane**. The preview pane will close.

NOTE

From this point on in the book, you will be working without the preview pane.

Using Outlook Today

One of the icons on the Outlook bar is labeled "Outlook Today." Outlook Today displays a snapshot of all the items you need during the day.

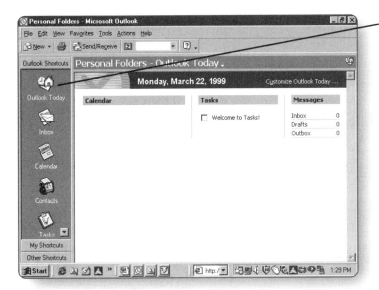

1. Click on the **Outlook Today icon**. The Information viewer will change to display the Outlook Today page.

Customizing Outlook Today

You can customize Outlook Today to display the folders you need, or to adjust the display of the calendar or task list. You can even designate Outlook Today as the default page that appears when Outlook starts.

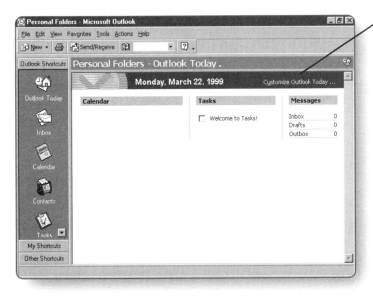

1. Click on **Customize Outlook Today** in the Information viewer. The Customize Outlook Today options window will appear.

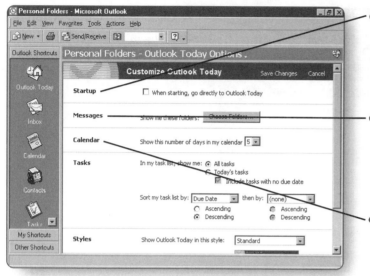

- **Startup**. Click on the check box to make Outlook Today your start page. Your start page will appear whenever you start up Outlook.

- **Messages**. Click on the Choose Folders button to select which e-mail will appear on the Outlook Today page.

- **Calendar**. Click on the drop-down arrow to select the number of days to appear in the calendar.

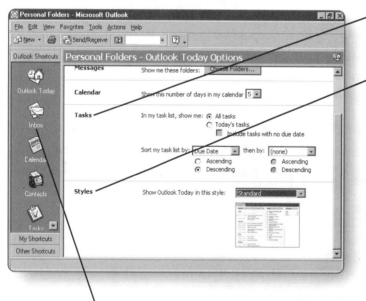

- **Tasks**. Click on an option button to select a simple task list or today's tasks.

- **Styles**. Click on the drop-down arrow to select a layout style for the Outlook Today page.

2. Click on **Save Changes** back at the top of the Customize Outlook Today screen. Your new settings will be saved.

3. Click on the **Inbox icon** on the Outlook bar. The Outlook Today window will close and the Inbox will display in the Information viewer.

Understanding Outlook Symbols

Outlook uses numerous symbols to represent different types of items. For example, a red exclamation point is used for high priority items, whereas a blue down-pointing arrow is used to identify low priority items. Symbols appear next to e-mail messages in the Inbox. You can learn more about the symbols in Outlook Help.

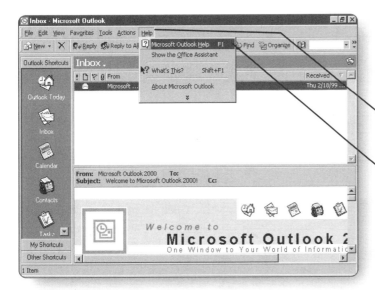

1. Click on **Help**. The Help menu will appear.

2. Click on **Microsoft Outlook Help**. The Office Assistant will appear.

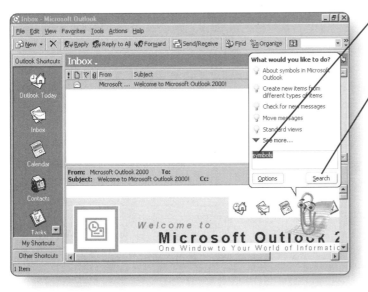

3. Type the **word Symbols** in the text box. The word will appear in the text box.

4. Click on the **Search button**. A list of topics will appear.

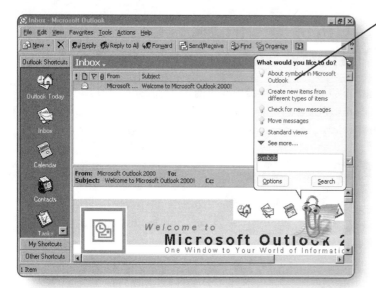

5. Click on **About symbols in Microsoft Outlook**. A Help window will open.

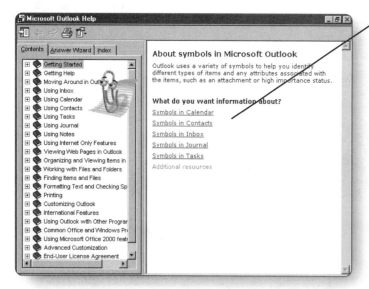

6. Click on **any topic** in the Microsoft Outlook window. The symbols used in Outlook will appear.

3

Getting the Help You Need

Outlook has so many features that you may need occasional assistance when you are first learning the program. Even after you learn to use Outlook, you'll find yourself checking the application's help often. Fortunately, Outlook gives you several ways to get
help while working with the application. In this chapter, you'll learn how to:

- Use the Office Assistant
- Search Contents and Index
- Get help on the Web

Introducing the Office Assistant

If you have used recent versions of Microsoft Office, you may already be familiar with the Office Assistant. The Office Assistant is a tool that provides an animated character that interacts with you to answer your questions about the application. The Office Assistant can be completely customized; in fact, if you get tired of the current one, you can even choose a different animated character (sometimes called an *actor*) for your Office Assistant.

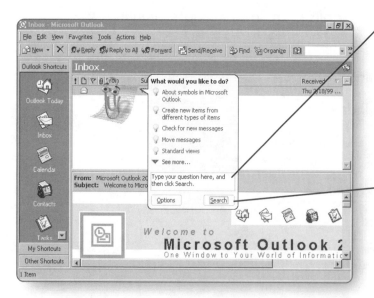

1. Click on **Help**. The Help menu will appear.

2. Click on the **Microsoft Outlook Help**. The Office Assistant will appear and present a message box asking what you want to do.

3. Click in the **text box**. The existing text will disappear and the insertion point will be in the text box.

4. Type your question. The question will appear in the text box.

5. Click on **Search**. The Office Assistant will respond with a list of topics that match the words in your sentence to answer your question.

TIP

You can type natural language questions, such as "How do I print?" to find help on a specific topic. You do not need to type punctuation or proper capitalization in your help queries.

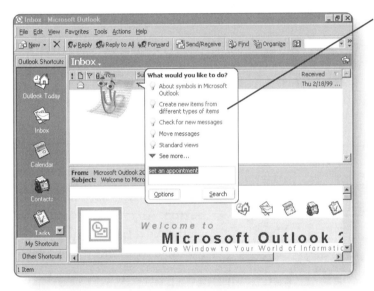

6. Click on **any topic** to get further help. A window will appear that expands on the topic that you've selected.

7. Click on the **Close button** when you are finished. The window will close.

Selecting an Office Assistant

When you start Outlook, you will meet Clipit, the default Office Assistant. If you get tired of this character, there are other assistants that you can choose from if they were installed during your installation of Outlook. Each assistant has its own personality, so you can pick the assistant that you will learn from the best.

The Office Assistants are a shared component of the Microsoft Office 2000 suite. If you would like to change your Office Assistant and you do not have the Office 2000 CD-ROM at hand, you can download additional Office Assistant characters from Microsoft's Web site at **http://www.microsoft.com**.

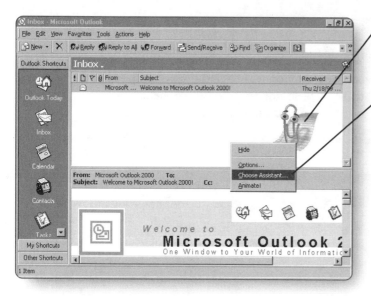

1. **Right-click** on the **Office Assistant**. A shortcut menu will appear.

2. **Click** on **Choose Assistant**. The Office Assistant dialog box will open.

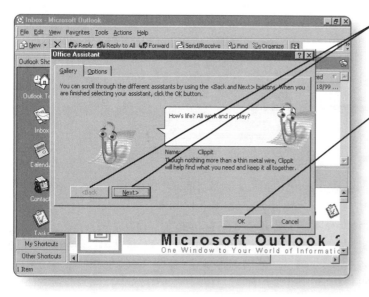

3. **Click** on the **Back or Next button**. As you continue clicking on the Next button, the available assistants will appear.

4. **Click** on **OK**. The dialog box will close and your Office Assistant will change to the one you've selected.

NOTE

You may be asked to insert your Office 2000 CD-ROM so that Office can install the files needed to use the Office Assistant you select.

Customizing the Office Assistant

As you work in Outlook, the Office Assistant will give you tips and suggestions to make your work easier. As you become more familiar with the application, you may need these tips less often. You can customize the Office Assistant so that it gives you only the information you need.

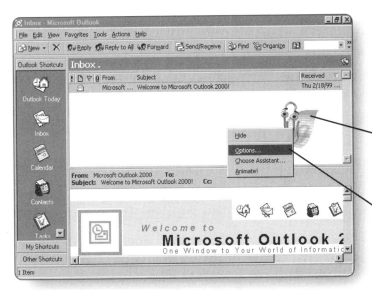

1. Right-click on the **Office Assistant**. A shortcut menu will appear.

2. Click on **Options**. The Office Assistant dialog box will open.

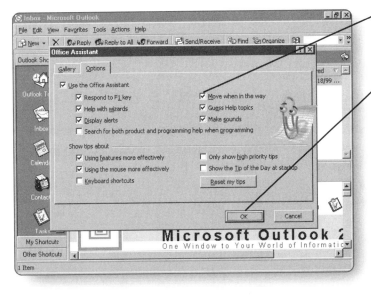

3. Click in the **check boxes** to select the options you want. The boxes will be checked.

4. Click on **OK**. The dialog box will close and your changes will be saved.

Hiding the Office Assistant

Sometimes the Office Assistant pops up when you don't really need it, or you just find the character distracting from the matter at hand. If so, you can hide the Office Assistant until you are ready to use it again.

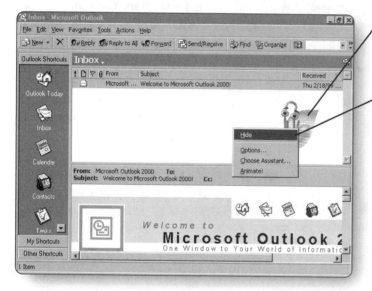

1. Right-click on **Office Assistant**. A shortcut menu will appear.

2. Click on **Hide**. The Office Assistant will perform an animated exit and disappear.

TIP

Right-click on the Office Assistant and click on Animate! to watch the Office Assistant's built-in animation effects. The effects appear in random order each time you select Animate!

Searching Contents and Index

Another way to get help is by using the online Help system provided with Outlook. You can either search through the reference by using the Index, or browse through the Table of Contents.

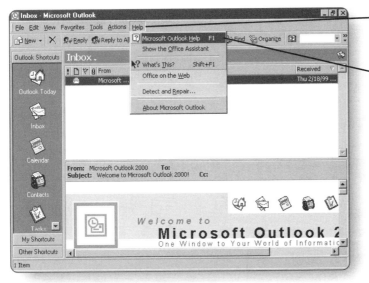

1. **Click** on **Help**. The Help menu will appear.

2. **Click** on **Microsoft Office Help**. The Office Assistant will appear.

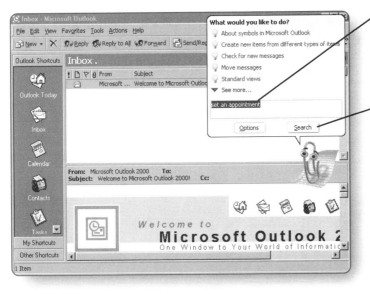

3. **Type a question** in the **Office Assistant text box**. The question will appear in the text box.

4. **Click** on **Search**. The Office Assistant will respond with a list of topics to answer your question.

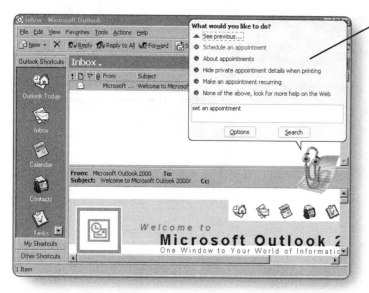

5. Click on any **topic**. The Microsoft Outlook Help window will appear, displaying details on the topic that you've selected.

6. Click on the **Show button**. The Help window will expand to show the Contents, Answer Wizard, and Index tabs.

7. Click on the **Contents tab** if it is not already selected. The tab will come to the front.

8. Double-click on any **topic**. You can continue until you find the item you want. If there are subtopics, more items will appear.

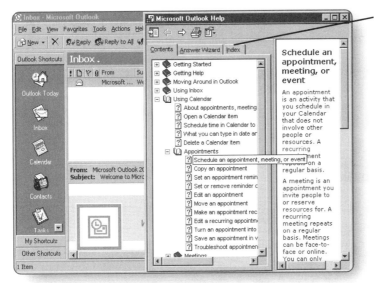

9. Click on the **Index tab**. The tab will come to the front.

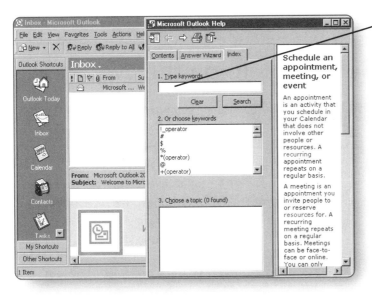

10. Type the first few **letters** of the topic for which you are searching in the first text box. The list will scroll to any words that begin with the letters you type.

11. Double-click on the **index entry** you want to view. The corresponding help topic will appear.

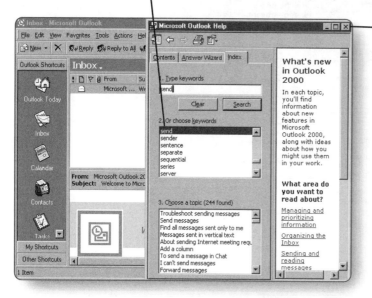

12. Click on the **Close button** to close the window. The Help window will close.

Getting Help on the Web

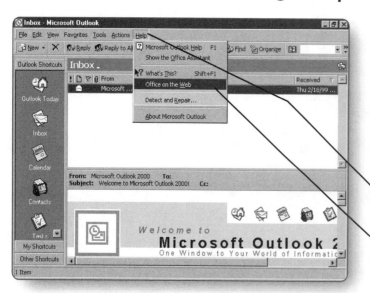

If you have access to the Internet, you can get help by using the Web and visiting Microsoft's Web site. Some topics available are frequently asked questions for Outlook, free stuff, and product news about Outlook.

1. Click on **Help**. The Help menu will appear.

2. Click on **Office on the Web**. Your Web browser will appear and will point to the Outlook support Web site.

3. **Click** on any **topic**. Details on the selected topic will appear in your browser.

4. **Click** on the **Close button** in your Web browser when you are finished. Your Web browser will close and Outlook will reappear.

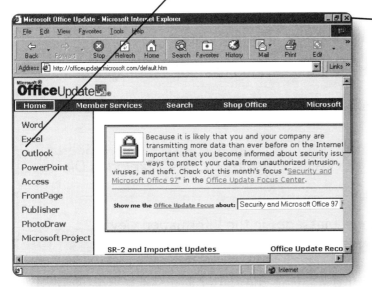

Part I Review Questions

1. How do you start Outlook? *See "Starting Outlook" in Chapter 1*

2. How do you exit Outlook? *See "Exiting Outlook" in Chapter 1*

3. How do you access a menu command? *See "Using Menus" in Chapter 2*

4. Name two methods for closing a dialog box. *See "Exploring Dialog Boxes" in Chapter 2*

5. How do you view e-mail messages in the Information viewer? *See "Using the Outlook Bar" in Chapter 2*

6. Name two methods for displaying the folder list. *See "Displaying the Folder List" in Chapter 2*

7. What feature in Outlook 2000 gives you a preview of your day? *See "Using Outlook Today" in Chapter 2*

8. What interactive feature in Outlook provides answers to your questions? *See "Using Office Assistant" in Chapter 3*

9. Where can you search online reference manuals for Outlook? *See "Searching Contents and Index" in Chapter 3*

10. How can you get up-to-date help from Microsoft? *See "Getting Help on the Web" in Chapter 3*

PART II

Communicating Via E-Mail and Faxes

4

Creating New Messages

Are you ready to let the world know that you're online? One of the first things you can do with Outlook is to communicate with others via e-mail. Using e-mail is a fast and effective way to send messages to people. In Outlook, you can completely customize your e-mail messages, automatically add a signature, and even send documents along with e-mail. In this chapter, you'll learn how to:

- Address and format an e-mail message
- Add an automatic signature and attach a file
- Check the spelling of a message
- Set message options
- Create draft messages

Addressing an E-mail Message

Every e-mail message must have an address so that Outlook knows how to deliver the message. An e-mail address can be a person's full name or some combination of their first and last name. Internet addresses have an @ symbol, such as president@whitehouse.gov.

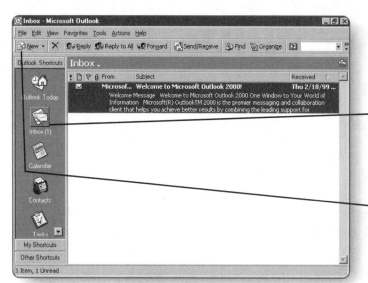

1. **Click** on the **Inbox icon** on the Outlook bar. The Inbox contents will appear in the Information viewer.

2. **Click** on the **New Mail Message button**. A new message will appear.

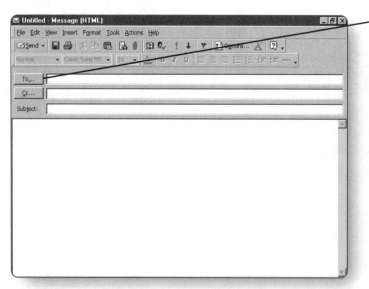

3. **Click** on the **To button** to access the Address Book. The Select Names dialog box will open.

NOTE

If you already know the e-mail address, you can type it directly in the text box.

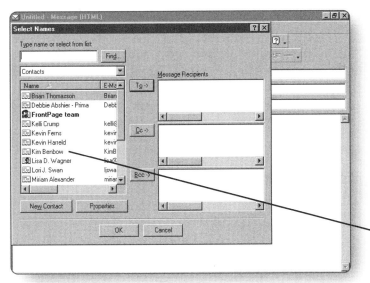

4. Click on a **name** from the list of addresses. The name will be selected.

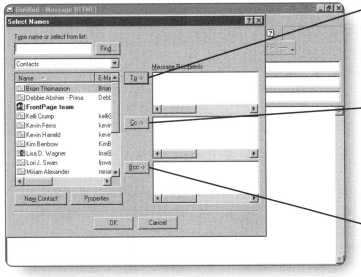

5a. Click on the **To button**. The message will be addressed to the selected individual.

OR

5b. Click on the **Cc button**. A copy of the message will be addressed to the selected individual.

OR

5c. Click on the **Bcc button**. A "blind" copy of the message will be addressed to the selected individual.

NOTE

CC and Bcc stand for "carbon copy" and "blind carbon copy." These terms are hold-overs from the days when duplicate copies of memos were created using carbon paper. A blind carbon copy is one that is send to another recipient without the original recipient's knowledge.

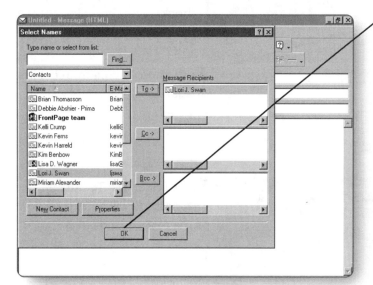

6. Click on **OK**. The Select Names dialog box will close.

TIP

You can send the message to multiple people by separating their names with semicolons or commas in the To text box.

Formatting a Message

You can type a message and send it immediately if you are pressed for time. However, if you have a few extra minutes, you can format your message so that the important points in the message stand out.

NOTE

By default, Outlook uses HTML format for all messages, enabling you to format your e-mail message like you would a Word document or Web page, using bold, italic, and other formatting options. However, some e-mail readers do not interpret HTML messages, and the reader's message may contain miscellaneous codes that make the message difficult to read. To send a plain-text message instead, click on Format, then click on Plain Text. The message title bar will change to indicate the new format. Your formatting buttons will be dimmed.

Formatting Text

Outlook has a Formatting toolbar with numerous options to change the look of your message.

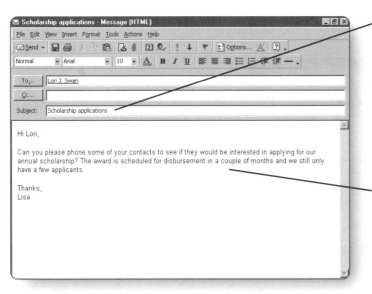

1. **Type** the **title** of the message in the Subject: text box. The title will appear in the text box.

2. **Press** the **Tab key**. The insertion point will move to the message text box.

3. **Type** a **message**. The message will appear in the text box.

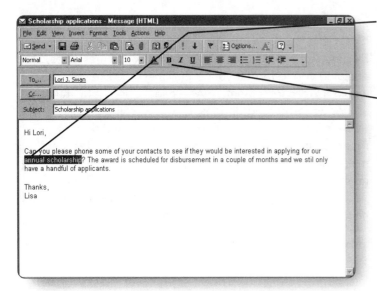

4. Click and **drag** the **mouse** over some text. The text will be selected.

5. Click on **any button or buttons** on the Formatting toolbar. The formatting will appear in the message.

The options are:

- **Font**. Click on the down arrow to the right of the font name to select a different font.

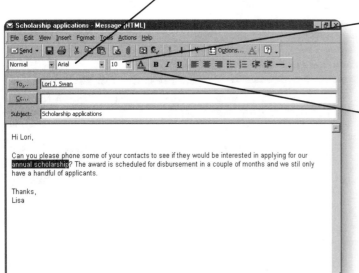

- **Font Size**. Click on the down arrow to the right of the font size to select a larger or smaller font size.

- **Font Color**. Click on the button to select a different font color. A color palette will appear. Click the desired color to select it and close the palette.

Bold. Click on the button to make the text bold.

Italic. Click on the button to make the text italic.

Underline. Click on the button to make the text underlined.

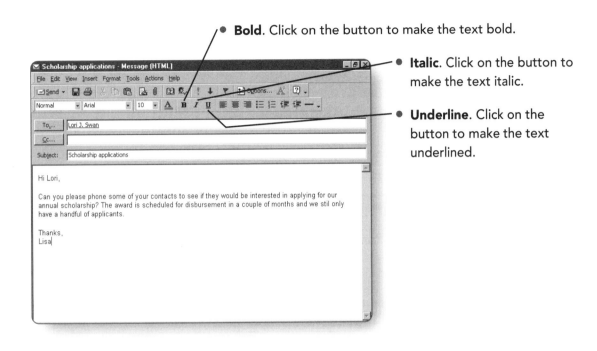

Formatting Paragraphs

You can also format entire paragraphs by clicking buttons on the Formatting toolbar.

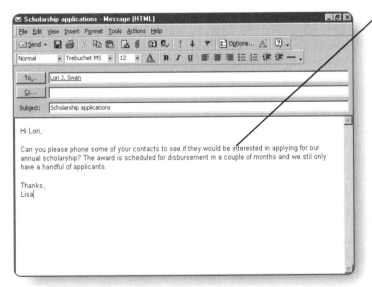

1a. **Click anywhere** in the paragraph you want to format. The insertion point will be in that paragraph.

OR

1b. **Click** and **drag** the **mouse** over several paragraphs to format more than one paragraph. The paragraphs will be highlighted.

The paragraph formatting options are:

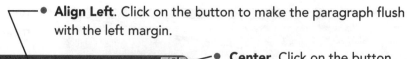

- **Align Left**. Click on the button to make the paragraph flush with the left margin.

- **Center**. Click on the button to make the paragraph centered.

- **Align Right**. Click on the button to make the paragraph flush with the right margin.

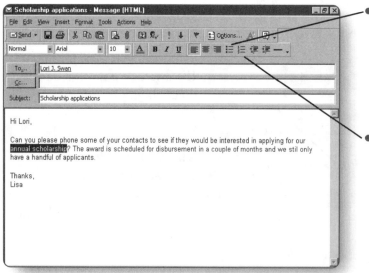

- **Bullets**. Click on the button to make a bulleted list. Each new paragraph you type will be bulleted. Click on the button again to turn off the bullets.

- **Numbering**. Click on this button to create a numbered list. Each new paragraph you type will be numbered sequentially. Click on the button again to stop numbering.

Decrease Indent. Click on the button to decrease the indent of the paragraph from the left margin.

Increase Indent. Click on the button to increase the indent from the left margin.

Horizontal Line. Click on this button to add a horizontal line below the selected paragraph.

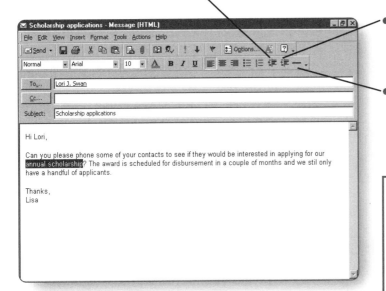

TIP

Click on the down arrow next to the Style drop-down list to assign preset paragraph styles to the selected text.

Adding an Automatic Signature

When you write a letter to someone, it's customary to add your signature to the bottom of the letter. E-mail is no different, but you have an advantage: Outlook's AutoSignature feature can add your signature automatically so that you don't have to sign your e-mail each time. You might also want to include other information such as your phone number or a favorite quote.

1. Click on **Insert**. The Insert menu will appear.

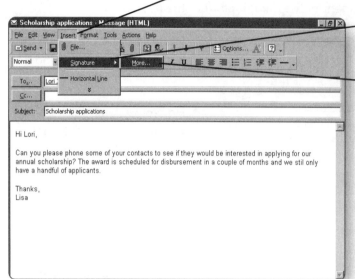

2. Click on **Signature**. The Signature submenu will appear.

3. Click on **More**. If you have established a signature, you will be presented with a list of available signatures. If not, a message will appear allowing you to do so.

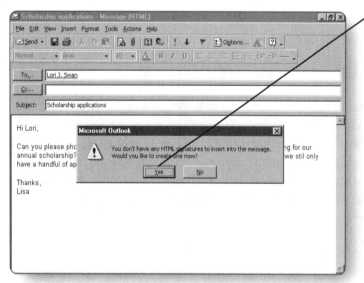

4. Click on **Yes** to create an automatic signature. The Create New Signature dialog box will open.

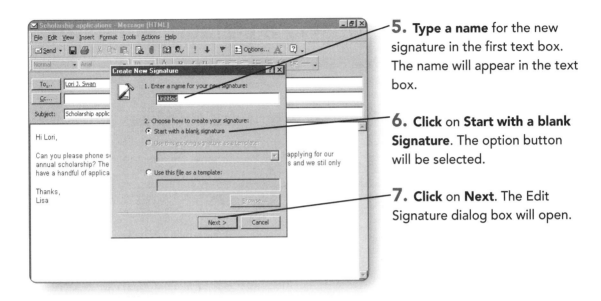

5. **Type a name** for the new signature in the first text box. The name will appear in the text box.

6. **Click** on **Start with a blank Signature**. The option button will be selected.

7. **Click** on **Next**. The Edit Signature dialog box will open.

8. **Click** on the **Font button** or the **Paragraph button** to establish special formatting for the signature.

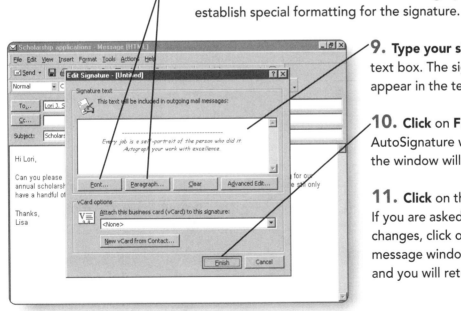

9. **Type your signature** in the text box. The signature will appear in the text box.

10. **Click** on **Finish**. Your AutoSignature will be saved and the window will close.

11. **Click** on the **Close button**. If you are asked to save changes, click on no. The message window will disappear and you will return to the Inbox.

Choosing a Default Signature

You can create multiple signatures in Outlook. Whenever you need a signature in your e-mail message, you can click on Insert, and then on Signature, and choose the signature you want. You can also choose a default signature that will automatically attach itself to any new, outgoing messages.

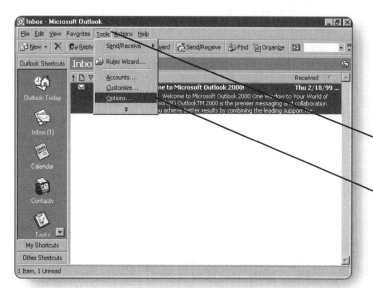

1. **Click** on **Tools**. The Tools menu will appear.

2. **Click** on **Options**. The Options dialog box will open.

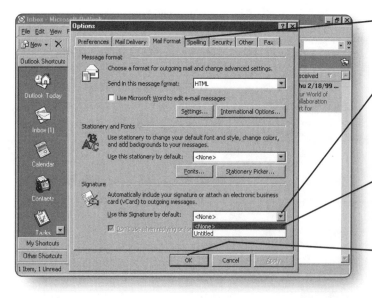

3. **Click** on the **Mail Format tab**. The tab will come to the front.

4. **Click** on the **down arrow** next to Use this Signature by default: list box. A drop-down list will appear.

5. **Click** on the **signature** you want to use. The signature will be highlighted.

6. **Click** on **OK**. The Options dialog box will close.

Checking the Spelling of a Message

Just because e-mail is fast doesn't mean it needs to be sloppy! Before sending your message, it's a good idea to check the spelling of the message.

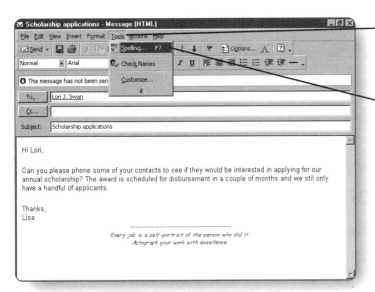

1. Click on **Tools** in the mail message. The Tools menu will appear.

2. Click on **Spelling**. The Spelling dialog box will open.

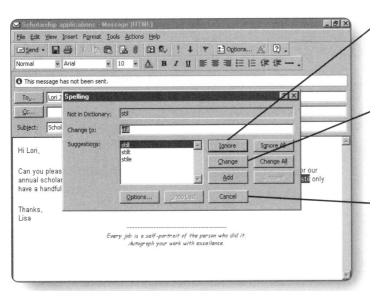

3a. Click on **Ignore** if you don't want to make the change.

OR

3b. Click on **Change** if you want to accept Outlook's proposed change. The change will be made in the message.

4. Click on **Close** when you're finished spell-checking the document. The Spelling dialog box will close.

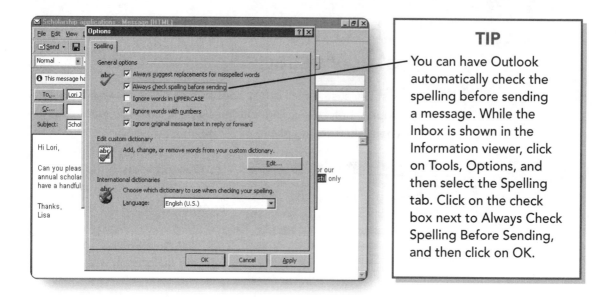

TIP

You can have Outlook automatically check the spelling before sending a message. While the Inbox is shown in the Information viewer, click on Tools, Options, and then select the Spelling tab. Click on the check box next to Always Check Spelling Before Sending, and then click on OK.

Setting Message Options

Before you send the message, there are many options that you can set. Options can change the importance or sensitivity of a message.

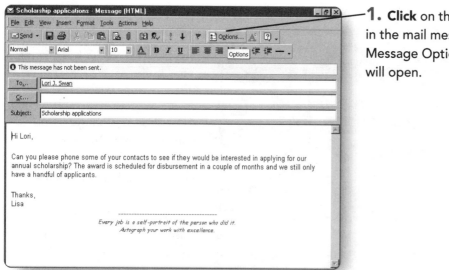

1. **Click** on the **Options button** in the mail message. The Message Options dialog box will open.

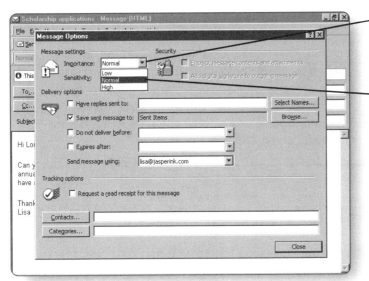

2. Click on the **down arrow** next to the Importance: list box. A drop-down list will appear.

3. Click on **Low, Normal, or High**. The importance level will be selected.

NOTE

A low-importance message will have a blue, down-pointing arrow, and a high-importance message will have a red exclamation point when delivered.

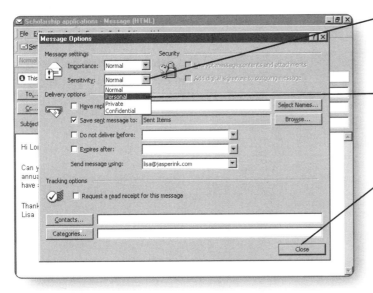

4. Click on the **down arrow** next to the Sensitivity: list box. A drop-down list will appear.

5. Click on **Normal, Personal, Private**, or **Confidential**. The option you select will appear in the edit box.

6. Click on the **Close button**. The Message Options dialog box will close and you will return to the message.

> ### NOTE
> Personal, Private, and Confidential messages will have a banner just below the To line at the top of the e-mail message with a note saying, "Please treat this message as Personal" (or Confidential or Private). Also, once you send a private message, the recipient will not be able to modify the contents.

Using Message Flags

You can add a message flag to an e-mail message. Message flags add notes to the message recipients, letting them know that a follow up is due by a certain date, or that no follow up is necessary.

1. Click on **Actions** in the mail message. The Actions menu will appear.

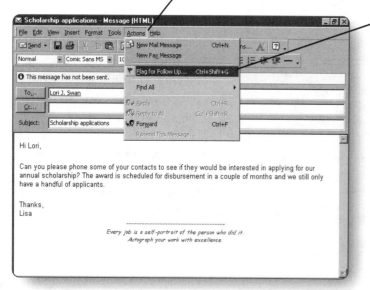

2. Click on **Flag for Follow Up**. The Flag for Follow Up dialog box will open.

3. Click on the **down arrow** to the right of the Flag to: list box. A drop-down list will appear.

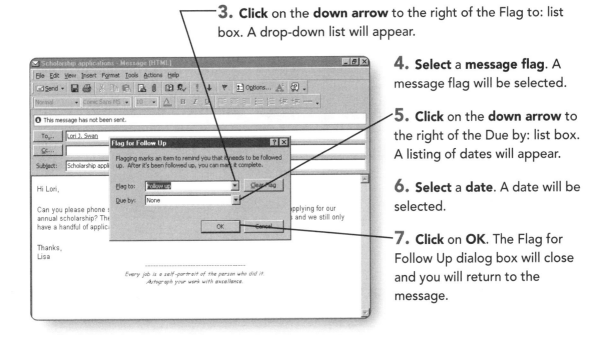

4. Select a **message flag**. A message flag will be selected.

5. Click on the **down arrow** to the right of the Due by: list box. A listing of dates will appear.

6. Select a **date**. A date will be selected.

7. Click on **OK**. The Flag for Follow Up dialog box will close and you will return to the message.

Creating a Draft Message

If you are composing a long e-mail and decide to finish it later, you can save the message as a draft.

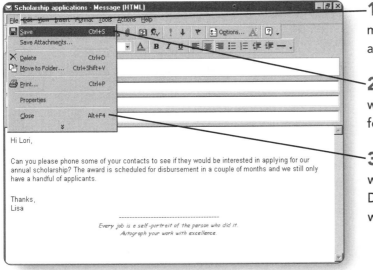

1. Click on **File** on an unsent message. The File menu will appear.

2. Click on **Save**. The message will be copied to the Drafts folder.

3. Click on **Close**. The message will close and be saved in the Drafts folder. You can finish it when you have more time.

Working with Draft Messages

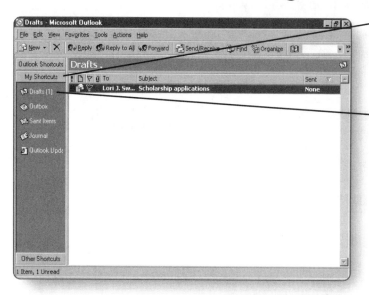

1. Click on the **My Shortcuts group** on the Outlook bar. The My Shortcuts group will be revealed on the Outlook bar.

2. Click on the **Drafts icon**. The contents of the Drafts folder will appear in the Information viewer.

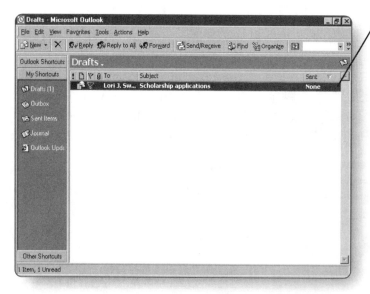

3. Double-click on the **draft message** in the Information viewer. The draft message will open. Once the message is open, you can continue working on the text until you are ready to send the message.

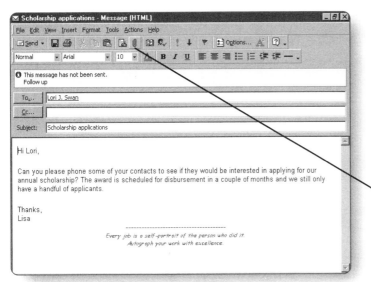

Attaching a File

Before you send a message, you may need to attach a file (document) to the e-mail message. Outlook gives you an easy way to attach files to e-mail messages.

1. **Click** on the **Insert File button**. The Insert File dialog box will open.

2. **Click** on the **file** you want to attach. The file will be selected.

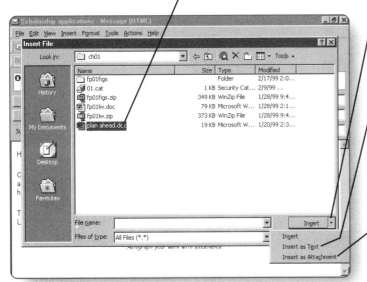

3. **Click** on the **down arrow** next to the Insert button. A drop-down list will appear. The Insert options include:

- **Insert as Text**. The file will be inserted as text in the body of the e-mail message. It's sometimes a good idea to use this option when sending files via the Internet.

- **Insert as Attachment**. The file will be inserted as an icon in the body of the message. When recipients receive e-mail messages, they can double-click on the icon to read the attachment.

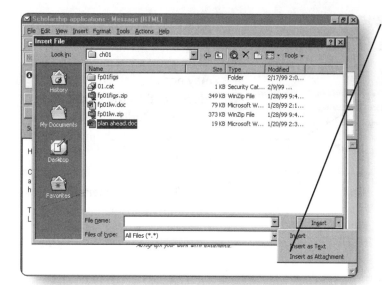

4. Click on the **insert option**. The file will be attached.

5

Sending and Tracking Messages

Once you have finished composing your e-mail message and setting options, it's a snap to send the message. Outlook will also allow you to view your sent messages, track the status of messages you've sent, and resend or forward them as many times as you like. In this chapter, you'll learn how to:

- Send a mail message
- View messages in the Sent Items folder
- Recall and resend a message
- Receive notification when a message is read
- Send replies to another individual
- Deliver a message at a specific time
- Expire a message

Sending a Mail Message

You've written the message, addressed it to the appropriate people, and set all the available options. You are now ready to send the message.

1. Click on the **Send button**. The message will be sent.

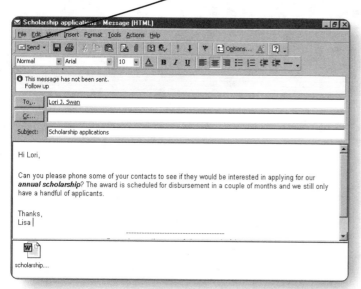

NOTE

When you send a message, it temporarily moves to the Outbox. Once the message has been sent, it moves to the Sent Items folder.

Viewing and Sorting Sent Messages

Trying to remember if you sent a message to someone can be tricky. Luckily, Outlook allows you to view all the messages you have sent, and it helps keep your messages organized.

1. Click on the **My Shortcuts button** on the Outlook bar. The contents of the My Shortcuts folder will appear in the Information viewer.

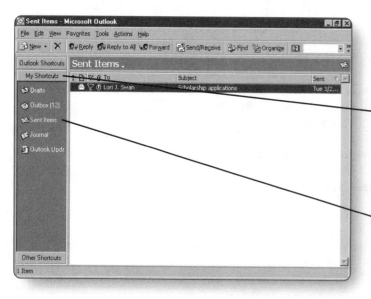

2. Click on the **Sent Items icon** on the Outlook bar. The contents of the Sent Items folder will appear in the Information viewer.

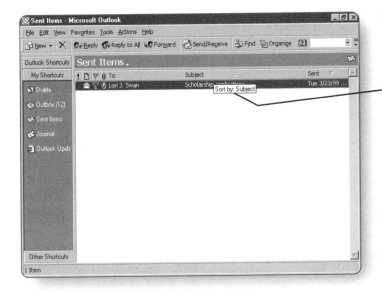

You can sort messages in the Sent Items folder to quickly locate them.

3. Click on **any column header**. The messages will be sorted by that field.

Recalling a Message

Ever had a sinking feeling as soon as you pressed the Send button? "I wish I hadn't sent that e-mail!" Outlook gives you a safety net with the Recall feature. Recall is also a good feature to use when you discover incorrect information in the message you just sent.

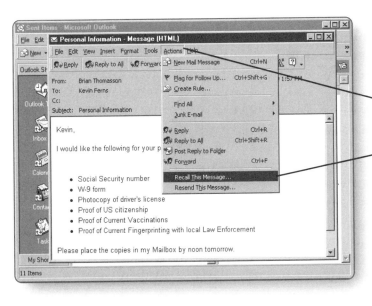

1. Click twice on a **message** in the Sent Items folder. The message will open.

2. Click on **Actions**. The Actions menu will appear.

3. Click on **Recall This Message**. The Recall This Message dialog box will open.

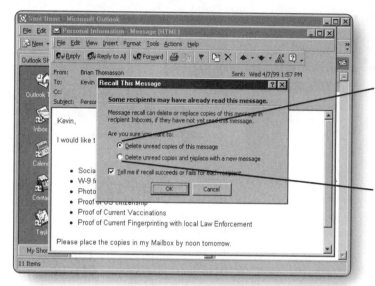

There are several options available when recalling a message. They are:

- **Delete unread copies of this message**. Outlook will delete any unread copies of the message from the recipient's Inbox.

- **Delete unread copies and replace with a new message**. A new message will open which will replace the message currently in the recipient's Inbox.

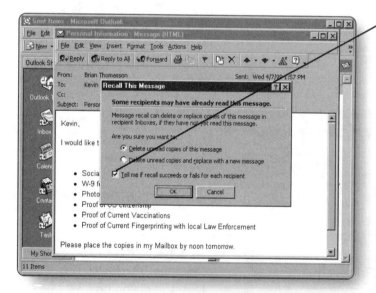

- **Tell me if recall succeeds or fails for each recipient**. Outlook sends you a new e-mail message informing you of success or failure of the attempt to recall the message.

NOTE

Recall failure occurs if the recipient has read the message before you attempt to recall it. If this occurs, the recipient receives a message warning them that you are attempting to recall the original message.

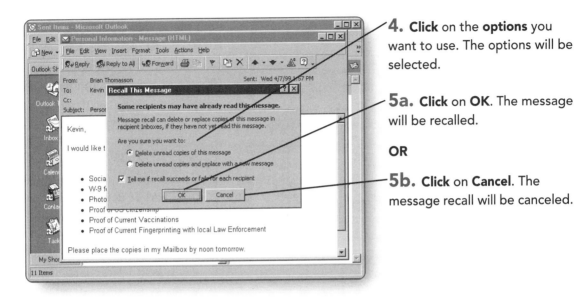

4. Click on the **options** you want to use. The options will be selected.

5a. Click on **OK**. The message will be recalled.

OR

5b. Click on **Cancel**. The message recall will be canceled.

Resending a Message

Sometimes message recipients may tell you that they didn't receive your message. Or you may send a message and then realize that you forgot to include an important recipient. Resending the message allows you to quickly handle both situations.

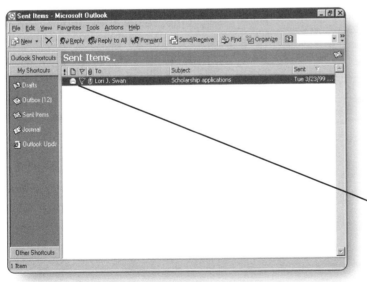

Also, if you are tired of typing the same messages week after week (for example, an e-mail message to the office asking for lunch orders, or a weekly status report), resending a message can save you valuable time. Messages can be edited before they are resent.

1. Click twice on the **message** in the Sent Items folder. The message will open.

2. Click on **Actions**. The Actions menu will appear.

3. Click on **Resend This Message**. The message will open as a new e-mail message.

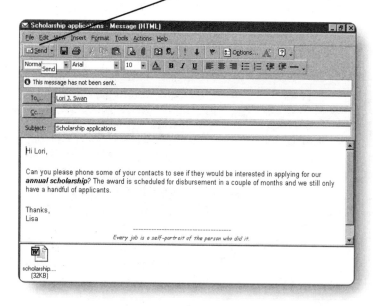

TIP

You can edit the message text, add or delete message recipients, and change message options before resending.

4. Click on the **Send button**. The message will be sent again.

NOTE

Resending a message will not remove the original message from the recipient's Inbox. You must recall a message to delete the original message.

Receiving Notification When a Message Is Read

Say you've sent an important e-mail message to someone and you want to follow up with a phone call. How do you know when they have read the message? It's easy! You tell Outlook to notify you when the message has been read.

1. Create a **new mail message**.

2. Click on **View**. The View menu will appear.

3. Click on **Options**. The Message Options dialog box will open.

NOTE

You must set the option to receive notification *before* the message is sent.

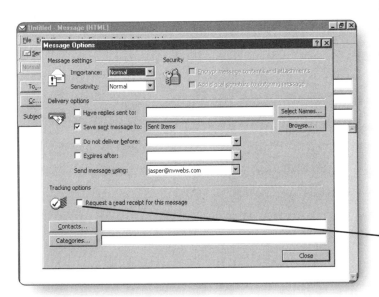

There are two notification options, depending on your configuration:

- **Request a delivery receipt for this message**. Outlook will notify you when the message has reached the recipient's Inbox. (This option is not available in the Internet Mail only configuration).

- **Request a read receipt for this message**. Outlook will notify you when the message has been opened.

NOTE

If the message is sent to someone outside of your company via the Internet, Outlook will only be able to tell you when the message has been delivered, not when it has been read.

TIP

If you use tracking options frequently, you can set all of your new messages to automatically have tracking. In the Inbox, click on Tools, Options, and click on the E-mail Options button. When the E-mail Options dialog box opens, click on the Tracking Options button and select the tracking options you want to use.

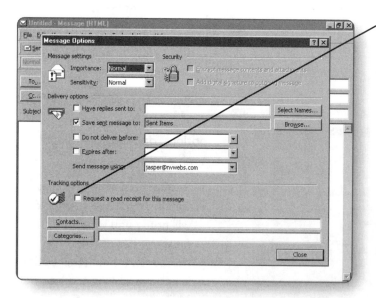

4. Click on the **tracking option**. The option will be selected.

Sending Replies to Another Individual

Normally, when people reply to an e-mail message, the reply is sent back to the message sender. However, you can have replies sent directly to another individual.

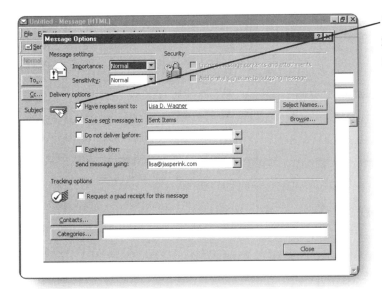

1. Click on the **Have Replies Sent to check box**. A check mark will be placed in the box.

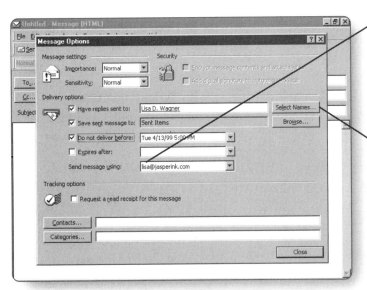

2a. Type the individual's **e-mail address** in the text box. The address will appear in the text box.

OR

2b. Click on the **Select Names button** and **select** the **individual's name** from the address book. The name will be selected.

Delivering a Message at a Specific Time

Messages are normally delivered as soon as you send them. However, you can delay the delivery of a message to a specific time. This feature works great if you are going to be out of the office and still want an e-mail delivered while you are gone.

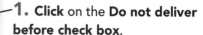

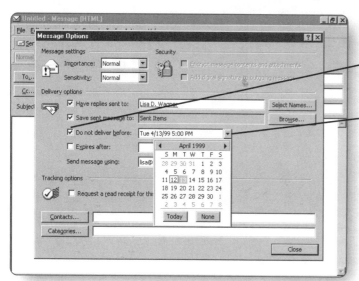

1. Click on the **Do not deliver before check box**.

2. Click on the **down arrow** to the right of the Do not deliver before check box. The Date Navigator will open.

3. Click on the **left or right arrow** on either side of the month. The month will change.

4. Click on the **date** you want when the correct month is displayed. The date will be highlighted.

TIP

You can type a different date or time directly into the Do Not Deliver Before text box.

NOTE

The message will remain in your Outbox until the specified delivery time. You can edit the message or delete the message from the Outbox.

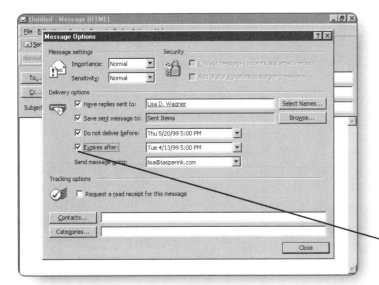

Expiring a Message

Have you ever been out of the office and returned to find a ton of out-of-date e-mail messages in your Inbox? It's considered good e-mail manners to expire your messages if they contain time-sensitive material.

1. **Click** on the **Expires after check box**.

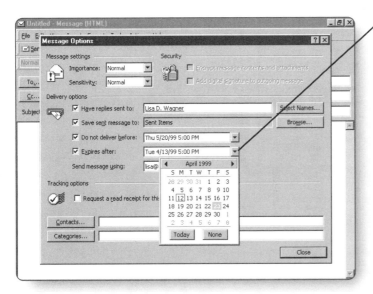

2. **Click** on the **down arrow** to the right of the Expires after check box. The Date Navigator will open.

NOTE

Expired messages remain in the recipient's Inbox, but they are highlighted with strikethrough formatting for easy identification.

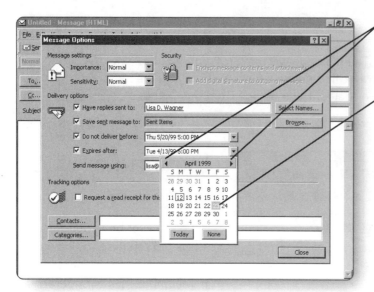

3. Click on the **left or right arrow** on either side of the month. The month will change.

4. Click on the **date** you want when the correct month is displayed. The date will be highlighted.

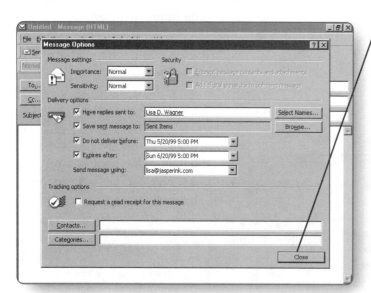

5. Click on the **Close button**. The Message Options dialog box will close and your unsent message will reappear.

6. Click on the **Close button** in the message window. The message will close.

6

Reading and Responding to Messages

You'll probably use e-mail more than any other feature in Outlook. Sending and receiving e-mail is now an integral part of doing business and communicating with others. Once you receive e-mail, you'll need to know what to do with it. In this chapter, you'll learn how to:

- ● Change how you view e-mail messages
- ● Use AutoPreview or the Preview Pane
- ● Read, reply, forward, delete, and print a message
- ● Navigate between e-mail messages

Changing How You View Your E-mail Messages

Views in Outlook provide you with different ways to look at information in a folder by putting it in different arrangements and formats. Use views to control how much detail appears in your e-mail messages.

1. Click on the **Inbox icon** on the Outlook bar. The Inbox contents will appear in the Information viewer.

2. Click on **View**. The View menu will appear.

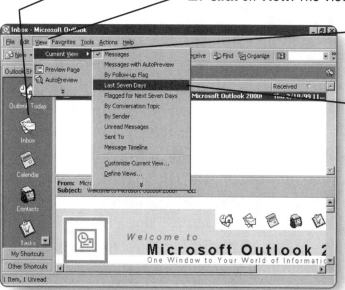

3. Click on **Current View**. The Current View submenu will appear.

4. Click on **any view**. Your e-mail messages will appear differently in the Information viewer.

TIP

If you find a view that is close to what you're looking for, you can click on View, Current View, and Customize Current View. From there, you can specify exactly how you want your e-mail messages to appear.

NOTE

Some views apply a filter. When a filter is applied, you will not see all of your e-mail messages. For example, if your view is set to Last Seven Days and you have messages in your Inbox more than seven days old, those messages will not appear in your Information viewer.

Using AutoPreview

AutoPreview is a way to quickly view the first three lines of an e-mail message without opening the message. Using AutoPreview saves you time and lets you open only the messages you want to read.

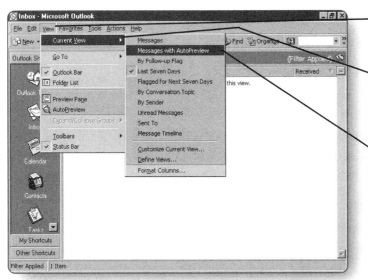

1. Click on **View**. The View menu will appear.

2. Click on **Current View**. The Current View submenu will appear.

3. Click on **Messages with AutoPreview**. Your Inbox will display up to the first three lines of e-mail messages you've received but have not yet read.

Using the Preview Pane

Another feature that lets you see a snapshot of your e-mail message is the Preview Pane. The Preview Pane divides the Information viewer in half—you can see the message header on the top half of the screen and the actual message on the bottom half of the screen.

1. **Click** on **View**. The View menu will appear.

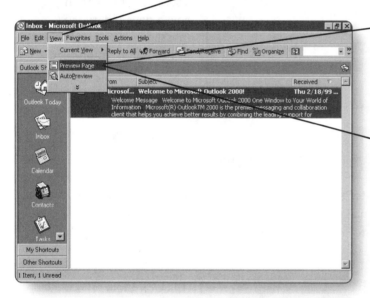

2. **Click** on **Preview Pane**. Your Information viewer will split, showing your regular Inbox view above and the body of the selected message below.

3. **Click** on **Preview Pane** again. It will turn off.

Responding to E-mail Messages

One great thing about e-mail is that there are so many options when you receive a message. You can reply to the sender of the message, or you can send your replies to everyone who received the message. You can forward the message on to someone else, and you can print the message for your files.

1. **Click twice** on a message in the Inbox. The message will open.

Choose one of the following options:

- **Reply**. Click on Reply to send a reply to the message sender.

- **Reply to All**. Click on Reply to All to send a reply to the message sender and all of the message recipients.

- **Forward**. Click on Forward to send the message to another person.

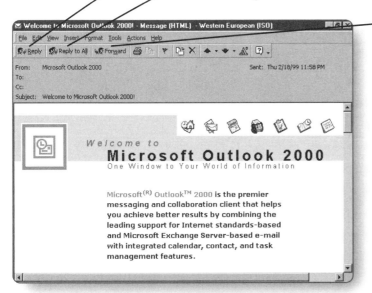

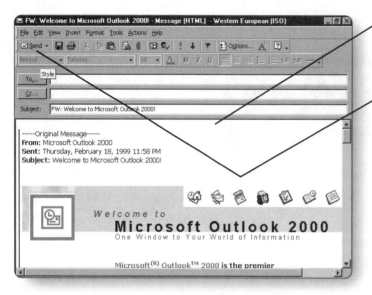

2. Type the **message text**. The message will appear in the text box.

3. Click on **Send**. Your message will be sent.

Printing a Message

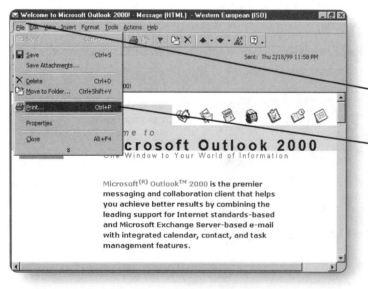

You can keep e-mail messages in your Inbox, or you can print messages for future reference.

1. Click on **File**. The File menu will appear.

2. Click on **Print**. The Print dialog box will open.

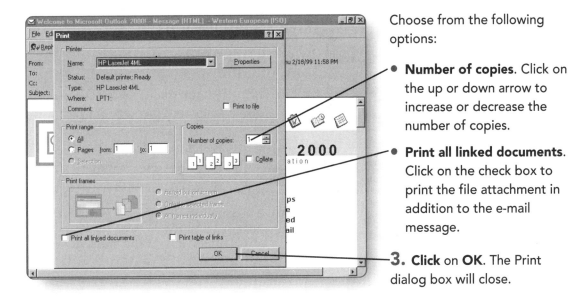

Choose from the following options:

- **Number of copies**. Click on the up or down arrow to increase or decrease the number of copies.

- **Print all linked documents**. Click on the check box to print the file attachment in addition to the e-mail message.

3. Click on **OK**. The Print dialog box will close.

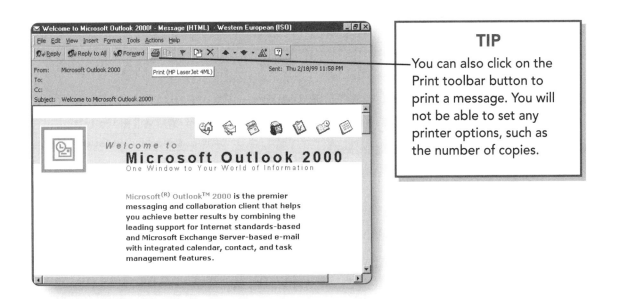

TIP

You can also click on the Print toolbar button to print a message. You will not be able to set any printer options, such as the number of copies.

Navigating between E-mail Messages

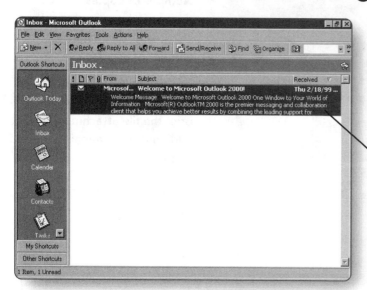

After a while, you will have numerous messages in your Inbox. Learning how to move around will help you locate the messages you want more quickly.

1. Click twice on any message in the Inbox. The message will open.

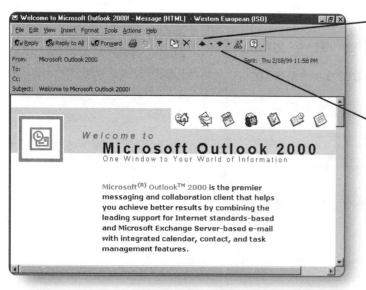

2a. Click on the **Previous Item button**. You will move to the previous e-mail message.

OR

2b. Click on the **Next Item button**. You will move to the next e-mail message.

There are down arrows to the right of the Next and Previous Item buttons. These give you more options so you can go to the next or previous item of a specific type.

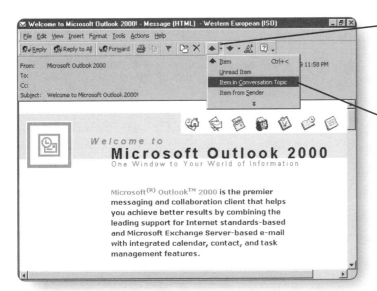

3. Click on the **down arrow** next to the Previous Item or Next Item buttons. A drop-down menu will appear.

4. Click on a **type**. You will move to the next or previous item of that type.

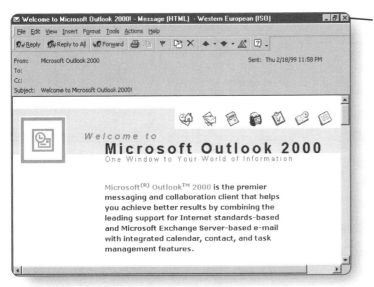

5. Click on the **Close button**. The message will close.

7

Managing Your Mail

You know how easy it is to let piles of paper stack up on your desk! Outlook gives you many tools to organize your messages so your Inbox remains uncluttered and you can easily locate the messages you need. In this chapter, you'll learn how to:

- Organize messages in folders
- Organize messages with color
- Control junk and adult-content mail
- Use the Rules Wizard
- Find, sort, and archive messages

Organizing Messages in Folders

Think of your Inbox as a drawer in a filing cabinet. Would you just toss all the messages into the drawer? No! You may read some mail immediately and throw it away, or you may need to store some messages while you wait for more information. Using electronic folders is an easy way to organize your messages, just as you would use file folders in a filing cabinet. Outlook lets you create new folders in your Inbox and moves messages into the folders manually or automatically.

1. Click on the **Inbox icon** on the Outlook Shortcuts bar. Outlook will display the contents of your Inbox in the Information viewer.

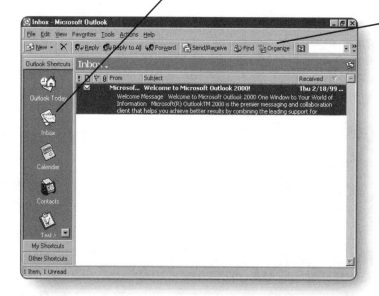

2. Click on the **Organize button**. The Ways to Organize Inbox pane will appear in the Information viewer.

3. **Click** on **Using Folders**. The Using Folders pane will come to the front.

4. **Click** on the **message** that you want to place in a folder. The message will be highlighted.

5. **Click** on the **down arrow** to the right of Move Message selected below to list box. A drop-down list will appear.

6. **Click** on the **folder** in which you want to store the message. It will be highlighted.

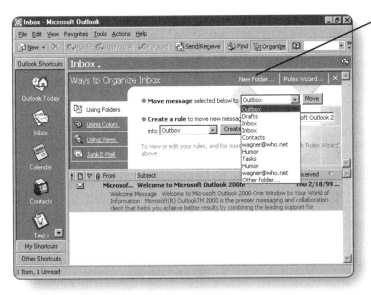

7. **Click** on the **New Folder button** if the folder does not exist. The Create New Folder dialog box will open.

8. Type the **name** of the new folder in the Name text box. The text will appear.

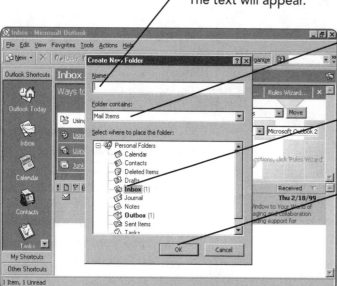

9. Click on **Mail Items** in the Folder contains: list box. It will be highlighted.

10. Click on **Inbox** under Select where to place the folder: list box. It will be highlighted.

11. Click on **OK**. The message will be moved to the new subfolder.

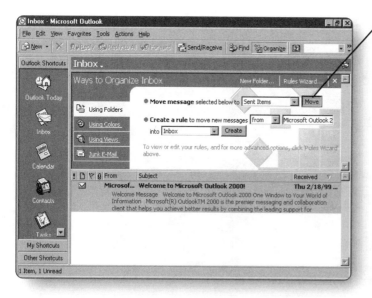

12. Click on the **Move button**. The selected message will be moved to the folder.

TIP

You can move multiple messages into a folder at once. When selecting the messages from the list of items in the Inbox, hold down the Ctrl key while you click on the messages.

Organizing Messages with Color

Another way to organize messages in the Inbox is by using color. If you are a visually oriented person, you'll appreciate this feature of Outlook. You can color messages sent to or received from a certain person.

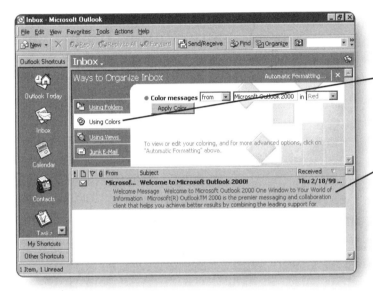

1. **Click** on **Using Colors**. Your organizer pane will change to allow you to organize messages by color.

2. **Click** on a **message** you want to color. It will be highlighted.

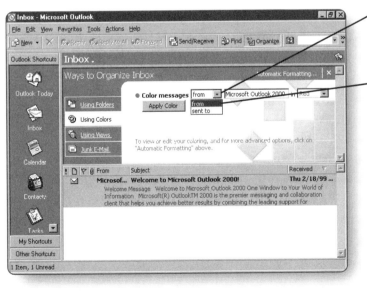

3. **Click** on the **down arrow** to the right of Color messages. A drop-down list will appear.

4a. **Click** on **from** to color messages from the sender of the selected message. The word will be highlighted.

NOTE

You can replace the selected sender by typing a new e-mail address in the edit box.

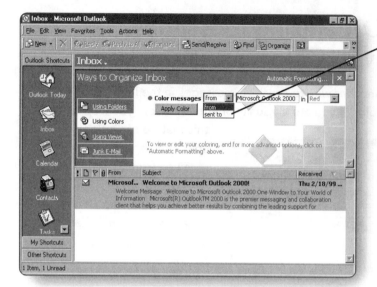

OR

4b. **Click** on **sent to** to color messages sent to the recipient of the selected message. The choice will be highlighted.

NOTE
You can replace the selected recipient by typing a new e-mail address in the edit box.

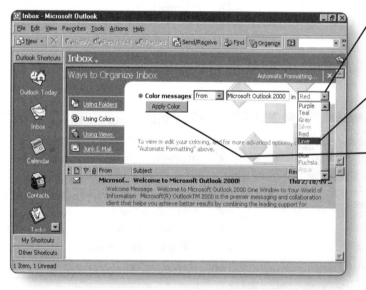

5. **Click** on the **down arrow** to the right of the color choices. A drop-down list will appear.

6. **Click** on a **color**. The color will be selected.

7. **Click** on the **Apply Color button**. Messages received from or sent to the individual you've selected will now be color-coded.

Controlling Junk and Adult-Content Mail

Ever heard of "spamming?" This is a term used to describe unsolicited e-mail that arrives in your Inbox. Unfortunately, once your e-mail address becomes public, you may frequently receive junk mail in your Inbox. Luckily, Outlook includes a special feature to control the junk and adult-content mail that you receive. You can automatically color, move, or delete any junk or adult-content e-mail.

1. **Click** on **Junk E-Mail**. Your organizer pane will change to allow you to control undesirable messages.

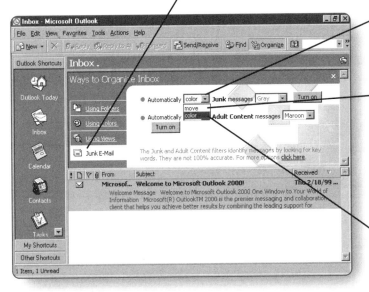

2. **Click** on the **down arrow** to the right of Automatically. A drop-down list will appear.

3a. **Click** on **move** to automatically move junk messages, and then **select** the **folder** in which it will be placed. The folder will be selected.

OR

3b. **Click** on **color** to automatically color junk messages, and then **select** a **color**. The color will be selected.

NOTE

If a junk e-mail folder does not exist, you may receive a message asking if you want to create one. Click on Yes to create the folder, or No to cancel.

TIP

Choosing to automatically move junk messages to the Deleted Items folder is the same as automatically deleting all junk e-mail.

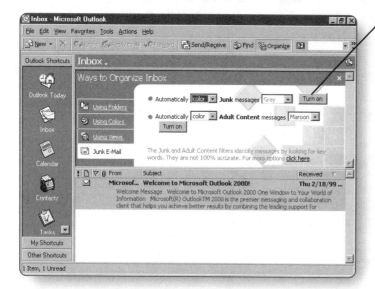

4. **Click** on the **Turn on button.** It will be activated.

When the junk e-mail rule is activated, the Turn on button changes to a Turn off button. To deactivate your rule, click on the Turn off button.

5. **Repeat steps 2 through 4** for Adult-Content e-mail.

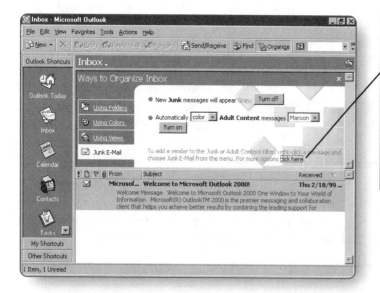

TIP

Outlook uses special rules to determine what is junk or adult-content e-mail. Click on For more options click here for more information about junk and adult-content mail.

Adding Names to the Junk E-mail List

Even after you have activated junk e-mail rules, certain junk messages may slip into your Inbox. You can quickly add the senders of these messages to your junk senders list.

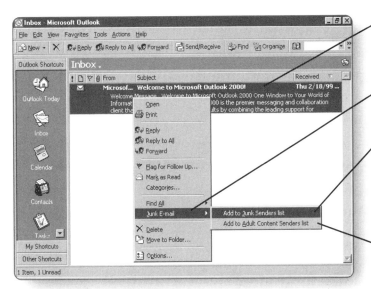

1. Right-click on the **offending message** in the Inbox. A shortcut menu will appear.

2. Click on **Junk E-mail**. The submenu will appear.

3a. Click on **Add to Junk Senders list**. The message will be added to the list.

OR

3b. Click on **Add to Adult Content Senders list**. The message will be added to the list.

NOTE

The Exceptions List is a built-in mail handling rule. You'll learn more about creating custom rules in the next section.

Making Exceptions to the Junk Senders List

There may be some cases in which Outlook mistakes legitimate mail for junk and inadvertently deletes normal messages. Fortunately, you can add a mistaken sender's address or domain name to the built-in Exceptions list to avoid future confusion.

1. Click on **Tools**. The Tools menu will appear.

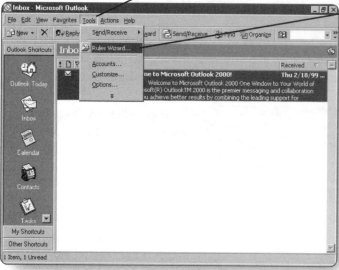

2. Click on **Rules Wizard**. The Rules Wizard dialog box will open, with the Exception List item showing.

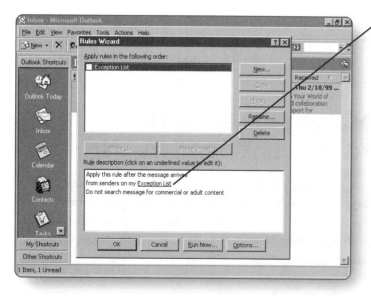

3. Click on **Exception List** in the Rule Description section of the dialog box to edit the list. The Edit Exception List dialog box will open.

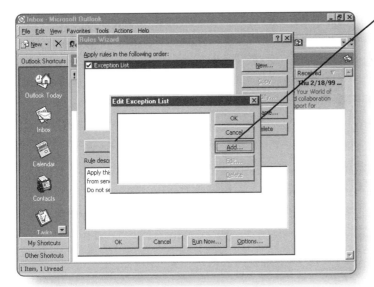

4. Click on **Add** to add a name. The Sender dialog box will open.

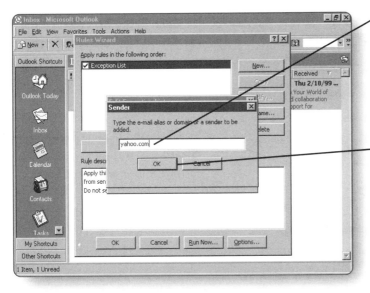

5. Type in a **domain name** (such as yahoo.com) or a specific e-mail address (bruce@yahoo.com) that you do not want to be handled as junk mail.

6. Click on **OK**. The dialog box will close.

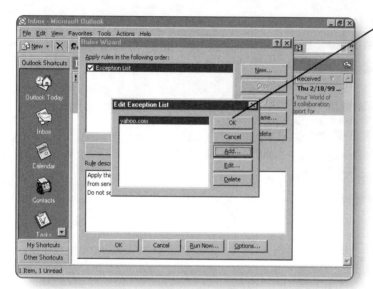

7. Click on **OK** again. The Rules Wizard will reappear.

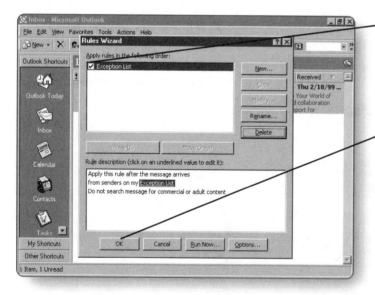

8. Click in the **box** next to the Exception List rule at the top of the dialog box. The box will be checked, and the Exception List rule will be enabled.

9. Click on **OK**. The Rules Wizard will close and your current folder will reappear.

Using the Rules Wizard

Previously, you created a rule to do something with junk or adult-content e-mail messages. Outlook has a Rules Wizard that walks you through the steps needed to create rules. Rules can be created to automatically move messages to a certain folder, automatically reply to messages, notify you when important messages arrive, and much more.

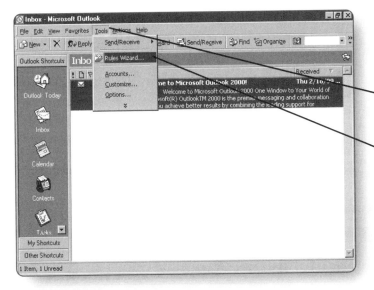

1. Click on **Tools**. The Tools menu will appear.

2. Click on **Rules Wizard**. The Rules Wizard dialog box will open.

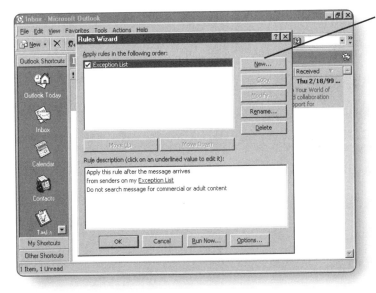

3. Click on the **New button**. The Rules Wizard will appear.

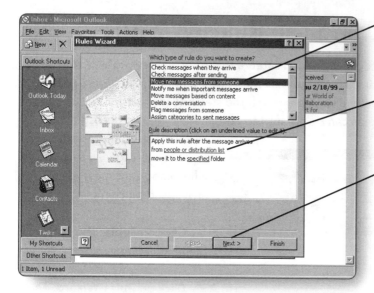

4. Click on the **type of rule** that you want to create. It will be highlighted.

5. Click on an **underlined option.** It will be highlighted and ready for you to edit.

6. Click on **Next.** The wizard will present you with a list of conditions for the rule.

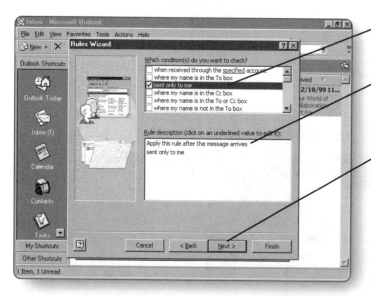

7. Click on a **check box** to select a condition.

8. Click on the **underlined options** to edit the rules description.

9. Click on **Next.** The wizard will present a list of options on how to handle the message.

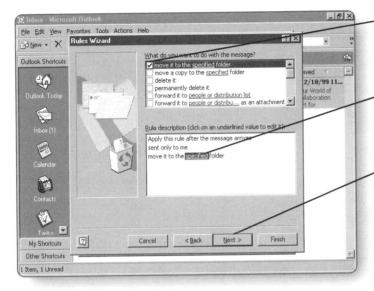

10. **Click** on a **check box** to select what Outlook should do with the message.

11. **Click** on the **underlined options** to edit the rules description.

12. **Click** on **Next**.

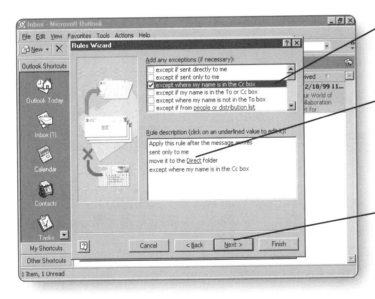

13. **Click** on a **check box** to select any exceptions. It will be highlighted.

14. **Click** on the **underlined options** to edit the rules description. The option will be highlighted and then change as edited.

15. **Click** on **Next**.

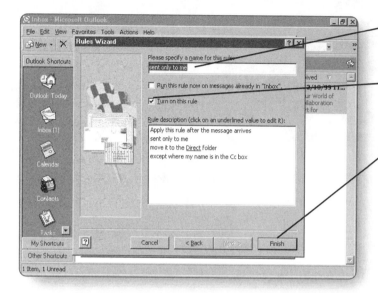

16. Type a **name** for the rule. It will be inserted.

17. Click on the **Turn on this rule check box** to turn the rule on or off.

18. Click on **Finish**.

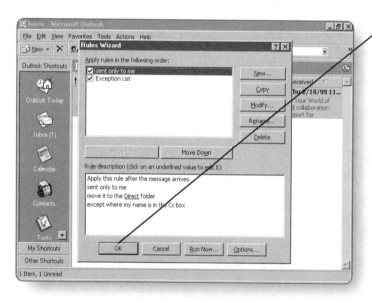

19. Click on **OK**. The Rules Wizard will close.

Finding Messages

After you have used Outlook for a while, you may have many messages stored in the Inbox or other folders. Outlook has extensive searching capabilities so you can always locate your messages.

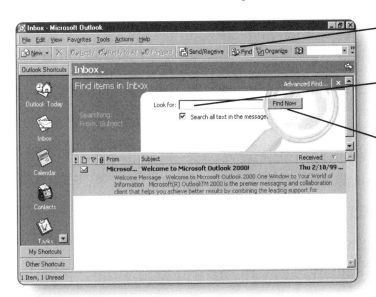

1. Click on the **Find button**. The Find pane will appear.

2. Type text in the Look for: text box. The text will appear.

3. Click on the **Find Now button**. All messages matching the typed text will be displayed in the Information viewer at the bottom section of the screen.

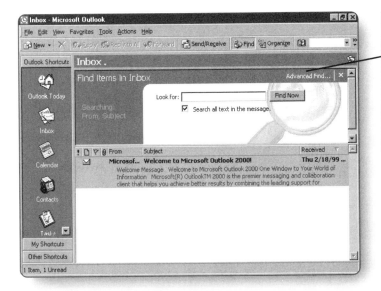

TIP

If you don't find the message, click on the Advanced Find option to specify even more criteria for searching.

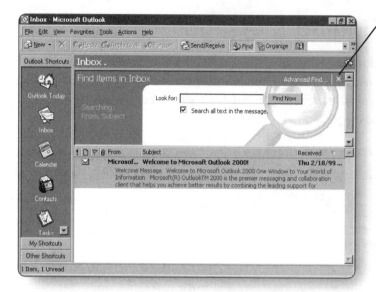

4. Click on the **Close button**. The Find window will close.

Sorting Messages

Another way to organize your e-mail is by sorting the messages in your Inbox. Incoming messages can be sorted by several criteria. You can view your messages in the order in which they were sent, by sender, or by several other options.

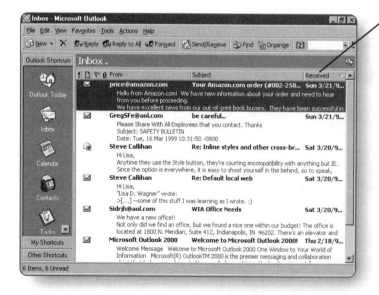

1. Click on the **Received column header** to sort all messages based on order received.

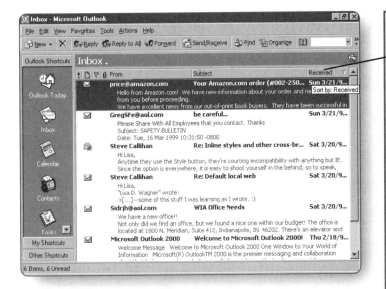

NOTE

The column headers are toggle buttons that let you sort in ascending or descending order. Click once on a column header to sort in ascending order; click again on the column header to sort in descending order. The small gray triangle to the right of the column header indicates ascending or descending order.

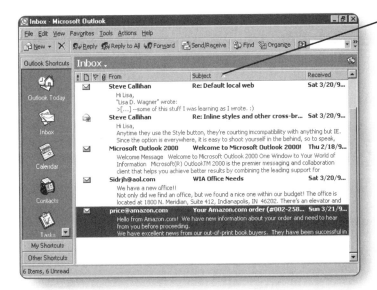

2. Click on the **Subject column header** to sort all messages based on subject.

TIP

You can use many fields to sort; however, not all of them appear in the Information viewer. Click on View, Current View, Customize Current View, and Fields to change which fields are displayed.

Archiving Messages Automatically

Outlook will occasionally poll your mailbox to determine whether it is time to archive. Archiving is the process of moving messages from the Inbox to another file. These messages are still available to you after they have been archived. Archiving helps to prevent cluttered or outdated materials from being stored in your everyday mailbox.

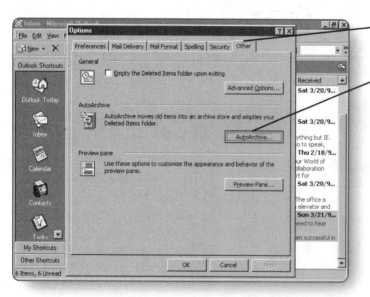

1. Click on **Tools**. The Tools menu will appear.

2. Click on **Options**. The Options dialog box will open.

3. Click on the **Other tab**. The tab will come to the front.

4. Click on the **AutoArchive button**. The AutoArchive dialog box will open.

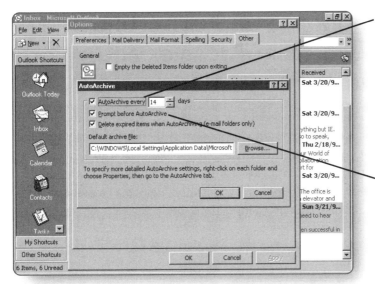

- **AutoArchive every 14 days**. Outlook will automatically archive according to the number of days set here. Click on the up or down arrows next to the number of days to increase or decrease the number of days.

- **Prompt before AutoArchive**. Before archiving, Outlook will display a message with an option to cancel that particular day's scheduled archiving.

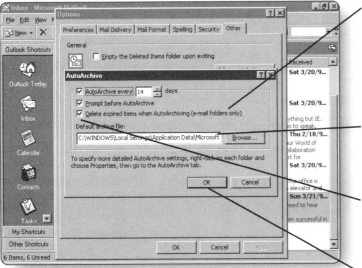

- **Delete expired items when AutoArchiving (e-mail folders only)**. Outlook will delete any expired e-mail messages instead of archiving the messages.

- **Default archive file**. The storage location for archived messages.

5. **Click** on the **options** that you want to use. They will be checked.

6. **Click** on **OK**. Your AutoArchive settings will update any changes.

Importing and Exporting Items from Archives and Other Programs

You may have messages or other items stored in archives or in mail folders from other applications, such as Outlook Express, that you want to bring into Outlook. You also can export Outlook items to these programs so you can work with them there. In this example, you will import any mail messages from your Outlook Express Inbox into Outlook.

1. Click on **File**. The File menu will appear.

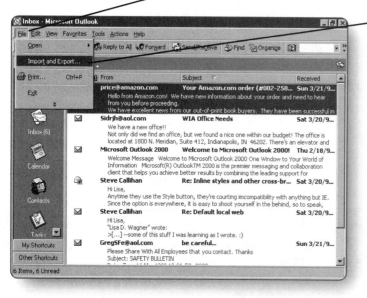

2. Click on **Import and Export**. The Import and Export Wizard will appear.

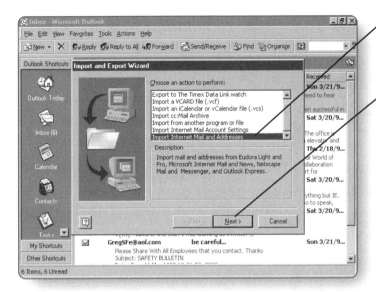

3. **Click** on the **action** you want to perform. It will be highlighted.

4. **Click** on **Next**. The Outlook Import dialog box will appear.

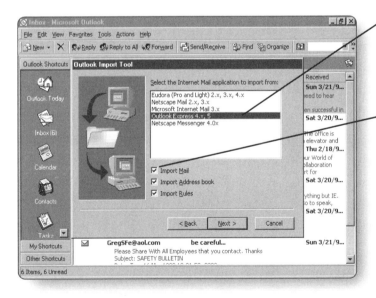

5. **Click** on the **program** from which you want to import the messages. The program will be highlighted.

6. **Click** on the **types of items** you want to import to select them. A check mark will appear next to the selected types.

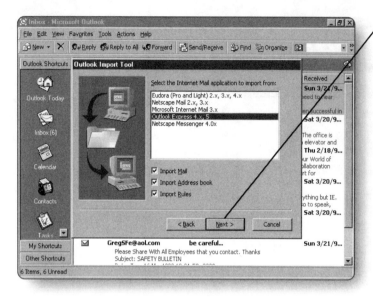

7. Click on **Next** and continue the import instructions as applicable for your selections.

8. Click on **Finish** when you reach the end of the Wizard. The Import and Export wizard will close and the items you selected will be imported.

8

Using the Address Book

Many e-mail addresses are long and filled with special symbols or characters. Outlook has an address book to keep all of your e-mail addresses handy. This reduces the chance of mistyping an address, which could send your e-mail message to the wrong person or cause a delay in delivery. The address book also gives you quick access to the e-mail addresses in your Contacts folder. In this chapter, you'll learn how to:

- Add new addresses
- Use the Contacts folder as your address book
- Use Personal Distribution Lists
- Edit Personal Distribution Lists
- Delete Address Book entries

Creating New E-mail Addresses

If you are sending an e-mail message to some people and think that you may need to write to them again, it's a good idea to add the addresses to your address book. If you work for a company, many e-mail addresses may already be stored in the Global Address List. In this section, you'll learn how to add an address to your Personal Address Book.

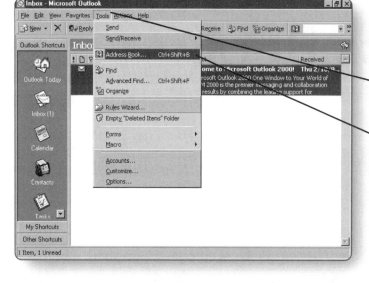

1. Click on **Tools**. The Tools menu will appear.

2. Click on **Address Book**. The Address Book window will appear.

NOTE

If your installation of Outlook is configured for Corporate and Workgroup use, your Address Book may look differently.

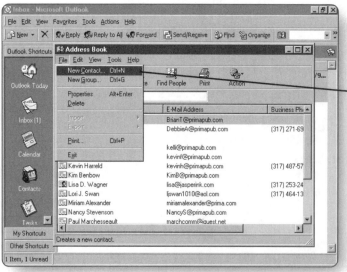

3. Click on **File**, and then on **New Contact**. The Properties dialog box for the new entry will open.

4. Type the **person's first, middle, and last name** as you would like it to appear in the address book. The full name will appear in the Display text box.

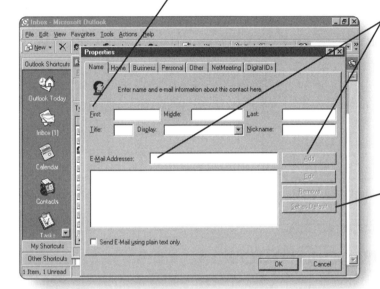

5. Type the **person's e-mail address** in the E-mail Addresses text box and **click** on **Add**. The new address will be added to the list of e-mail addresses for this contact.

TIP

If you have more than one e-mail address for this contact, click on the preferred one and click on Set as Default. Outlook will automatically use the default address each time unless you specify otherwise.

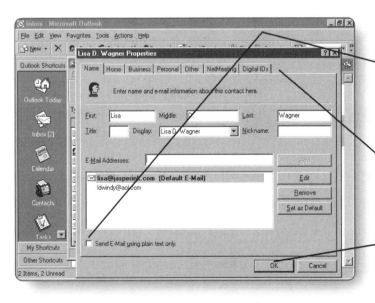

6. Click on **Send E-Mail using plain text only** if you know that the recipient cannot receive messages in other formats.

7. Click on the **other tabs** to enter additional information if desired, such as a street address or phone number.

8. Click on **OK**. The Address Book will reappear.

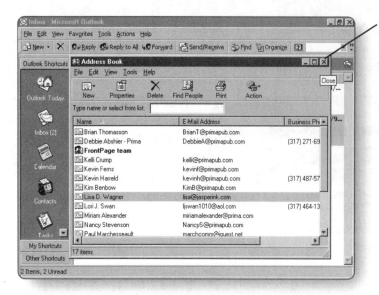

9. Click on the **Address Book Close button**. You will return to the Inbox.

Using Groups

You know that you can send a message to multiple people by typing their names in the To box. If you send messages to the same group of people on a regular basis, creating an e-mail group will save you time and will guarantee that you don't forget anyone.

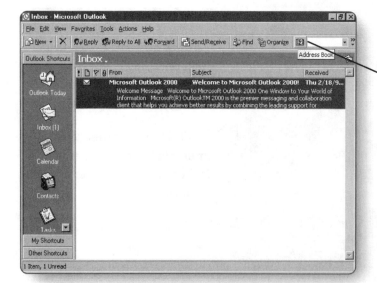

1. Click on the **Address Book button**. The Address Book window will appear.

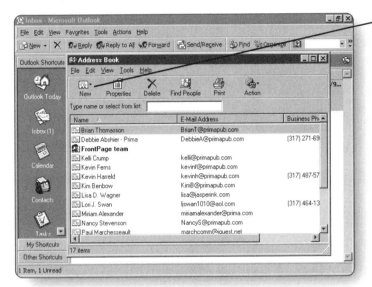

2. Click on the **New button**. The Properties dialog box for the new box will open.

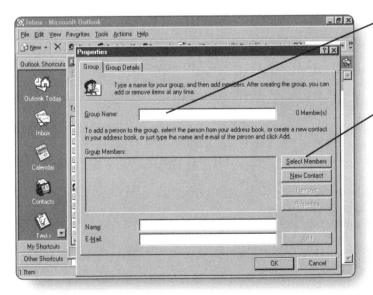

3. Type a **name** for the new group in the Group Name: text box. The name will appear in the box.

4. Click on **Select Members** to add existing e-mail addresses to your new group. The Select Group Members dialog box will open.

5. Click on a **name** in the list on the left. The name will be selected.

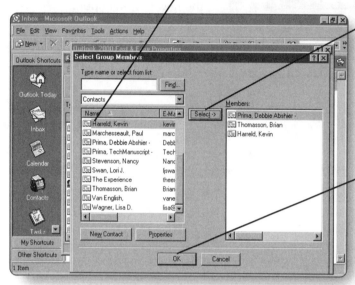

6. Click on the **Select button**. The name will appear in the Members list on the right.

7. Repeat steps 5 and 6 until all of the members are included in the Group list.

8. Click on **OK**. The Address Book will reappear and your new group will appear on the list.

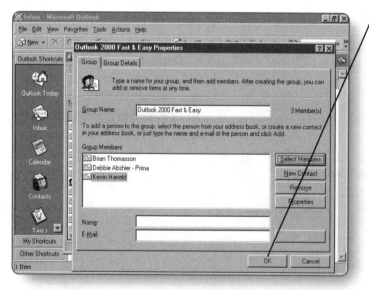

9. Click on **OK**. The Properties dialog box will close.

Editing E-mail Groups

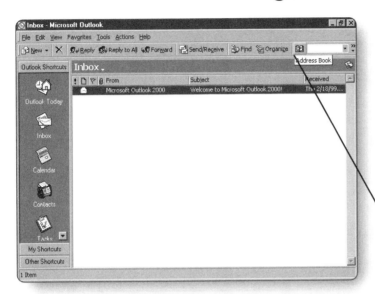

When you store your Group Lists in the Personal Address Book, it is your responsibility to keep them up to date. For example, if you have a list with members of a committee, you will need to edit the list as new members join and others leave the committee.

1. Click on the **Address Book button**. The contents of your Personal Address Book will appear.

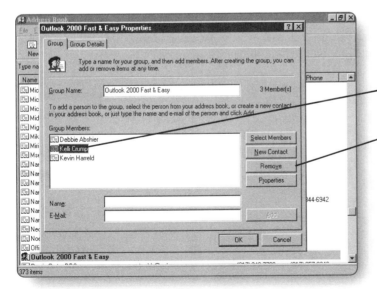

2. Click twice on the **group** you want to edit. The Properties dialog box will open.

3. Click on a **name**. The name will be selected.

4. Click on the **Remove button**. The name will be removed from the Group list.

> ### NOTE
> Removing a name from this list does not remove it from the Address Book or other groups, just the group you're working with.

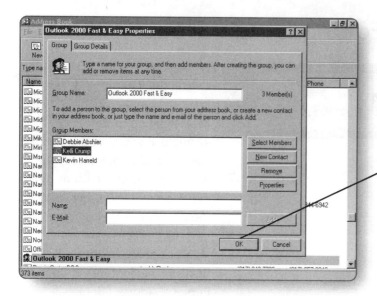

TIP

Click on New Contact to create a new contact not already in your address book.

5. Click on **OK**. The Address Book will reappear.

Deleting Address Book Entries

You may create an e-mail group for a project and no longer need the group when the project is complete. It's easy to delete entries from the Personal Address Book.

1. Click on the **entry** in the Address Book that you want to delete. It will be selected.

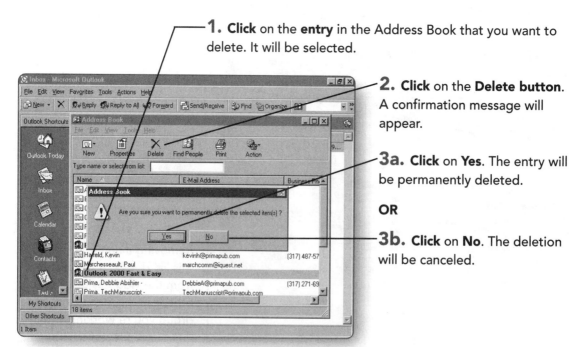

2. Click on the **Delete button**. A confirmation message will appear.

3a. Click on **Yes**. The entry will be permanently deleted.

OR

3b. Click on **No**. The deletion will be canceled.

9

Sending and Receiving Faxes

Outlook 2000 includes a special feature that enables you to send faxes using your modem. With a few minor differences, you use the same steps to send a fax as you would to send an e-mail message. You can also receive faxes from any fax machine and view them from your Outlook Inbox. In this chapter, you'll learn how to:

- Install and set up Outlook's faxing software
- Create a fax
- Attach a document to a fax
- Add fax numbers to your contacts
- Send a fax from within another application
- View and print a fax that you received

Installing Symantec WinFax Starter Edition

Before you can send or receive faxes in Outlook, you need to install and configure your faxing service if it has not already been set up for you.

Running the Setup Wizard

The first time you start Outlook, the Symantec WinFax Starter Edition Setup Wizard runs. The wizard steps you through setting your modem information and cover page preferences.

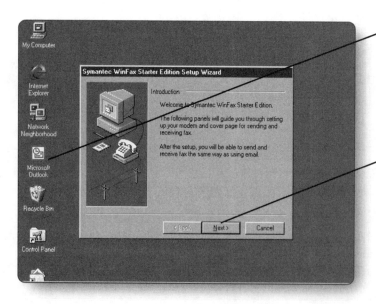

1. Double-click on the **Outlook shortcut** on the desktop. Outlook will launch and the Symantec WinFax Starter Edition Setup Wizard will appear.

2. Click on **Next**. The User Information page will appear.

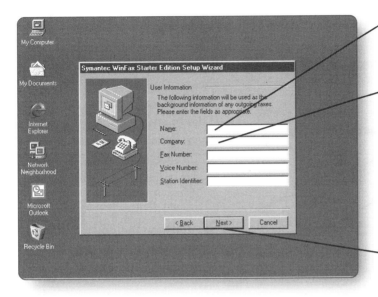

3. **Click** in the **Name: text box**.

4. **Type** your **name**.

5. **Press tab** to move to the next text box.

6. **Type** your **company name**, if any.

7. **Complete** the **remaining fields**.

8. **Click** on **Next**. The Address Information page will appear.

9. **Repeat steps 3–5** to complete the remaining wizard pages.

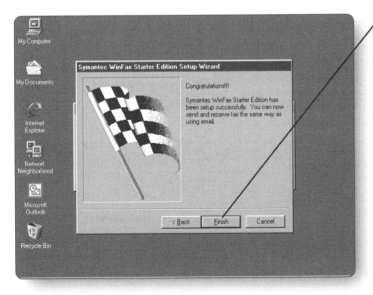

10. **Click** on **Finish** to complete the setup. The Setup Wizard will close. Outlook will open and display the contents of your Inbox.

NOTE

You may be prompted to register your version of WinFax Starter Edition. If so, click on Next to complete the wizard, or click on Skip to close the wizard and register later.

Creating a New Fax

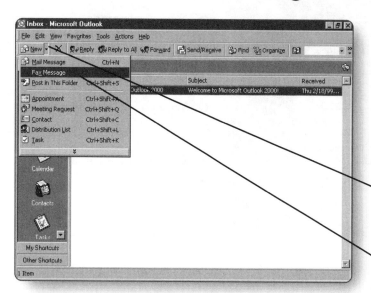

You can create and send faxes quickly and easily in Outlook, using nearly the same steps you take to create and send e-mail messages. The biggest difference is in the way Outlook handles the message after you click Send.

1. **Click** on the **down arrow** next to the New button. A drop-down menu will appear.

2. **Click** on **Fax Message**. A new, blank fax window will appear.

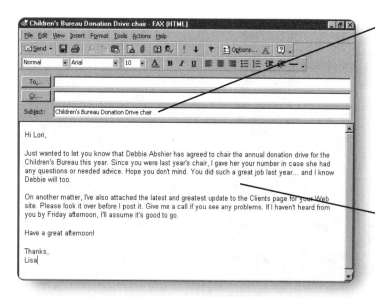

2. **Click** in the **Subject: text box**.

3. **Type** a **subject** for your fax message.

4. **Press** the **Tab key** to move the cursor to the message window.

5. **Type** your **message**. The information you type here will appear on the cover page of the fax.

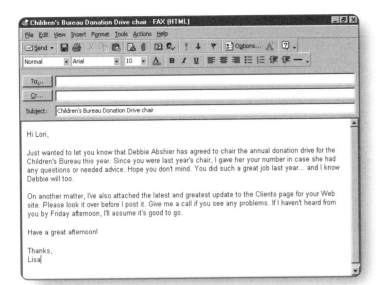

6. Format the **text** as desired and check for spelling errors. (See Chapter 4, "Creating New Messages," for help.)

NOTE

If your fax is complete with just a message on the cover page, you can skip the next section. If you want to attach a document to the fax cover page, continue to the next section.

Faxing an Office Document

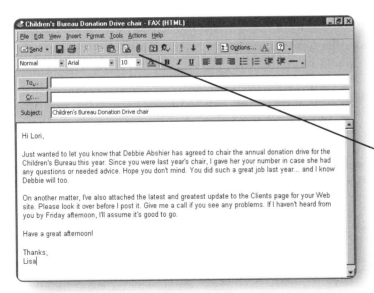

Outlook can convert any Office document to a faxable format. The recipient will receive a printed copy of the document on his or her fax machine along with your cover page.

1. Click on the **Insert File button**. The Insert File dialog box will open.

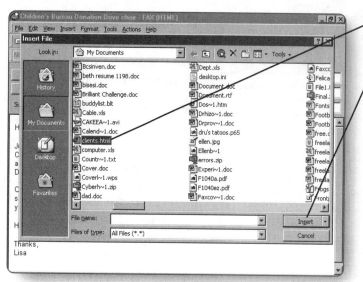

2. Click on the **file** you want to attach. It will be selected.

3. Click on **Insert**. The dialog box will close and the file will appear in a window at the bottom of the message.

TIP

If you need to create a new contact, see Chapter 8, "Using the Address Book."

Entering the Fax Number

Every fax must have a telephone number to dial to send the fax. You can store fax numbers in your Contacts or Address Book, along with that person's name, e-mail address, and other important information.

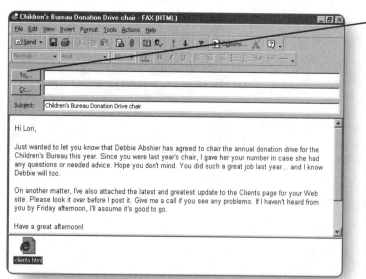

1. Click on the **To button** to access the Address Book. The Select Names dialog box will open.

NOTE

If you're certain the person's fax number is already in the address book, you can type the name directly in the text box.

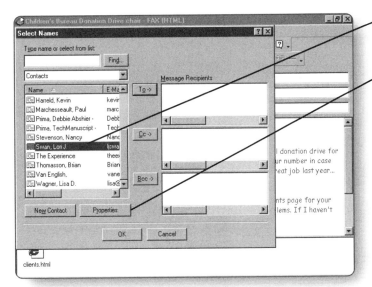

2. Click on a **name** from the list. It will be highlighted.

3. Click on **Properties**. The Properties dialog box for that name will open.

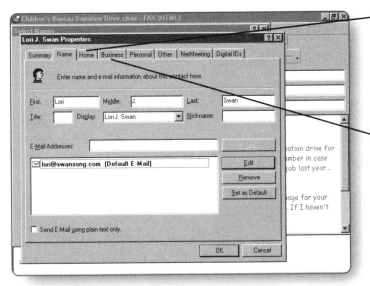

4a. Click the **Home tab** to enter a home fax number. The Home tab page will come to the front.

OR

4b. Click the **Business tab** to enter a business fax number. The Business tab page will come to the front.

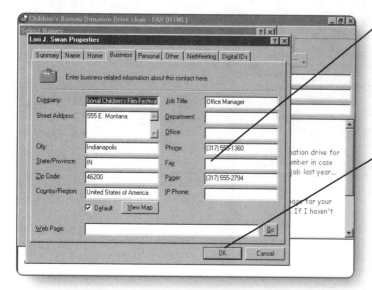

5. **Click** in the **text box** next to Fax.

6. **Type** the **number**. Include the area code if it is different than yours.

7. **Click** on **OK**. The fax number will be saved in the address book. The Properties dialog box will close and the Select Names dialog box will reappear.

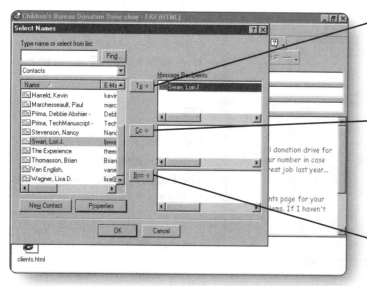

8a. **Click** on the **To button**. The fax will be addressed to the selected individual.

OR

8b. **Click** on the **Cc button**. A carbon copy of the fax will be addressed to the selected individual.

OR

8c. **Click** on the **Bcc button**. A blind carbon copy of the fax will be addressed to the selected individual.

NOTE

The terms *carbon copy* (Cc) and *blind carbon copy* (Bcc) are holdovers from the days when memos and letters were duplicated by placing a sheet of carbon paper between two sheets of paper. Traditionally, you "cc" someone as a matter of courtesy or information. A Blind cc is a copy sent to a third recipient without the original receiver's (the name or names in the To and Cc boxes) knowledge.

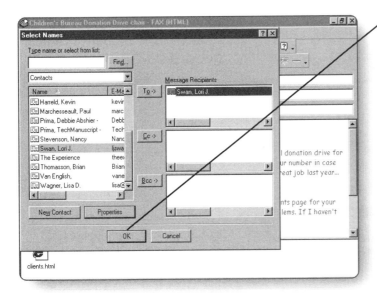

9. Click on **OK**. The Select Names dialog box will close. The fax recipients will appear in the appropriate boxes.

NOTE

You can send a fax to multiple people by separating their names with semicolons or commas in the To text box. You also can use faxes with e-mail addresses in the same message. When sending, Outlook will send the message to each individual as either an e-mail or a fax, depending on the information you specified.

NOTE

You can set sending options for your fax, such as a specific delivery time or the importance or sensitivity level. For more information, see Chapter 4, "Creating New Messages."

Sending the Fax

After you've written the fax, attached any appropriate documents, addressed it to the appropriate people, and set all of the available options, your fax is ready to send.

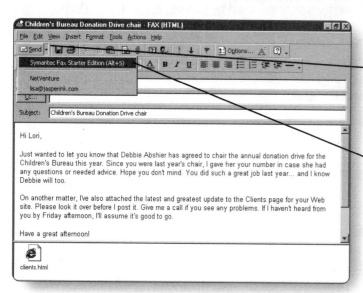

1. Click on the **down arrow** next to Send to choose the fax service. A list of available services will appear.

2. Click on **Symantec Fax Starter Edition**. Outlook will close the fax window and begin sending the fax.

If you attached a document, Outlook will notify you as it converts the document into a fax. After a few moments, Outlook will ask you to verify the fax number.

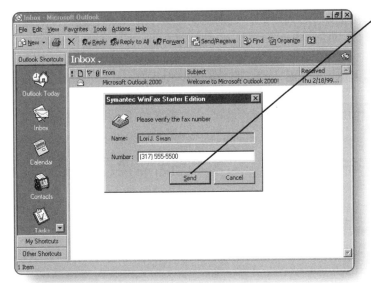

3. Click on **Send** after you verify the number. Outlook will close the message box and begin dialing. A status message will appear to let you know how the fax is progressing. When the process is complete, the status message will close and Outlook will return you to the Inbox.

NOTE

When you send a fax, it temporarily moves to the Outbox. After the fax has been sent, it moves to the Sent Items folder, where a copy of the fax is stored along with other e-mails and faxes you've sent.

Faxing a Document Directly from Another Application

If you have an Office document that you want to fax to someone, you don't have to go to the trouble of opening Outlook and creating a new fax message. Instead, save time by faxing the document directly from within the application you're working in. In the following steps, you learn to fax a document from within Microsoft Word.

1. Click on **Save**. Word saves any recent changes you made to the document.

2. Click on **File**. The File menu will open.

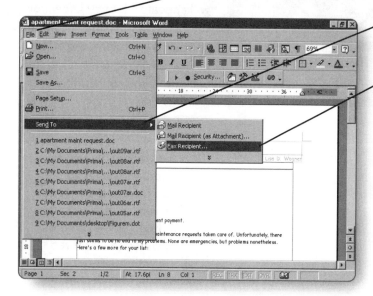

3. Click on **Send To**. The Send To submenu will open.

4. Click on **Fax Recipient**. The Fax Wizard will appear.

5. Click on **Next**. The first Wizard screen will appear.

6. Complete the **Wizard** and **click** on **Finish**. Outlook will close the Wizard and send the fax. A status message will appear to let you know how the fax is progressing. When the process is complete, the status message will close and Word will return you to the open document.

Receiving a Fax

Using Outlook, you can receive a fax with your modem. Any faxes you receive will appear in your Inbox along with your incoming messages, appointment requests, and other items you receive. You can view and print any fax you receive, or forward it to another person, much like an e-mail message.

NOTE

Outlook must be running before you can receive a fax. You can minimize Outlook to run in the background if you want to use other applications while you wait for the fax.

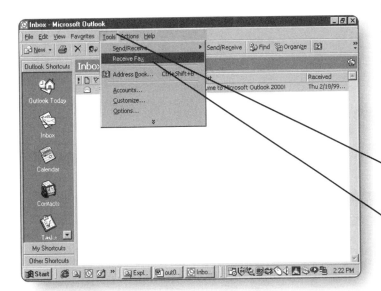

1. Open Microsoft Outlook if it is not already open.

2. Click on **Tools**. The Tools menu will appear.

3. Click on **Receive Fax**. Outlook will initialize your modem and prepare to receive a fax from an outside caller.

When Outlook detects a call, a status message will appear while the fax is being received. When complete, the new fax moves to your Inbox and appears as an unread message.

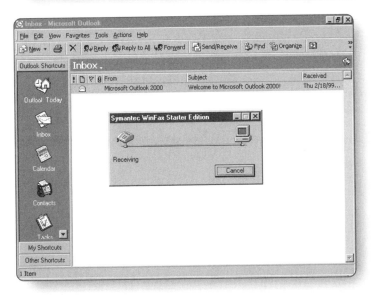

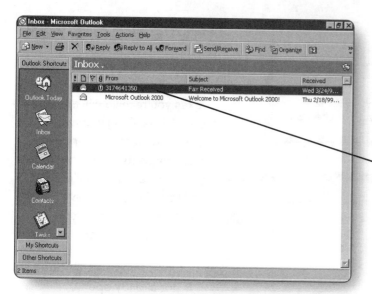

Viewing and Printing a Fax

After you receive a fax, you can open it to view its contents or print it for future reference.

1. Click twice on the **fax message** in the Inbox. The fax will open and a status report will appear.

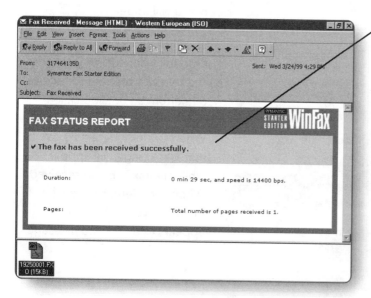

2. Double-click on the **attached document** to view the fax. The Quick Fax Viewer will open and the faxed document will appear.

NOTE

You may be prompted to either open the file or save it to disk. If so, click on Open It and click on OK.

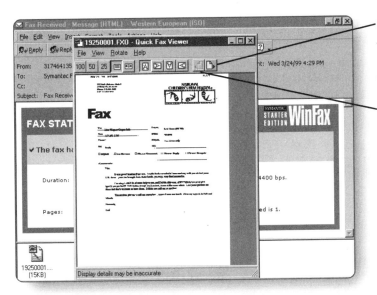

3a. Click on the **Next button** to see additional pages.

OR

3b. Click on the **Previous button** to see preceding pages.

4. Click on the **View buttons** to get a closer look at the document. You can choose from the following options:

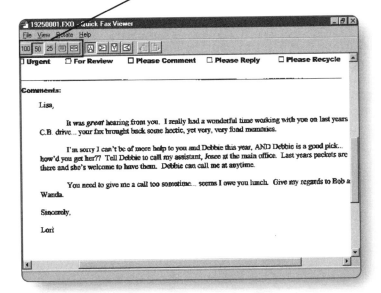

- **100%.** The fax will appear at its actual size.

- **50%.** The fax will appear at 50% of its actual size.

- **25%.** The fax will appear at 25% of its actual size.

- **View Whole Page.** Quick Fax Viewer will display the entire first page of the fax.

- **View Page Width.** Quick Fax Viewer will adjust the view to fill the Viewer window.

5. Click on the **Rotate button** to adjust the orientation of a fax that was received sideways or upside down. You can choose from the following Rotate options:

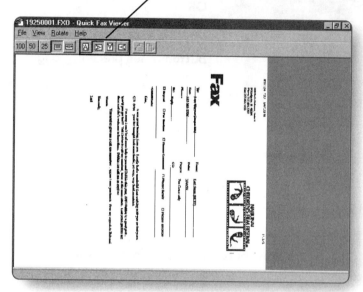

- **None**. Does not rotate (or restore the original orientation).

- **Rotate 90**. Rotates the fax 90 degrees clockwise.

- **Upside Down**. Rotates the fax 180 degrees clockwise.

- **Rotate 270**. Rotates the fax 270 degrees clockwise.

6. Click on **File, Print** to print the fax. The Print dialog box will open.

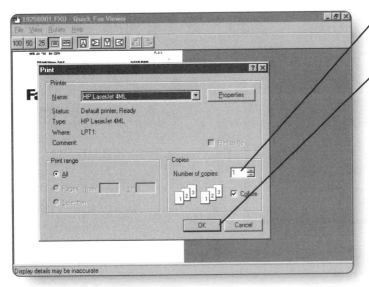

7. Enter the **number of copies** to print.

8. Click on **OK**. Outlook will print the fax.

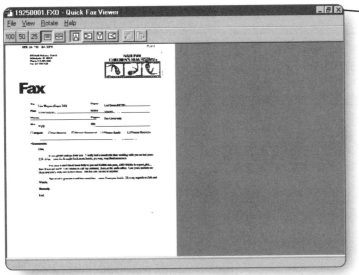

9. Click on the **Close button**. Outlook will close the viewer and the fax status report will reappear.

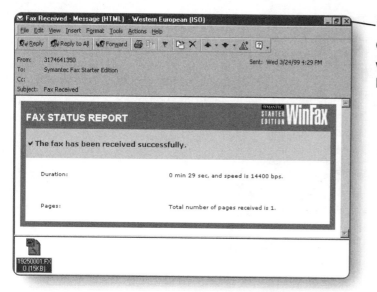

10. **Click** on the **Close button**. Outlook will close the message window and return you to the Inbox.

Changing Your Fax Options

You can change your fax settings at any time. If your fax number or contact information changes, for example, you can update your original settings easily.

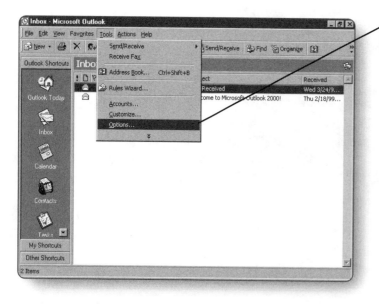

1. **Click** on **Tools, Options**. The Options dialog box will appear.

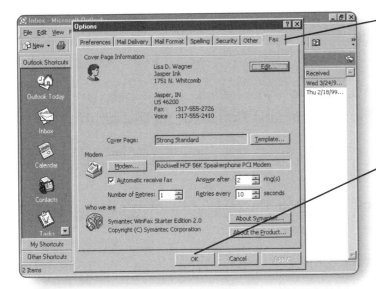

2. Click on the **Fax tab**. The available faxing options and settings will appear in the dialog box.

3. Edit your settings as needed.

4. Click on **OK**. The dialog box will close and your settings will be updated.

Part II Review Questions

1. How do you insert an automatic signature into your e-mail message? *See "Adding an Automatic Signature" in Chapter 4*

2. How do you send an e-mail message? *See "Sending a Mail Message" in Chapter 5*

3. How do you recall a message from the recipient's Inbox? *See "Recalling a Message" in Chapter 5*

4. How do you deliver a message at a specific time? *See "Delivering a Message at a Specific Time" in Chapter 5*

5. Name two methods for previewing the content of an e-mail message without opening the message. *See "Using AutoPreview" in Chapter 6*

6. Name three choices for responding to an e-mail message? *See "Responding to E-mail Messages" in Chapter 6*

7. How do you add an address to the Address Book from a message you have received? *See "Using Addresses from Messages You Have Received" in Chapter 8*

8. How do you add names to the junk e-mail list? *See "Adding Names to the Junk E-mail List" in Chapter 7*

9. How do you attach a document to a fax? *See "Faxing an Office Document" in Chapter 9*

10. How do you adjust the orientation of a fax that was received upside down? *"See Viewing and Printing a Fax" in Chapter 9*

PART III

Scheduling with the Calendar

10

Viewing Your Calendar

When scheduling appointments, it's sometimes necessary to see what is going on around the same time period but in a different calendar format. Outlook keeps your calendar of appointments and provides you with the flexibility to view your calendar in many different ways. In this chapter, you'll learn how to:

- Show different calendar views
- Use Organize to select different calendar views
- Create your own views
- Use the Date Navigator
- Move to dates in the past or future

Showing Different Calendar Views

There are three primary calendar views in Outlook: daily, weekly, and monthly. To choose any of these views, click on the corresponding toolbar button or menu command. Use views to control what appears on your screen.

1. **Click** on the **Calendar icon** on the Outlook bar. The Outlook calendar view will show in the Information viewer.

2. **Click** on **View**. The View menu will appear.

3. **Click** on **Day**, **Work Week**, **Week**, or **Month**. Your calendar will change accordingly.

TIP

The Standard toolbar contains buttons to quickly select these views.

Using Organize to Change Views

Outlook has a feature called Organize that lets you arrange your calendar. There are two ways to organize the calendar: by categories or by views. *Categories* are words or phrases (such as Business or Personal) that are used to keep track of items in Outlook. Use categories to organize your Christmas card mailing list, expense-related contacts, suppliers and vendors, or other details.

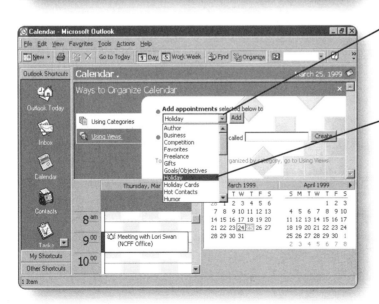

1. Click on **Organize**. The Ways to Organize Calendar pane will appear.

2. Click on **Using Categories**. The Organize pane will change, allowing you to organize your appointments by category.

3. Click on **any item(s)** in the calendar. The item(s) will appear selected.

4. Click on the **down arrow** next to Add appointments selected below to. A drop-down list will appear.

5. Click on **any category** in the drop-down list. It will be highlighted.

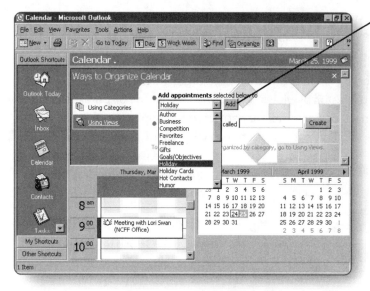

6. Click on the **Add button**. A message saying "Done!" will appear to the right of the Add button and the appointment(s) you've selected will be added to the category you chose.

Adding Categories

Outlook comes with numerous categories, but you can always add more.

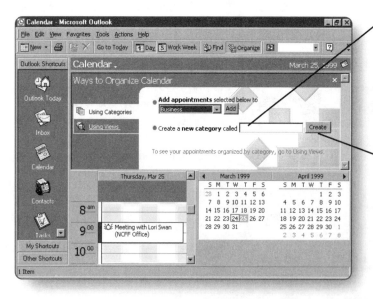

1. Click in the **text box** next to Create a new category called.

2. Type the **name** of the new category. The name will appear in the text box.

3. Click on **Create**. A message saying "Done!" will appear to the right of the Create button and your category will be created. Once this is done, you can add calendar items to the new category.

Changing Your Calendar View

By changing your calendar view, you can control the look of the calendar. Some views apply filters, which will display only certain items in the calendar, such as active appointments.

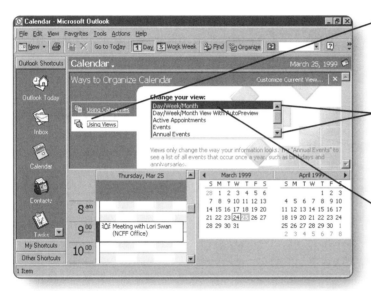

1. Click on **Using Views**. Your Organize pane will change, allowing you to organize your appointments visually.

2. Click on the **up or down arrows** to scroll through the list of views. Scroll until you find your selection.

3. Click on **any view**. The view will change accordingly.

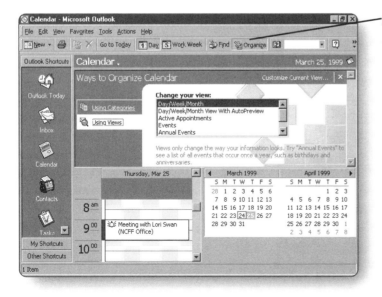

4. Click on **Organize**. The Organize pane will close.

Creating Your Own Views

If the Outlook views do not provide the options you want, you can create your own views.

1. Click on **View**. The View menu will appear.

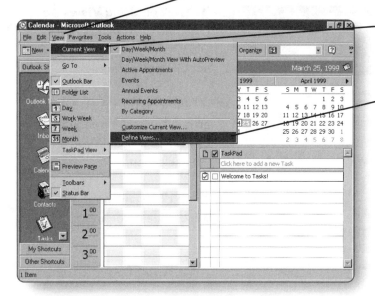

2. Click on **Current View**. The Current View submenu will appear.

3. Click on **Define Views**. The Define Views for Calendar dialog box will open.

4. Click on **New**. The Create a New View dialog box will open.

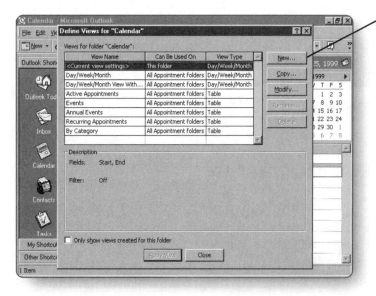

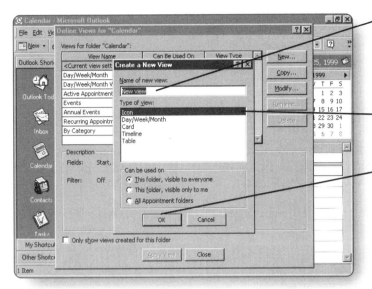

5. Type the **name** of the new view. The name will appear in the Name of new view: text box.

6. Click on a **type of view**. The view will be selected.

7. Click on **OK**. The View Settings dialog box will open.

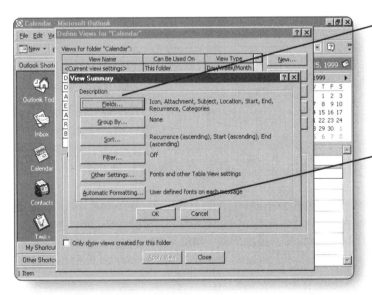

8. Click on the **description buttons** to choose the view settings. Adjust as many of these settings as you like. The dialog box will change to reflect your settings.

9. Click on **OK**. The View Settings dialog box will close.

10. **Click** on the **Close button**. The Define Views dialog box will close and the calendar will reappear in the Information viewer.

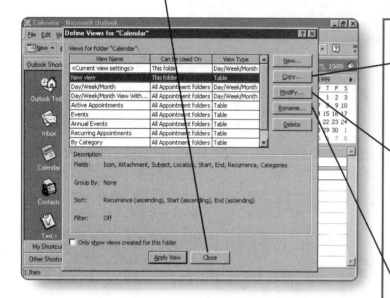

TIP

To copy an existing view and make changes to the copy, click on **Copy**, then follow the previous steps 5-10.

To change the settings for an existing view, click on **Modify**, then follow the previous steps 8 through 10 to modify the entry.

To change the name of an existing view, click on **Rename**, then enter the new name for the view and click on OK, then follow the previous steps 9 and 10.

Using the Date Navigator

The Date Navigator appears in the right corner of the calendar. A red box appears around today's date, and any day with items scheduled appear in bold. You can use the Date Navigator to jump to any date in the calendar to schedule an appointment or an event.

Viewing Different Months

1. **Click** on **any date**. You will jump to the date.

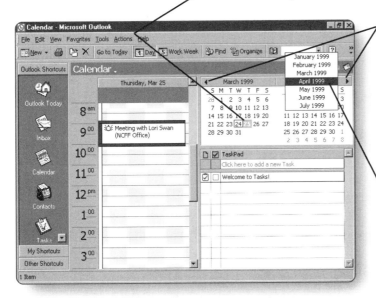

2a. **Click** on the **left or right arrow** next to the month to move backward or forward one month. The calendar will change to show the previous or following month.

OR

2b. **Click** on the **current month button** and select a new month from the pop-up list. The calendar will change to show the selected month.

Using the Date Navigator to Select a Series of Days

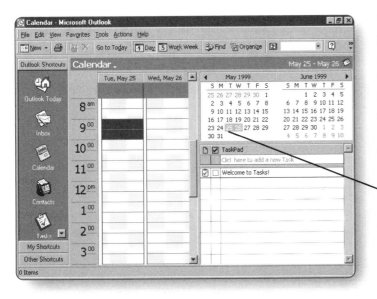

The Date Navigator can also be used to change the days that display on the calendar. If one of the pre-defined day, week, or month views doesn't fit your needs, you can use the Date Navigator to customize the days that display in the calendar.

1. **Click** on the **beginning date** in the Date Navigator. The date will be selected.

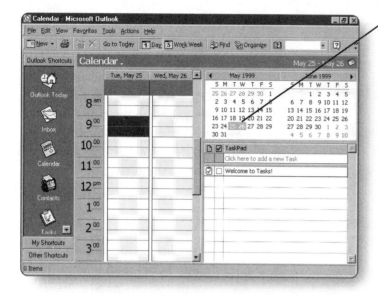

2. **Press** and **hold** the **Shift key** and **click** on the **ending date** in the Date Navigator. All dates from the initial date to the ending date will be selected, and you will see those days in the Information viewer.

Using the Date Navigator to Select Non-Contiguous Days

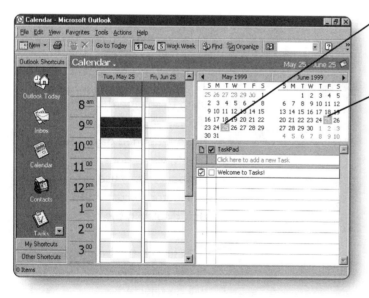

1. **Click** on the **beginning date** in the Date Navigator. It will be selected.

2. **Press** and **hold** the **Ctrl key** and **click** on **non-contiguous days** in the calendar. Only those days will be selected.

Going to a Specific Date

If the date you want doesn't appear in the Date Navigator, you can use the Go to Date feature to display it. Go to Date can also be used when you do not know the exact calendar date, but you know that it occurs three weeks from today or on a certain holiday.

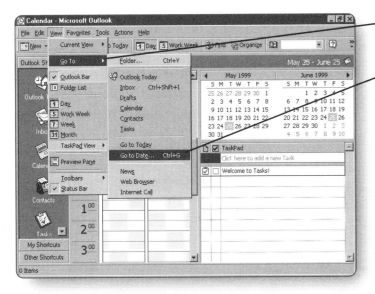

1. **Click** on **Go To**. The Go To menu will appear.

2. **Click** on **Go to Date**. The Go To Date dialog box will open.

NOTE

You may need to expand the menu to see the Go To Date command.

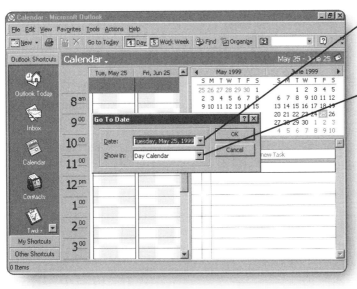

3. **Click** on the **down arrow** to the right of the Date: list box and select a particular date.

4. **Click** on the **down arrow** to the right of the Show in: list box and select a view.

If you don't know the particular date, there are numerous phrases you can type in the Date: list box on the Go To Date dialog box. Here are a few you might find helpful:

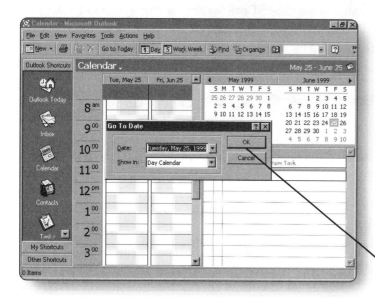

- **Dates**. You can type "5 weeks from today," "1st week in September," or "3 wks ago."

- **Description of Dates**. You can type "now," "today," "yesterday," or "last week."

- **Holidays**. You can type any holidays that occur at the same time every year, such as President's Day, Boxing Day, or Cinco de Mayo.

5. Click on **OK**. The Go To Date dialog box will close and you will return to the Calendar.

TIP

After using the Date Navigator, you may need to return to today's date. Click on the Go to Today button to return the calendar to the current date.

11

Scheduling Appointments

It's difficult to remember and keep track of all the appointments and obligations on your calendar. When you use Outlook to manage your appointments, you can keep them all in one location and quickly edit or delete them, should the appointment be changed or canceled. In this chapter, you'll learn how to:

- Create an appointment
- Set up a reminder
- Move an appointment to a different date or time
- Schedule a recurring appointment
- Delete an appointment

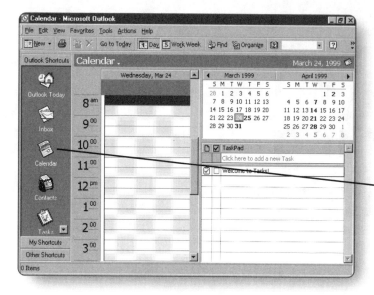

Creating an Appointment

When you want to schedule an appointment in Outlook, you first select the date and then create the appointment.

1. Click on the **Calendar icon** on the Outlook bar. The Calendar will show in the Information viewer.

2. Click on **File**. The File menu will appear.

3. Click on **New**. The New submenu will appear.

4. Click on **Appointment**. The Appointment dialog box will open.

5. **Click** in the **Subject: text box**.

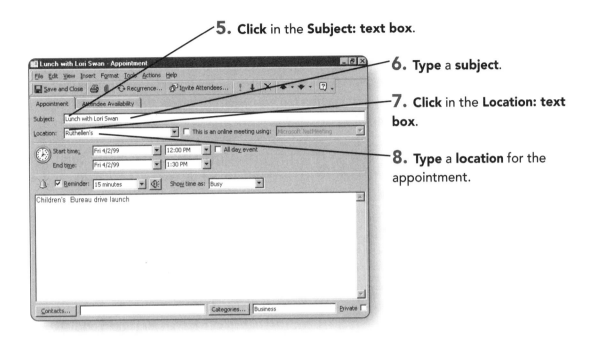

6. **Type** a **subject**.

7. **Click** in the **Location: text box**.

8. **Type** a **location** for the appointment.

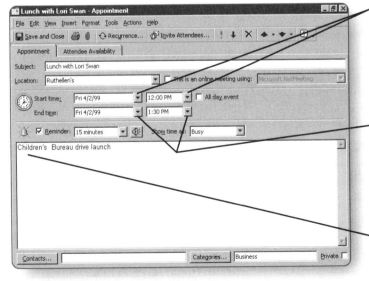

9. **Click** on the **down arrows** next to the Start time: list boxes and click on a starting date and time. A date and time will be selected.

10. **Click** on the **down arrows** next to the End time: list boxes and click on an ending date and time. An end time will be selected.

11. **Click** on the **notes section** and **begin typing** to add any notes or comments related to the appointment. The notes will appear in the window.

Setting a Reminder

A reminder is a great way to guarantee that you won't miss any important appointments. Once a reminder is activated, you can dismiss the reminder or click on the Snooze button and have the reminder pop up again later.

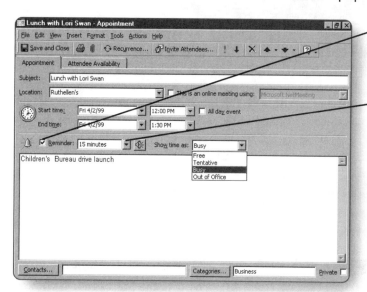

1. Click on the **Reminder: check box**. A check mark will be placed in the box.

2. Click on the **down arrow** next to Reminder. A list of times will appear.

3. Select the **amount of time** the Reminder should appear prior to the appointment. The reminder will be selected.

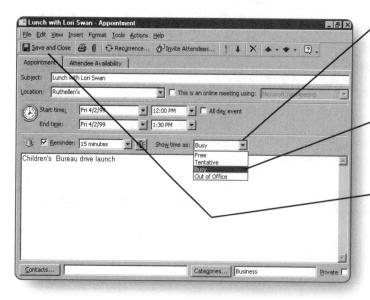

4. Click on the **down arrow** next to the Show time as: list box. A list of options will appear.

5. Click on **Free, Tentative, Busy,** or **Out of Office**. The choice will be selected.

6. Click on **Save and Close**. The appointment will be saved and closed.

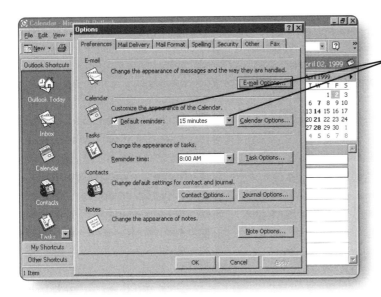

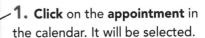

TIP

You can set the default reminder time by choosing Tools, Options, and selecting the Preferences tab. Turn the default reminder off or on and set the default reminder time.

Moving the Appointment to a Different Date and Time

Once you have scheduled an appointment, it's easy to change the time or day of the appointment. Appointments can be dragged to any day on the Date Navigator to reschedule the appointment.

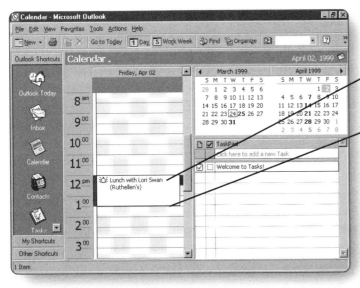

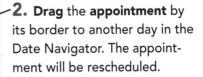

1. Click on the **appointment** in the calendar. It will be selected.

2. Drag the **appointment** by its border to another day in the Date Navigator. The appointment will be rescheduled.

Changing Appointment Times

You can change the appointment time by dragging the appointment boundaries on the calendar.

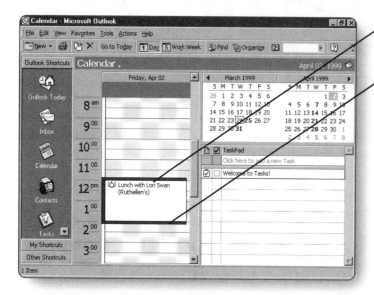

1. **Click** on the **appointment** in the calendar. It will be selected.

2. **Move** the **mouse pointer** over the top or bottom border of the appointment. The mouse pointer will change to a double-headed arrow.

3. **Click** and **drag** either **border** to increase or decrease the length of the appointment. The appointment will be changed.

TIP

You can change the starting and ending times of the appointment by placing the mouse pointer over the left border of the appointment. The pointer changes to a four-sided arrow, and you can click and drag the appointment to a different time.

NOTE

Another way to change the date, time, or duration of an appointment is to double-click on the appointment. When the appointment window opens, make the necessary changes, and then save and close the appointment.

Scheduling a Recurring Appointment

A *recurring appointment* is an appointment that occurs more than once at a regular time. The appointment can occur every day, week, month, or year. Outlook even lets you designate how the appointment occurs (for example, the first Thursday of every month or the 15th of every month).

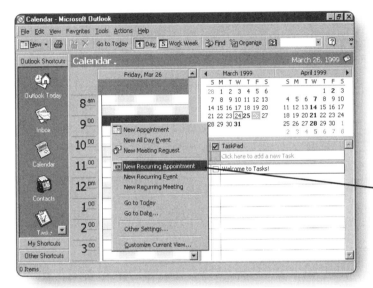

1. Right-click on the **calendar**. A shortcut menu will appear.

2. Click on **New Recurring Appointment**. The Appointment Recurrence dialog box will open.

3. Click on the **down arrow** to the right of the Start: list box and click on a start time. The starting time will be selected.

4. Click on the **down arrow** to the right of the End: list box and click on an ending time. The ending time will be selected.

5. Click on the **down arrow** to the right of the Duration: list box and click on a duration. The duration will be indicated.

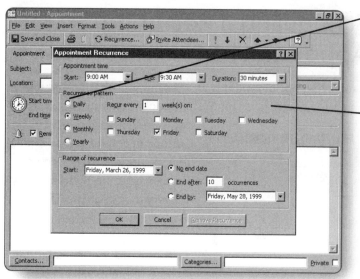

6. Click on **one of the four Recurrence pattern option buttons.** The option will be selected.

7. Click on the **options** to the right of the recurrence pattern to establish the pattern. The pattern will be selected.

NOTE

The window next to the recurrence pattern changes depending on the recurrence pattern that you select. Your screen may not look like the figure if you have selected a different recurrence pattern.

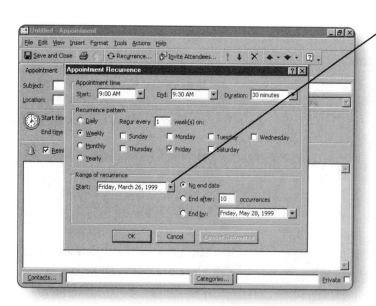

8. Click on the **down arrow** to the right of the Start: list box to establish the beginning range of recurrence.

There are several options for ending the appointment. They are:

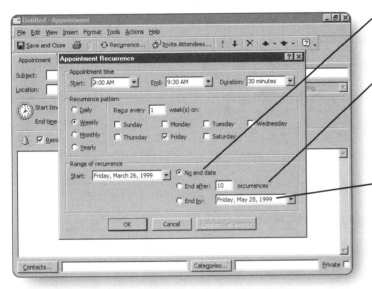

- **No end date**. The appointment will be repeated indefinitely on the calendar.

- **End after "x" occurrences**. The appointment will be repeated on the calendar for a specific number of occurrences.

- **End by**. The appointment will not appear on the calendar after a certain date.

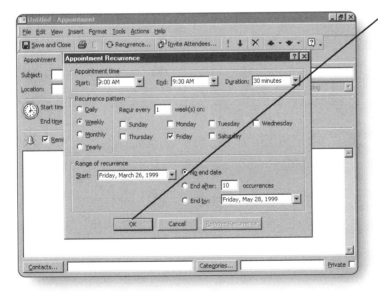

9. Click on **OK**. The Appointment Recurrence dialog box will close.

You can now follow the same steps that you followed earlier to fill in the Appointment window. Remember to save and close the appointment when you are finished.

Deleting an Appointment

If an appointment is canceled, it's important to delete the appointment from your calendar. If you work with others who may be viewing your calendar to schedule a meeting, it's best to delete appointments as soon as possible.

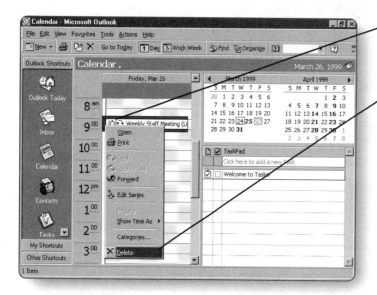

1. **Right-click** on the **appointment** in the calendar. A shortcut menu will appear.

2. **Click** on **Delete**. The appointment will be deleted.

NOTE

If you are deleting a recurring appointment, a message will ask if you want to delete all occurrences of the appointment or just the one occurrence.

12

Planning an Event

You have already learned how to schedule appointments. *Events* are special types of appointments that last 24 hours or more. Events are a great way to record such calendar items as birthdays, anniversaries, trade shows, or vacations. In this chapter, you'll learn how to:

- Create an event
- View and modify an event
- Schedule a recurring event
- Edit a recurring event
- Delete a recurring event

Creating an Event

Events can be split into two categories: an *annual event* or a *standard event*. A birthday is a perfect example of an annual event. It occurs on a particular day and it lasts all day. An example of a standard event is a seminar. A seminar can last one or several days. Events can be added to the calendar as easily as appointments.

1. **Click** on the **Calendar icon** on the Outlook bar. The contents of your Calendar will appear in the Information viewer.

2. **Right-click** on the **daily appointment area** of the calendar. A shortcut menu will appear.

3. **Click** on **New All Day Event**. The Event window will appear.

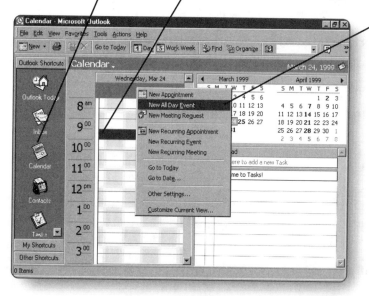

4. Click in the **Subject: text box**.

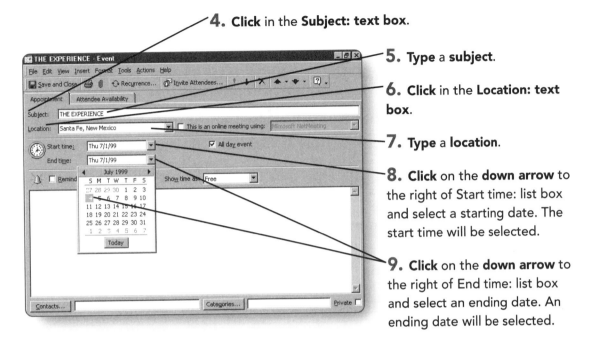

5. Type a **subject**.

6. Click in the **Location: text box**.

7. Type a **location**.

8. Click on the **down arrow** to the right of Start time: list box and select a starting date. The start time will be selected.

9. Click on the **down arrow** to the right of End time: list box and select an ending date. An ending date will be selected.

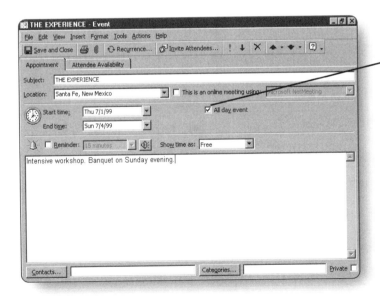

NOTE

The All day event check box is automatically selected for events. If you remove the check mark from the All day event check box, the event will automatically be changed to an appointment.

10. Click on the **Reminder check box** to set a reminder. A check mark will be placed in the box.

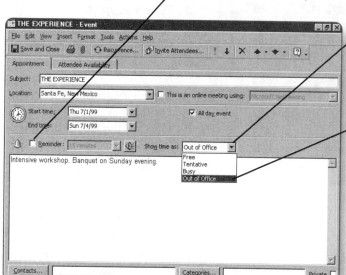

11. Click on the **down arrow** to the right of the Show time as: list box. A list of options will appear.

12. Click on **Free, Tentative, Busy,** or **Out of Office**. The choice will be selected.

NOTE

By default, events appear as free time on your calendar, while appointments appear as busy time.

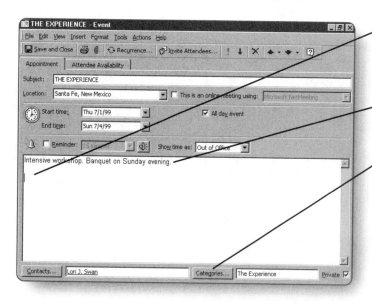

13. Click in the **text area**. An insertion point will be in the text area.

14. Type any **notes** regarding the event.

15. Click on the **Categories button** and add categories to the event, if desired. The categories will be selected.

16. Click on the **Save and Close button**. The event will be scheduled.

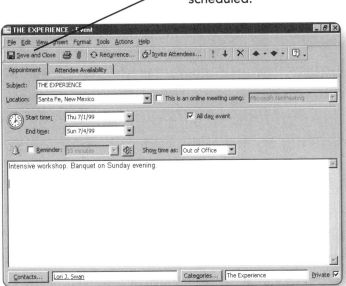

Viewing and Modifying Events

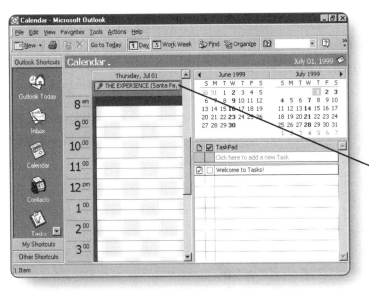

Events do not always appear in the same area as appointments. In Day view, they appear in the banner area, underneath the date. If you are in a monthly view, a shaded box surrounds events.

1. Click twice on the **event**. The Event window will appear.

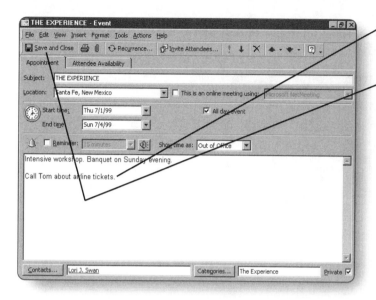

2. Type any **changes** to modify the event. The text will appear.

3. Click on the **Save and Close button**. Your changes will be saved and the Event window will close.

Scheduling a Recurring Event

An annual event, such as a birthday, is an example of a recurring event. Events can recur daily, weekly, monthly, or yearly.

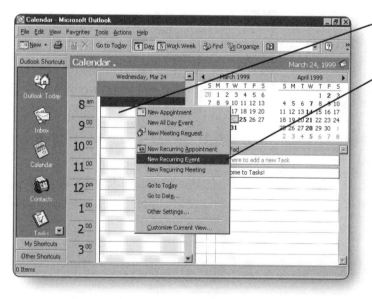

1. Right-click on the **calendar**. A shortcut menu will appear.

2. Click on **New Recurring Event**. The Appointment Recurrence dialog box will open.

3. Click on the **down arrow** to the right of the Start: list box and select a start time. A start time will be selected.

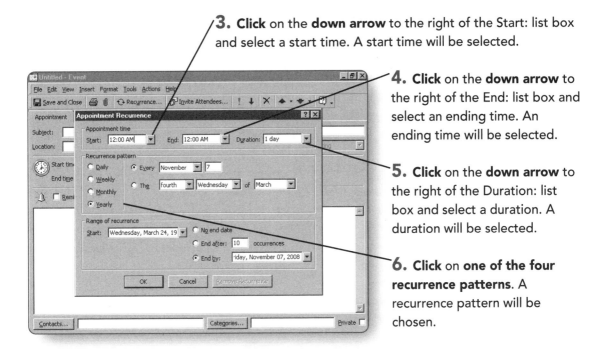

4. Click on the **down arrow** to the right of the End: list box and select an ending time. An ending time will be selected.

5. Click on the **down arrow** to the right of the Duration: list box and select a duration. A duration will be selected.

6. Click on **one of the four recurrence patterns**. A recurrence pattern will be chosen.

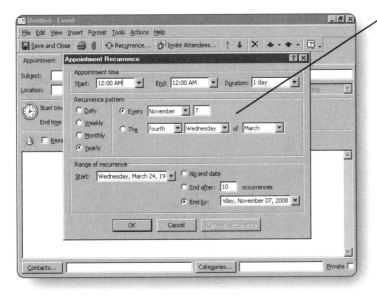

7. Click on the **options** to the right of the recurrence pattern to establish the pattern. An option will be selected.

NOTE

The windows next to the recurrence pattern change depending on the recurrence pattern selected. Your screen may not look like the figure if you have selected a different recurrence pattern.

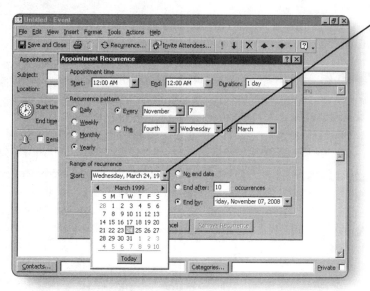

8. Click on the **down arrow** to the right of the Start: list box to establish the beginning range of recurrence.

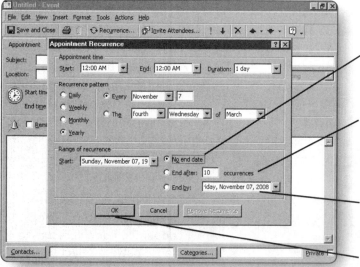

There are several options for ending the event. They are:

- **No end date**. The event will be repeated indefinitely on the calendar.

- **End after "x" occurrences**. The event will end after a specified number of occurrences.

- **End by**. The event will end by a certain date.

9. Click on **OK**. The Appointment Recurrence dialog box will close.

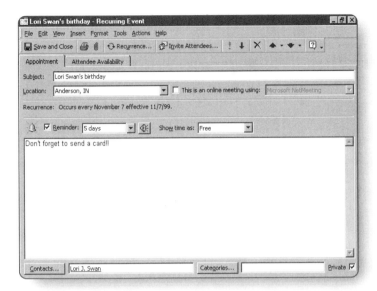

You can follow the same steps you followed earlier to fill in the Event window. Remember to save and close the event when you are finished.

> **NOTE**
> Recurring events are indicated on the calendar with a circular arrow icon.

Editing a Recurring Event

After an event has been scheduled, you may find that you need to make changes to a single instance of the event, or to the entire series. Outlook allows you to edit the event and to change the recurrence pattern.

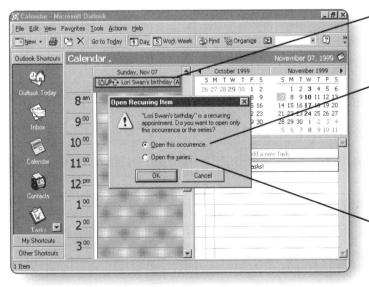

1. **Click twice** on the **event**. The Open Recurring Item dialog box will open.

2a. **Click** on the **Open this occurrence option button** to edit a single occurrence of the event. The option will be selected.

OR

2b. **Click** on the **Open the series option button** to edit the series of recurring events. The option will be selected.

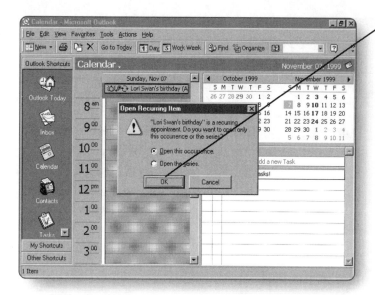

3. Click on **OK**. Either that occurrence of the event or the entire series will open, depending on your choice in step 2.

4. Click on the **Recurrence button** to change the recurrence pattern of the series. The Appointment Recurrence dialog box will open.

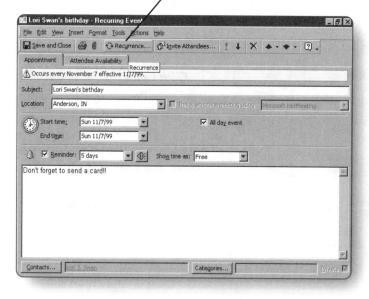

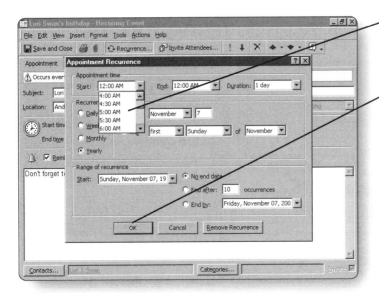

5. Type any **changes** to the recurrence pattern. The changes will be made.

6. Click on **OK**. The Appointment Recurrence dialog box will close.

7. Click on the **Save and Close button**. Your changes will be saved and the window will close.

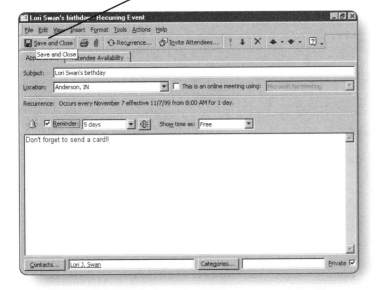

Deleting Recurring Events

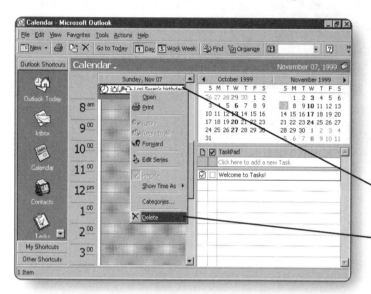

Once an event has been scheduled, you may have reason to delete the event. Do you have to search through the entire calendar, deleting each event? Of course not! Outlook can easily handle the situation for you.

1. Right-click on the **event**. A shortcut menu will appear.

2. Click on **Delete**. The Confirm Delete dialog box will open.

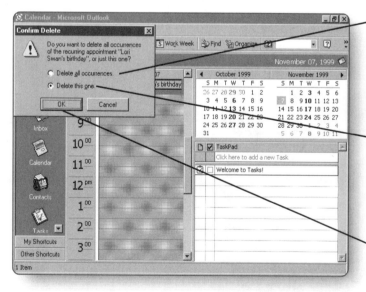

3a. Click on the **Delete all occurrences option button** to delete all instances of the event. The option will be selected.

OR

3b. Click on the **Delete this one option button** to delete the one selected instance of the event. The option will be selected.

4. Click on **OK**. Either this single event or every recurrence of it will be deleted, depending on the option you chose in step 3. The Confirm Delete dialog box will close.

13

Requesting a Meeting

Have you ever tried to coordinate a meeting with several people? Normally, several calls or e-mails fly back and forth before you can find a time that is convenient for everyone. If you are using Outlook on a network, you can use some powerful tools that are included in the program to take all of the hassle out of scheduling a meeting. In this chapter, you'll learn how to:

- Plan, reschedule, or cancel a meeting
- Create or respond to a new meeting request
- Include resources in the meeting request
- Schedule a recurring meeting
- Turn an appointment into a meeting

Planning a Meeting

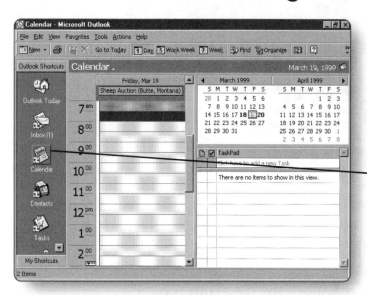

The most difficult part of scheduling a meeting is finding a time when everyone can attend. You can use the Plan a Meeting feature to quickly determine the best time for the meeting.

1. Click on the **Calendar icon** on the Outlook bar. The contents of your calendar will appear in the Information viewer.

2. Click on **Actions**. The Actions menu will appear.

3. Click on **Plan a Meeting**. The Plan a Meeting dialog box will open.

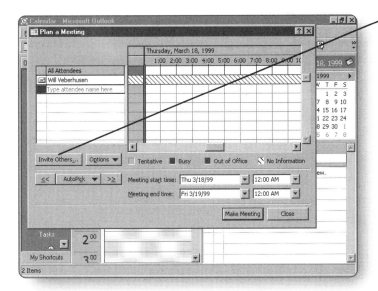

4. Click on the **Invite Others button**. The Select Attendees and Resources dialog box will open.

5. Click on a **name** in the address list to select the individual. The individual will be selected.

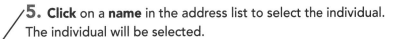

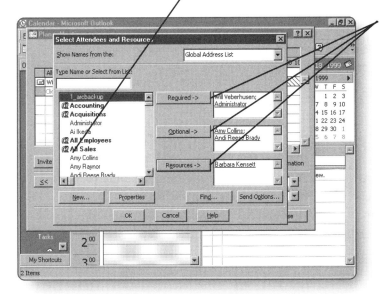

6. Click on **Required, Optional, or Resources**. The name will appear in the appropriate list.

NOTE

A resource can be a conference room or a piece of audiovisual equipment. If selected, resources will appear in the Location text box in the Meeting Request. The people who are required or optional will appear in the To line of the meeting request.

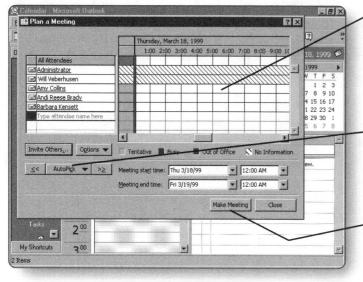

7a. **View** the **free and busy times** for each attendee. This is done manually for each attendee.

OR

7b. **Click** on the **AutoPick button**. Outlook will search for the next available free time for all attendees.

8. **Click** on the **Make Meeting button** when you have found a suitable meeting time. A new meeting request will appear.

> **TIP**
> If you don't want to use the Plan a Meeting feature, you can send a meeting request by clicking on the Calendar icon and then clicking on Actions, New Meeting Request.

Creating a Meeting Request

Now that you've planned your meeting, it's time to invite everyone. A meeting request is a lot like an e-mail message, but it has the added advantage of coordinating with the calendar.

1. **Type** a **subject** for the meeting in the Subject: text box.

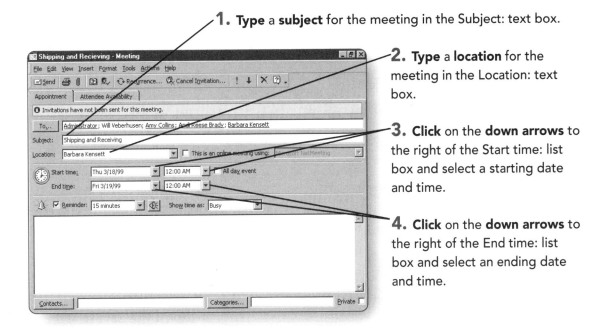

2. **Type** a **location** for the meeting in the Location: text box.

3. **Click** on the **down arrows** to the right of the Start time: list box and select a starting date and time.

4. **Click** on the **down arrows** to the right of the End time: list box and select an ending date and time.

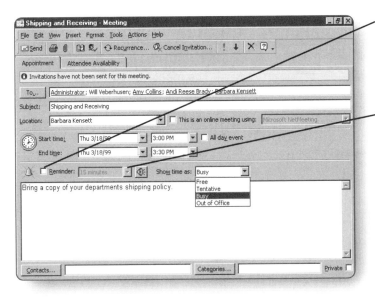

5. **Click** on the **Reminder: check box** to activate a meeting reminder. A check mark will be placed in the box.

6. **Click** on the **down arrow** next to Reminder. A list of times will appear.

7. **Select** the **amount of time** the Reminder should appear prior to the appointment. The reminder will be selected.

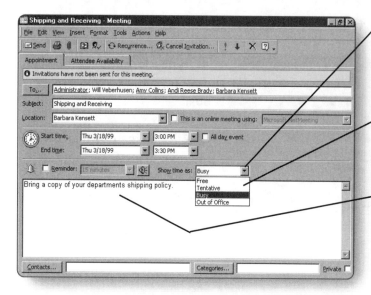

8. **Click** on the **down arrow** to the right of the Show time as: list box. A list of options will appear.

9. **Click** on **Free, Tentative, Busy,** or **Out of Office**. The choice will be selected.

10. **Type any notes** in the message text area. The text will appear in the text area.

> ### TIP
> Click on the Categories button if you want to add categories to the meeting request.

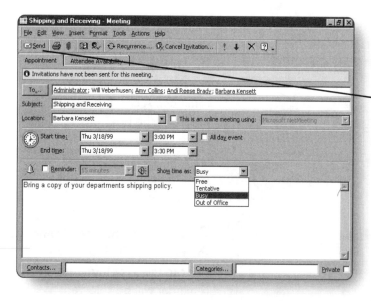

11. **Click** on the **Send button.** The meeting request will be sent.

Scheduling a Recurring Meeting

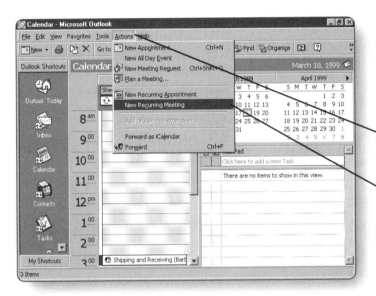

You can take any meeting and turn it into a recurring meeting. A recurring meeting can occur on any series of days, weeks, months, or years.

1. Click on **Actions**. The Actions menu will appear.

2. Click on **New Recurring Meeting**. The Appointment Recurrence dialog box will open.

3. Click on the **down arrow** to the right of the Start: list box and select a start time.

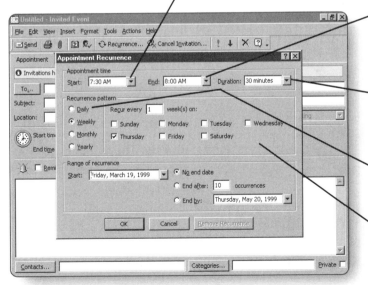

4. Click on the **down arrow** to the right of the End: list box and select an end time.

5. Click on the **down arrow** to the right of Duration and select a duration.

6. Click on **one of the four recurrence patterns**.

7. Click on the **options** to the right of the recurrence pattern to establish the pattern.

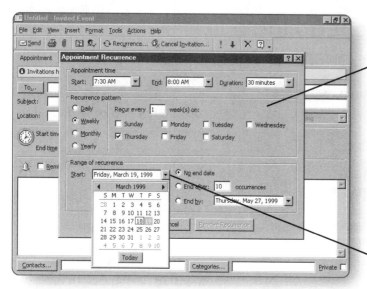

NOTE

The windows next to Recurrence pattern change depending on the recurrence pattern selected. Your screen may not look like the figure if you have selected a different recurrence pattern.

8. Click on the **down arrow** to the right of the Start: list box to establish the beginning range of recurrence.

There are several options for how the recurring meeting will appear on the calendar. They are:

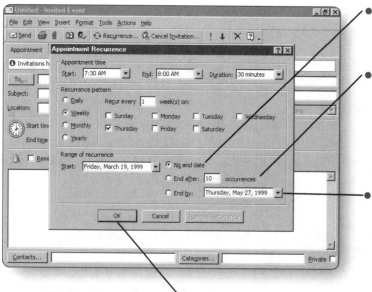

- **No end date**. The meeting will be repeated indefinitely on the calendar.

- **End after "x" occurrences**. The meeting will not appear on the calendar after a specified number of occurrences. The default number of occurrences is 10.

- **End by**. The meeting will not appear on the calendar after a certain date.

9. Click on **OK**. The Appointment Recurrence dialog box will close.

You can follow the same steps that you followed previously to fill in the meeting request. Remember to send the meeting request when you are finished.

Responding to a Meeting Request

When you receive a meeting request, you have three choices. You can accept, decline, or tentatively accept. If you accept or tentatively accept the meeting request, the meeting will automatically be added to your calendar. If you decline the request, the meeting will not be added to your calendar.

1. Click on the **Inbox icon** on the Outlook bar. The contents of your Inbox will appear in the Information viewer.

2. Click twice on the **meeting request**. The request will appear.

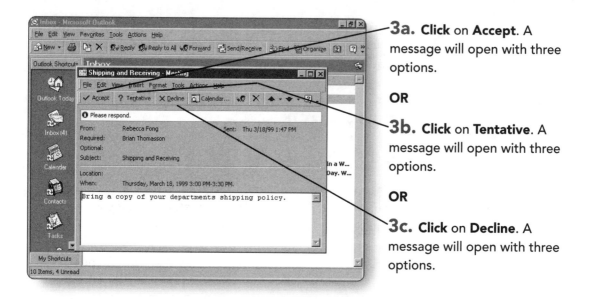

3a. Click on **Accept**. A message will open with three options.

OR

3b. Click on **Tentative**. A message will open with three options.

OR

3c. Click on **Decline**. A message will open with three options.

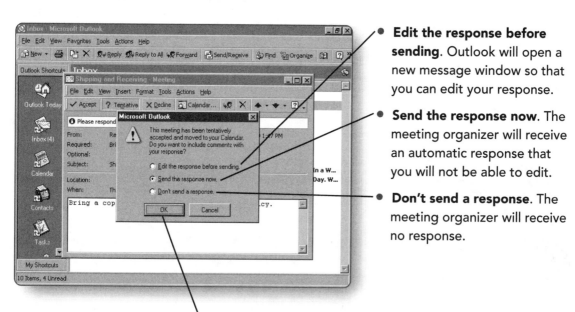

- **Edit the response before sending.** Outlook will open a new message window so that you can edit your response.

- **Send the response now.** The meeting organizer will receive an automatic response that you will not be able to edit.

- **Don't send a response.** The meeting organizer will receive no response.

4. Click on **OK**. The message window will close, and your choice will be registered. Also, your response will be sent to the sender unless you chose "Don't send a response" from the previous list.

Rescheduling a Meeting

Sometimes a meeting may need to be rescheduled. Outlook gives you a fast and easy way to inform everyone of the change.

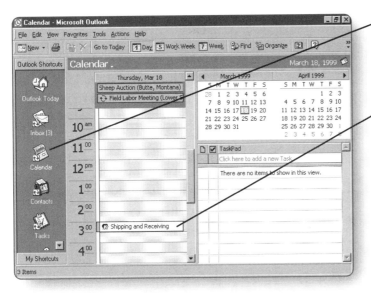

1. Click on the **Calendar icon** on the Outlook bar. The Calendar will appear in the Information viewer.

2. Click twice on the **meeting** in the calendar you want to edit. The Meeting window will appear.

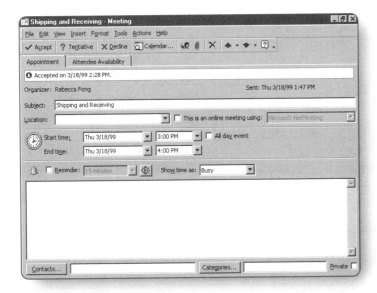

3. Type any **changes**, such as start time, end time, or location. The changes will be indicated.

4. Click on **Save and Close**. A message box will open.

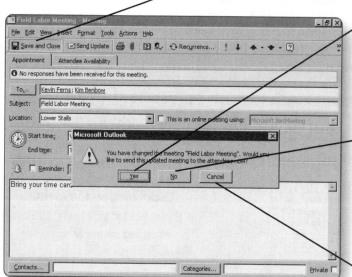

5a. Click on **Yes**. The change will be made and Outlook will send a message to update meeting attendees of the change.

OR

5b. Click on **No**. The change will be made, but Outlook will not send a message to update the meeting attendees of the change.

OR

5c. Click on **Cancel** to cancel any changes. The changes will be discarded.

Canceling a Meeting

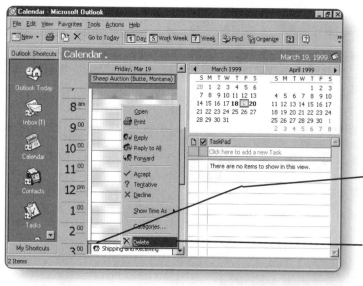

When a meeting has been canceled, it is important to update your calendar so that your schedule will be accurate. Canceling the meeting will also update the calendars of the people that you invited to the meeting.

1. Right-click on the **meeting** in the calendar. A shortcut menu will appear.

2. Click on **Delete**. A confirmation message box will open.

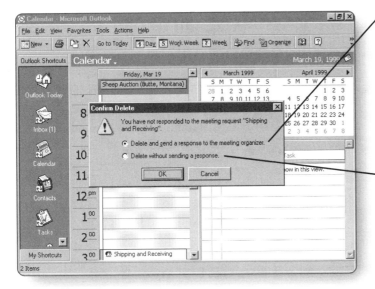

3a. **Click** on **Delete and send response to the meeting organizer** to notify the attendees. The cancellation will be sent and the meeting will be deleted from your calendar.

OR

3b. **Click** on **Delete without sending a response** to cancel the meeting without notifying attendees. The meeting will be deleted from your calendar.

NOTE

If you send a cancellation, the attendees will be notified with an e-mail message. When they receive the message, they can click on the Remove from Calendar button to delete the canceled meeting from their calendar.

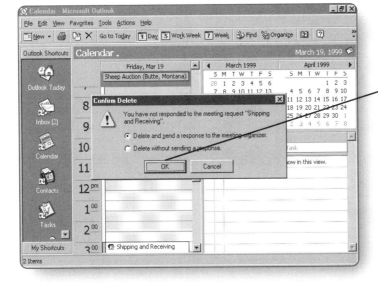

4. **Click** on **OK**. The meeting will be deleted and a cancellation may or may not be sent, depending on the choice you made in step 3.

Turning an Appointment into a Meeting

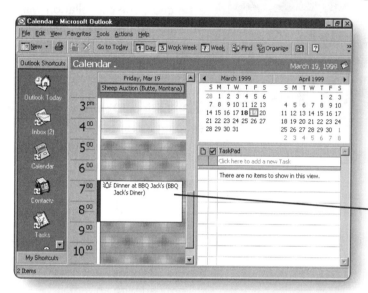

An appointment affects only your calendar, whereas a meeting involves other people. Occasionally you might have an appointment on your calendar and realize that other people need to be invited. You can easily turn the appointment into a meeting by inviting others.

1. Click twice on the **appointment** in the calendar. The Appointment window will appear.

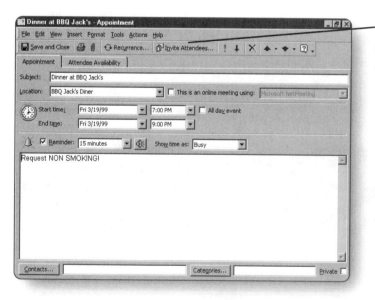

2. Click on **Invite Attendees**. A new Meeting window will appear.

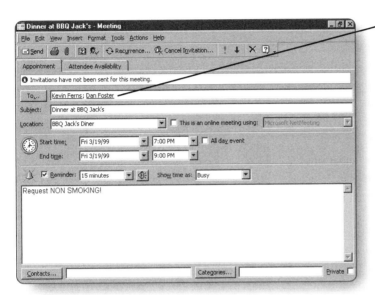

3. Type the **names** of the people who you want to invite in the To text box.

4. Type any changes to the appointment, if desired. The changes will be made.

5. Click on **Send**. An invitation to the meeting will be sent to those people you typed in the To text box.

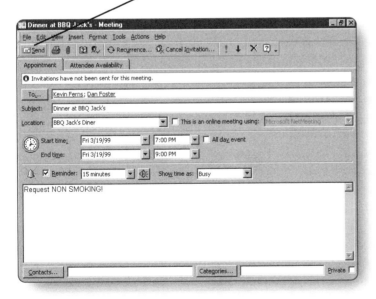

14

Requesting an Online Meeting

If you've ever spent time in an Internet chat room, you have some idea of what an online meeting is like. Many companies are setting up online meetings to have people in different cities attend meetings without incurring the high cost of travel. During an online meeting, you can hold conversations, share documents, look at videos, and even speak to others. In this chapter, you'll learn how to:

- Request and attend an online meeting
- Make any meeting an online meeting

Requesting an Online Meeting

Filling in an online meeting request is not much different than a regular meeting request. You simply choose a convenient time for everyone and invite others to attend. The main difference is the location—instead of gathering together in a room, people can attend the meeting from their home, office, or any place they have a computer.

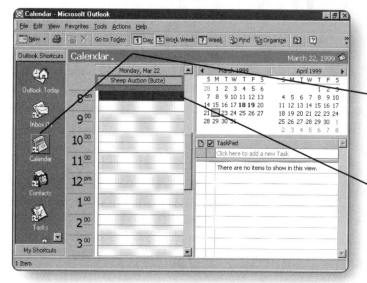

1. Click on the **Calendar icon** on the Outlook bar. The Calendar will appear in your Information viewer.

2. Right-click in a **blank area** of the calendar. A shortcut menu will appear.

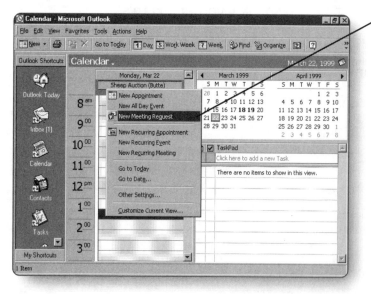

3. Click on **New Meeting Request**. The Meeting window will appear.

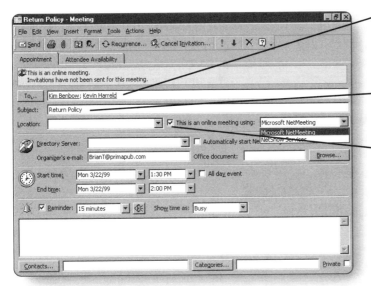

4. **Type** the **e-mail addresses** of the people you would like to attend.

5. **Type** the **subject** in the Subject: text box.

6. **Click** on the **check box** next to This is an online meeting using:, if it is not selected. A check mark will be placed in the box and the dialog box will change to present online meeting options.

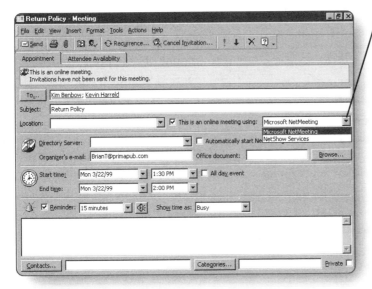

7. **Click** on the **down arrow** next to **This is an online meeting using: list box** and select the online meeting software you want to use. These options will be selected.

TIP

Microsoft NetMeeting and NetShow are free programs. They can be downloaded from the Microsoft Web site at www.microsoft.com.

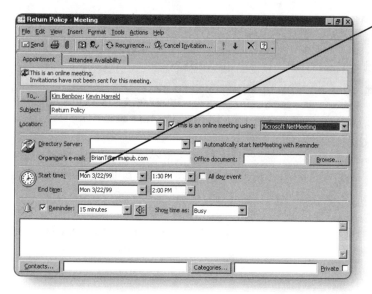

8. Click on the **Start time: list box** and the **End time: list box** to select starting and ending times for the meeting. The times will be selected.

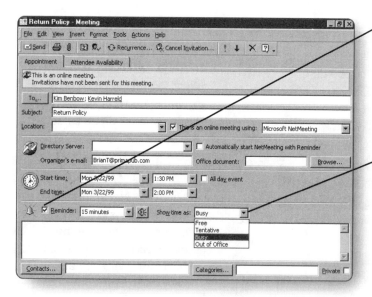

9. Click on the **Reminder: check box** and select the amount of time prior to the meeting for which Outlook should send a reminder. A reminder will be set.

10. Click on the **down arrow** next to the Show time as: list box and select how Outlook should display the time. The time will be selected.

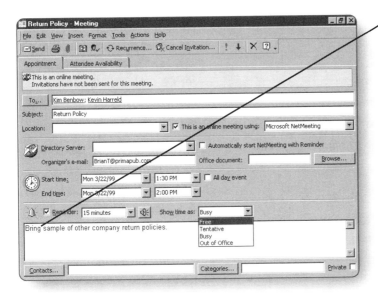

11. **Click** in the **text area** and **type** any **notes** regarding the meeting.

12. **Click** in the **Directory Server: list box** and **type** a directory server name.

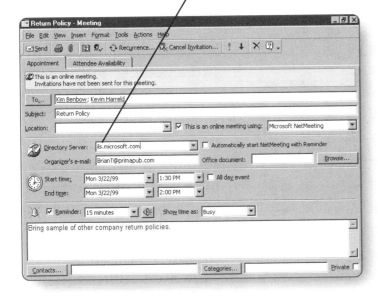

NOTE

The directory server information is very important. All meeting attendees must be logged on to the same server in order to participate. If you are asked to attend a meeting, you will be told which directory server to use. If you are organizing the meeting, you can choose any directory server you like. Some directory servers are ils.microsoft.com, uls.microsoft.com, or ils.four11.com.

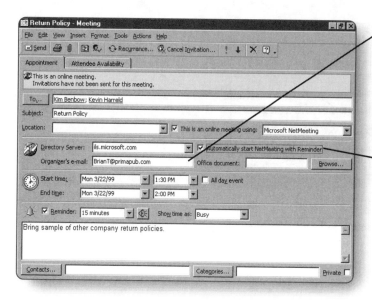

13. If you are organizing the meeting for someone else, **click** in the **text box** next to Organizer's e-mail: and type the name of the meeting organizer. The new name will appear.

14. **Click** on the **check box** next to Automatically start NetMeeting with Reminder. A check mark will be inserted into the check box.

15. **Click** on **Send**. Invitations will be sent to those invitees who are currently online.

Attending an Online Meeting

When you have been invited to an online meeting, you can respond just as you would for another meeting. An online meeting may already be in progress when you are invited, so it is a good idea to respond to the meeting organizer as quickly as possible.

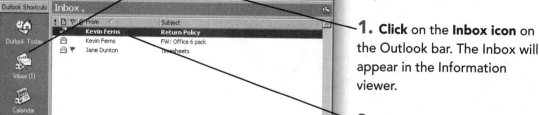

1. **Click** on the **Inbox icon** on the Outlook bar. The Inbox will appear in the Information viewer.

2. **Click twice** on the **meeting request**. The request will appear.

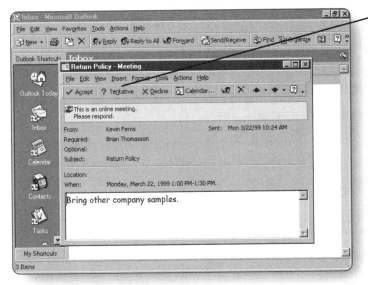

3. **Click** on **Accept**, **Tentative**, **or Decline** to place the meeting in your calendar. Once the meeting is on your calendar, you will be ready to join the online meeting.

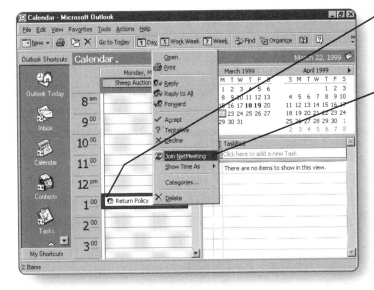

4. **Right-click** on the **meeting** in the calendar. A shortcut will appear.

5. **Click** on **Join NetMeeting**. Microsoft NetMeeting will open.

TIP

If you set a reminder, the reminder will automatically include a Join button that you can click on.

Making Any Meeting an Online Meeting

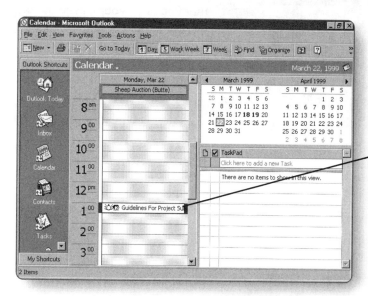

If you have a meeting scheduled and your room reservation is bumped, don't panic! Once a meeting is on the calendar, it's easy to turn it into an online meeting.

1. **Click twice** on any **meeting** in the calendar. The Meeting window will appear.

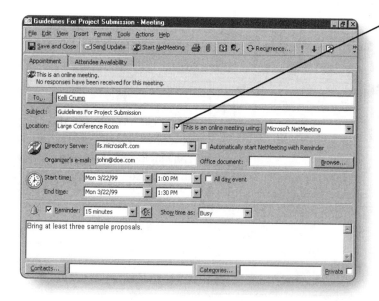

2. **Click** on the **check box** next to This is an online meeting using: and enter the necessary information.

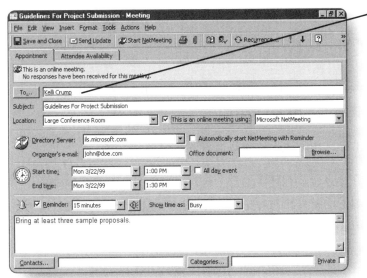

3. Click in the **To text box** and **type** the **name** or **e-mail address** of the person(s) you want to invite.

4. Click on the **Send Update button**. The meeting attendees will be informed of the change.

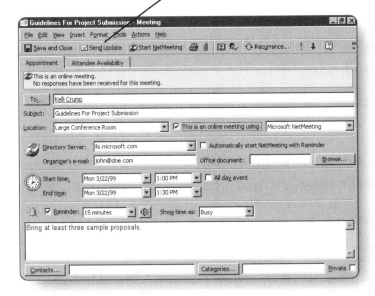

Part III Review Questions

1. What are the four calendar display options? *See "Showing Different Calendar Views" in Chapter 10*

2. How can you find out the date of a holiday? *See "Going to a Specific Date" in Chapter 10*

3. How do you change the default reminder time for all appointments? *See "Setting a Reminder" in Chapter 11*

4. Name two ways to change the date of an appointment. *See "Moving the Appointment to a Different Date and Time" in Chapter 11*

5. Where do events appear in the calendar? *See "Viewing and Modifying Events" in Chapter 12*

6. How would you record a birthday on the calendar? *See "Scheduling a Recurring Event" in Chapter 12*

7. How can you have Outlook determine the next available free time for all meeting attendees? *See "Planning a Meeting" in Chapter 13*

8. Name three possible responses to a meeting request. *See "Responding to a Meeting Request" in Chapter 13*

9. Where does an online meeting take place? *See "Requesting an Online Meeting" in Chapter 14*

10. How do you change a meeting to an online meeting? *See "Making any Meeting an Online Meeting" in Chapter 14*

PART IV

Keeping in Touch with Contacts

15

Creating New Contacts

If you've looked at any business cards recently, you've probably noticed how much information is being included on the card. Everyone seems to have multiple phone numbers, e-mail addresses, street addresses, and even a Web page! Creating contacts in Outlook is a great way to keep all this information organized and have it available when you need to get in touch with someone. In this chapter, you'll learn how to:

- Create a new contact
- View the address map
- Create a new contact from the same company
- Add a contact from an e-mail message

Creating a New Contact

It's a good idea to create a new contact record as soon as you meet someone, even if you don't have all the information that you need. You can always go back later and update the contact as you receive more details.

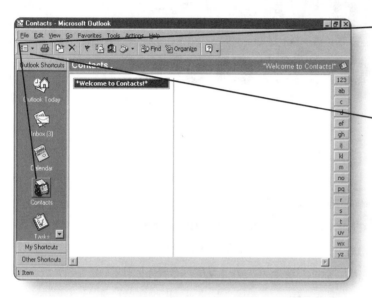

1. **Click** on the **Contacts icon** on the Outlook Shortcuts bar. Your contacts will appear in the Information viewer.

2. **Click** on the **New Contact button**. A new, blank Contact window will appear.

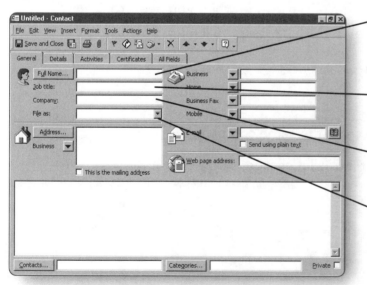

3. **Click** in the **Full Name: text box** and **type** the **name** of the individual.

4. **Click** in the **Job title: text box** and type a **job title**.

5. **Click** in the **Company: text box** and type a **company name**.

6. **Click** on the **down arrow** next to the File as: list box and **select a filing scheme** from the drop-down list.

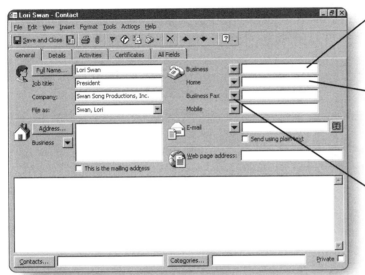

7. **Click** in the **text box** next to Business and **type** a **business telephone number**.

8a. **Click** in any of the other **phone number fields** and **type** a **telephone number**.

OR

8b. **Click** on any of the **down arrows** next to the numbers and **select** a **different type of number**.

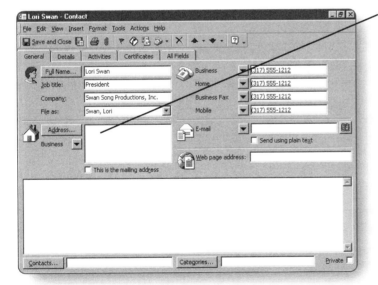

9. **Click** in the **Address text box** and **type** the **address**.

NOTE

If you do not type the address in a format that Outlook can understand, a Check Address dialog box may appear when you exit the Address field. At this point you can fill in more address information and click on OK.

10. **Click** on the **down arrow** next to Business and **select a different type of address**, if necessary.

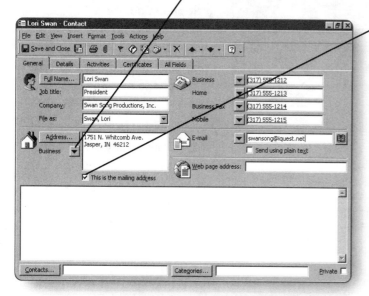

11. **Click** in the **check box** next to This is the mailing address. The address in the Address text box will appear as the mailing address.

NOTE

Mailing addresses are used in other programs, such as Word, when inserting an address from the contact list on an envelope or label.

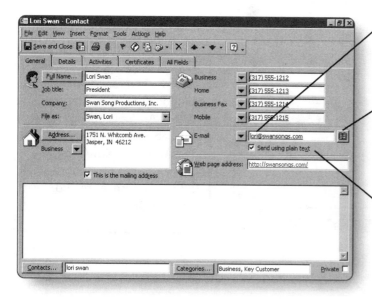

12a. **Click** in the **E-mail text box** and **type** an **e-mail address**.

OR

12b. **Click** on the **Address Book icon** and **select** an **e-mail name** from the list that appears.

13. **Click** on the **box** next to Send using plain text if your contact's e-mail software does not support HTML. A check mark will appear in the box.

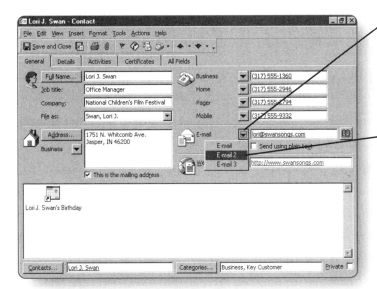

14. **Click** on the **down arrow** next to E-mail to add another e-mail address, if necessary. You can store up to three e-mail addresses for each contact.

15. **Click** on **E-mail 2** or **E-mail 3**. Your selection will appear in the list box and the insertion point will be in the text box.

16. **Type** the additional **e-mail address**. The address will appear in the text box.

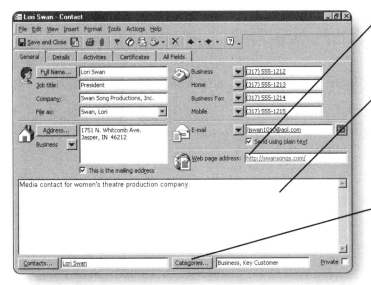

17. **Click** in the **Web page address: text box** and **type** a **Web page address**.

18. **Click** in the **comment text box area** and **type** any **comments** or notes about the contact. The text will appear in the comments area.

19. **Click** on **Categories**. The Categories dialog box will open.

20. Click in the **check box** next to any category. The category will be added to the contact.

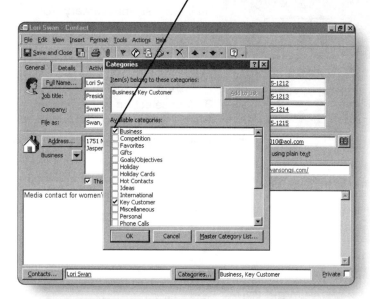

TIP

You can add multiple categories to a contact, or add your own categories. To add a new category, type a category in the Item(s) Belong to these categories: text box and click on the Add to List button.

21. Click on **OK**. The Categories dialog box will close and you will return to the Contact window.

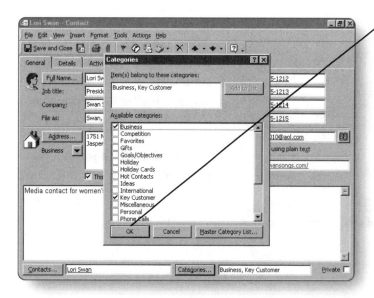

There are many more fields of information that can be added to the contact. Similar fields are organized together on the tabs of the Contact window.

- **Details**. Enter information about the contact's birthday, anniversary, spouse's name, or department.

- **Activities**. Record details about letters, e-mails, or phone calls sent to the contact.

- **Certificates**. If you have added additional security, you can load security IDs in this tab.

- **All Fields**. Enter additional fields of information for the contact.

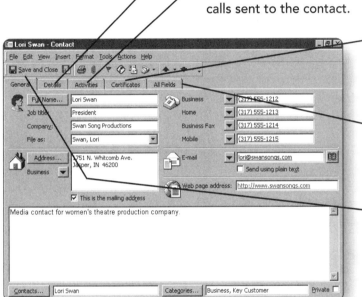

22. Click on **Save and Close**. The contact will appear in the contact list.

Viewing the Address Map

Have you ever needed quick directions to an address? Or perhaps you know where an address is, but you need to locate nearby streets or cities. The new Address Map feature allows you to do all these things and more.

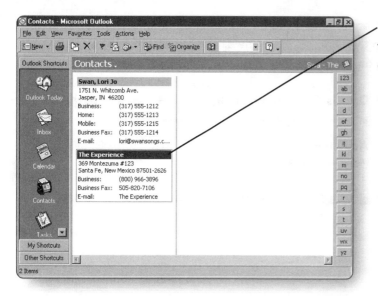

1. Double-click on a **contact** in the Information viewer. The contact will open.

2. Click on the **down arrow** beneath the Address button. A drop-down list will appear. You can store up to three addresses for each contact.

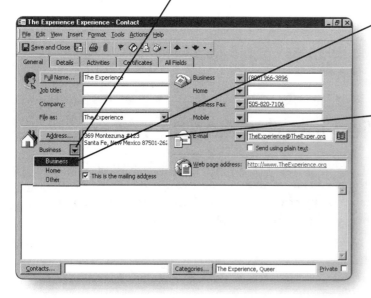

3. Click on **Business**, **Home**, or **Other**. The option will be selected and the insertion point will be in the text box.

4. Type the **address**. The address will appear in the text box.

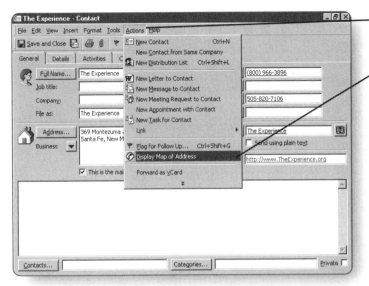

5. **Click** on **Actions**. The Actions menu will appear.

6. **Click** on **Display Map of Address**. Outlook will point your Internet browser to the page on the Outlook Web site that contains a detailed street map of the contact's address.

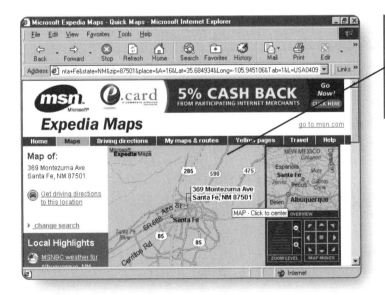

NOTE

You must have Internet access to connect to the map.

Creating a New Contact from the Same Company

Often, there will be several contacts that have similar information. People who work for the same company often have the same business telephone numbers and addresses. Instead of typing repetitive information, let Outlook do the work for you!

1. **Click** on **any contact** in the Information viewer.

2. **Click** on **Actions**. The Actions menu will appear.

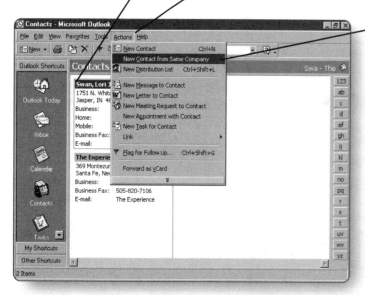

3. **Click** on **New Contact from Same Company**. Outlook will open a new contact and fill in the address, business phone, and company name information from the original contact you selected.

NOTE

Outlook will not copy non-business information, such as home address or home phone numbers, when you create a new contact using this method.

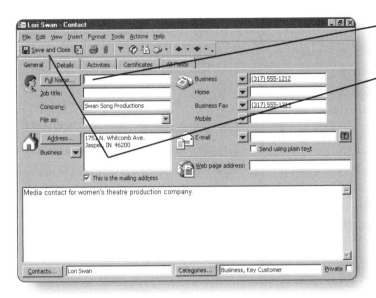

4. Type any **new contact information**.

5. **Click** on **Save and Close**. The contact will be saved and the window will close.

Adding a New Contact from an E-mail Message

What if you receive an e-mail message from someone and decide to add them to the contact list? You don't have to retype the e-mail address — Outlook can take the information and create a new contact for you.

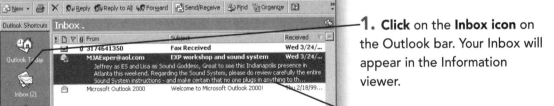

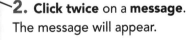

1. **Click** on the **Inbox icon** on the Outlook bar. Your Inbox will appear in the Information viewer.

2. **Click twice** on a **message**. The message will appear.

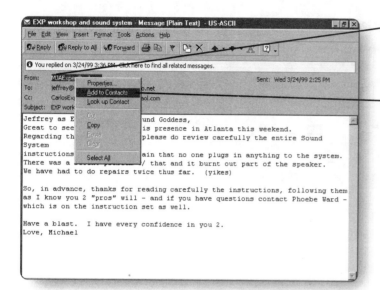

3. Right-click on the **e-mail address** in the From: line. A shortcut menu will appear.

4. Click on **Add to Contacts**. The Contact window will appear.

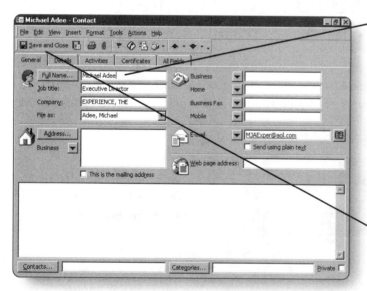

5. Type the **necessary information** for the contact in the appropriate text boxes.

NOTE
The e-mail address will automatically be added to the contact record.

6. Click on **Save and Close**. The contact will be saved and the window will close.

16

Working with Contacts

Outlook makes it easy to quickly draft a letter, send e-mail, or explore a Web page with the information stored in the contact record. In this chapter, you'll learn how to:

- Edit and print contacts
- Send an e-mail message to a contact
- Write a letter to a contact
- Explore a contact's Web page
- Dial a contact

Editing a Contact

It's rare to have all of the data you need when you initially create a contact. As you receive more details, you can add, edit, or delete any information in the contact record.

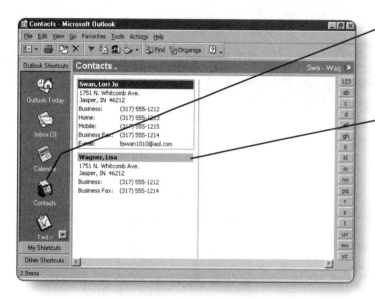

1. Click on the **Contacts icon** on the Outlook bar. Your Contacts will appear in the Information viewer.

2. Click twice on any **contact**. The contact will appear.

TIP

If your Contacts list is lengthy, you can quickly move to the contact you want to edit by clicking the alphabetical tabs at the far right edge of the information viewer.

---

3. Type any changes to the contact. The changes will be made.

4. Click on **Save and Close**. The contact will close and the changes you've made will be saved.

Printing a Contact

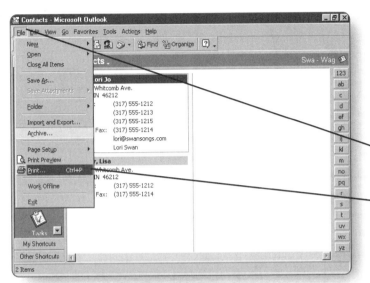

If you need a contact list, it's easy to generate a printout. Outlook gives you the option of printing one contact, selected contacts, or all the contacts in your list.

1. **Click** on **File**. The File menu will appear.

2. **Click** on **Print**. The Print dialog box will open.

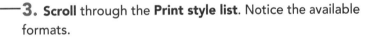

3. **Scroll** through the **Print style list**. Notice the available formats.

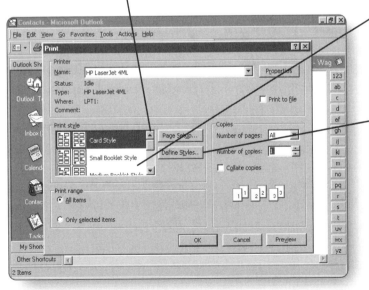

4. **Select** a **print style**. Your choice will be highlighted.

TIP

A print style can be edited if the style does not meet your needs. Click on Define Styles and select the print style you want to modify. Click on Edit and make any changes to the font size or style, shading, paper size, and headers or footers.

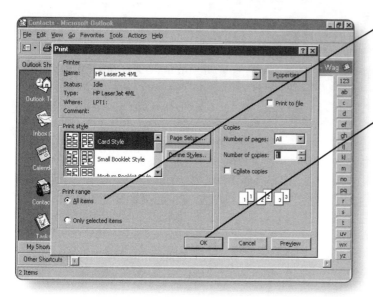

5. **Click** on the **option buttons** for All items or Only selected items. The option will be selected.

6. **Click** on **OK**. The Print dialog box will close and Outlook will print your option selection in step 4.

Sending an E-mail to a Contact

Once you have recorded an e-mail address, it's easy to send an e-mail message to the contact. Outlook allows you to store up to three e-mail addresses for a contact, so you can easily reach someone with multiple addresses.

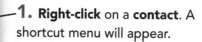

1. **Right-click** on a **contact**. A shortcut menu will appear.

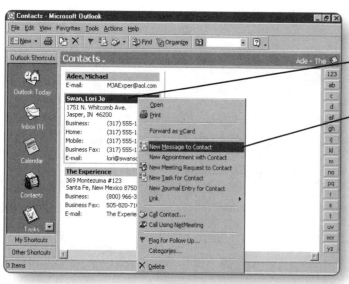

2. **Click** on **New Message to Contact**. If the contact has an e-mail address, an e-mail message window will open already addressed to that person.

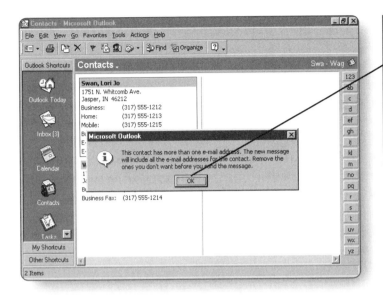

NOTE

If a contact has more than one e-mail address, you will receive a message from Outlook. All e-mail addresses for the contact will be included in the To text box, and you can delete the addresses you don't need.

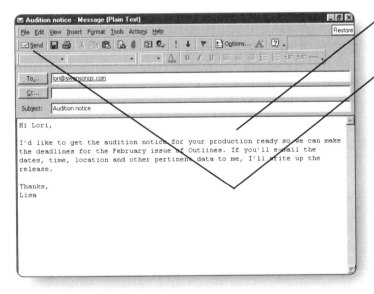

3. Type the **message**. The text will appear.

4. Click on **Send**. The message will be sent.

Writing a Letter to a Contact

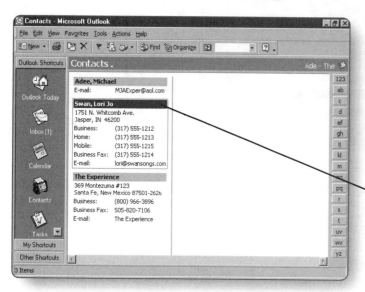

Once you have a postal address for a contact, you can use it to send a letter. Outlook has three addresses: Business, Home, and Other. The address that is marked as the mailing address will be used when sending a letter.

1. Click on a **contact**. The contact will be selected.

2. Click on **Actions**. The Actions menu will appear.

3. Click on **New Letter to Contact**. The Letter Wizard will open.

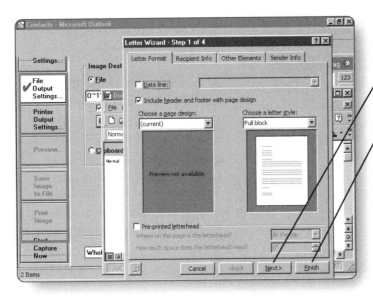

4. Select the **options** for the letter. They will be selected.

5. Click on **Next** to move through the Letter Wizard.

6. Click on **Finish** when you are finished with the Letter Wizard.

NOTE

In Word, you can access the addresses in the Contact list by clicking on the Address Book button in the Envelopes and Labels dialog box.

Creating a Mail Merge with Contacts

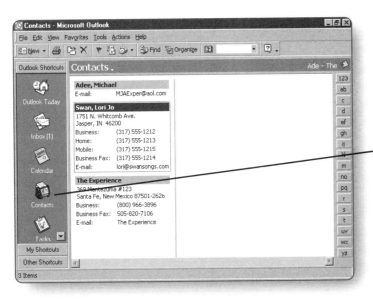

When you need to get the same information to a lot of people, a mail merge is often the best way to go. Outlook's Mail Merge feature makes composing form letters easier than ever.

1. Click on the **Contacts icon** on the Outlook bar. Your Contacts will appear in the Information viewer.

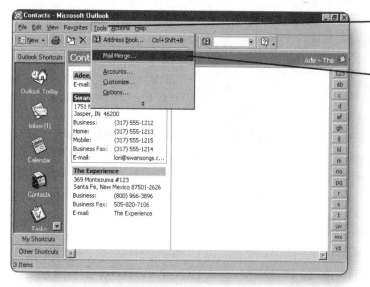

2. **Click** on **Tools**. The Tools menu will appear.

3. **Click** on **Mail Merge**. The Mail Merge Contacts dialog box will open.

4. **Click** on a **selection** under Contacts to choose which contacts to include in the merge. The options include:

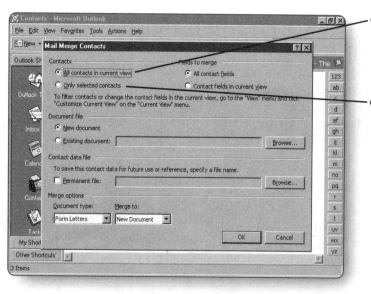

- **All Contacts in current view**. Use all the contacts that are showing in the information viewer.

- **Only Selected Contacts**. Use only the contacts currently selected in the Information viewer.

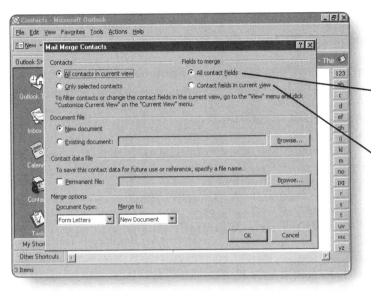

5. Click on a **selection** under Fields to Merge. The options include:

- **All Contact Fields**. Uses all the fields from the Outlook Contacts dialog box.

- **Contact Fields in Current View**. Uses only the fields that are showing in the Information viewer.

6. Click on a **selection** under Document File. The contact information will be merged into a new or existing document.

- **New Document**. Creates a new document in Microsoft Word and inserts your selected Contact fields to use in the merge.

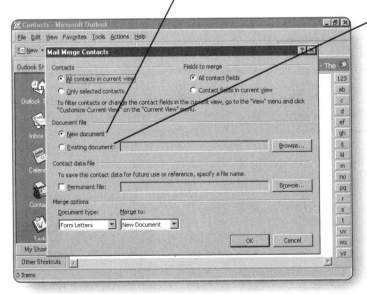

- **Existing Document**. Opens an existing document that already contains the desired merge fields. Click on the Browse button to locate the document on your computer.

TIP

For detailed instructions on working with merge fields and documents, open Microsoft Word and press F1 to get help from the Office Assistant.

7. Click on a **selection** under Document Type. The options include:

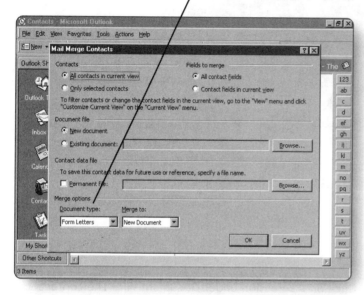

- **Form Letters**. Formats the merged document to use for creating a letter to multiple contacts.

- **Mailing Labels**. Formats the merged document to use for label sheets.

- **Envelopes**. Formats the merged document to use for addressing envelopes.

- **Catalogs**. Formats the merged document to use for creating catalogs. This is convenient if you use your Contacts list to track inventory and products.

8. Click on a **selection** under Merge To. The options include:

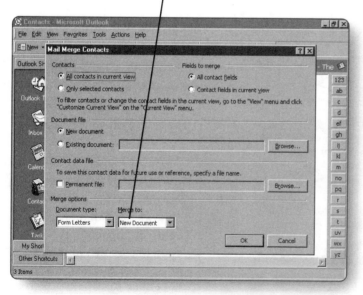

- **New Document**. Merges the information into a new document that can be saved and edited.

- **Printer**. Sends the merge directly to the printer. Does not save the merged document.

- **Fax**. Sends the merge directly to the fax modem using Outlook.

- **E-Mail**. Sends the merge directly to a new e-mail message using Outlook.

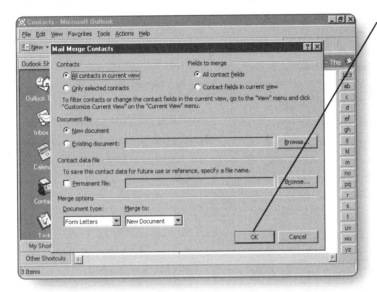

9. Click on **OK**. The dialog box will close and the merge will be created. Depending on your selections, Word may open and present the Office Assistant, the Mail Merge Helper, or both.

Exploring a Contact's Web Page

Many businesses have pages on the Web that people can access to quickly locate information about their company.

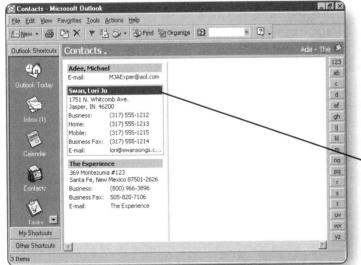

Individuals are also creating their own pages and loading them on the Internet. Fortunately, Outlook allows you to keep a link to a Web page in the contact record, making it easy to visit a Web page at any time.

1. Double-click on a **contact** in the Information viewer. The contact will open.

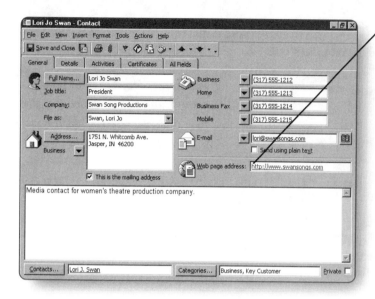

2. Click on the **hyperlink** next to Web page address. Outlook will point your Internet browser to that page.

3. Click on **Close** when you are finished exploring. The browser will close and the contact will reappear.

NOTE

You must have Internet access and a Web browser to explore a contact's Web page.

Tracking Contact Activities

Outlook can help you keep track of all the activity surrounding each person in your Contacts folder. It uses the Contacts and Journal features together to log all incoming and outgoing mail, phone calls, and related documents for each contact.

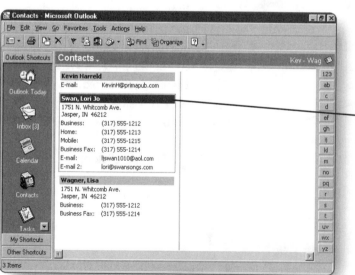

1. Click twice on the **contact** you want to track in the Information viewer. The contact will open.

2. Click on the **Activities** tab. The contact's Activities page will appear.

3. Click on the **down arrow** next to Show. A list of activity types will appear. They include:

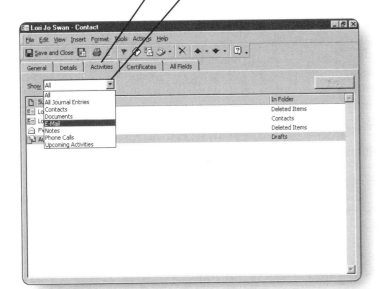

- **All**. Displays all the activities related to this contact.

- **All Journal Entries**. Displays all the journal entries related to this contact.

- **Contacts**. Displays other contacts linked to this contact.

- **E-mail**. Displays all the e-mail sent to and received from the contact.

- **Notes**. Displays all notes related to this contact.

- **Upcoming Activities**. Displays all activities related to this contact that are currently scheduled in the calendar.

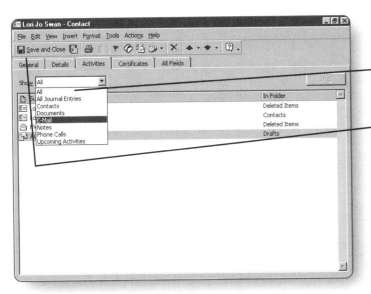

4. Click on **All** to see activities of all types.

5. Click on **Save and Close**. The Contacts folder will reappear in the Information viewer.

Calling a Contact

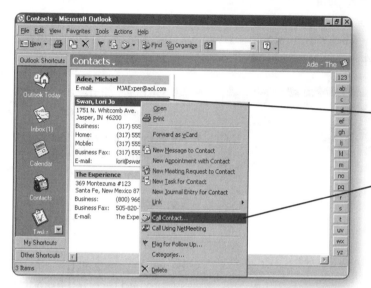

You can use Outlook's AutoDialer feature to automatically dial a contact's phone number or fax line.

1. **Right-click** on the **contact** you want to call. A shortcut menu will appear.

2. **Click** on **Call Contact**. The New Call dialog box will appear.

Outlook enables you to choose which number and set calling options easily:

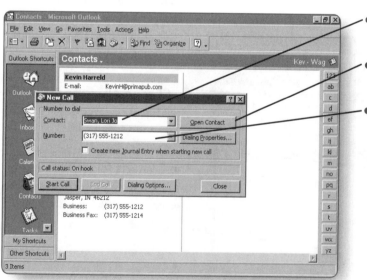

- **Contact**. Type the name of the contact you want to dial.

- **Open Contact**. View the full contact dialog box.

- **Number**. Choose which number to dial, depending on what is available in the contact's information.

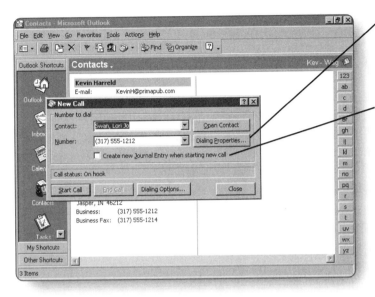

- **Dialing Properties**. Edit the dialing properties, such as long distance calling card information.

- **Create new Journal Entry when starting new call**. Log this call in the Journal for tracking purposes.

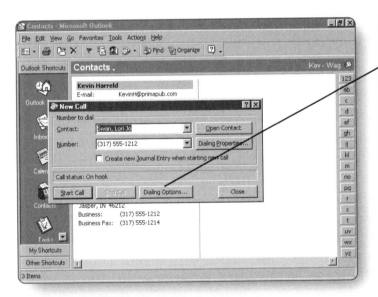

TIP

Click on Dialing Options to set advanced features for the call, such as speed dialing and modem properties.

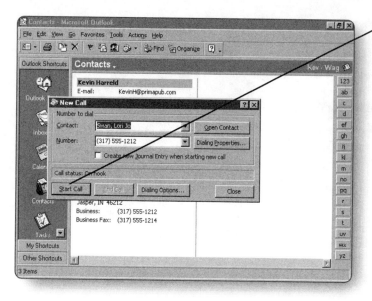

3. Click on **Start Call** to make the call. Outlook will dial the selected phone number.

4. When the phone begins to ring, **click** on **Talk** and pick up the receiver. Your call will be connected and you can begin talking.

17

Organizing Contacts

After you have entered numerous contact records, you may need to organize them. Contacts can be organized by categories, by names, by location, and more. You can also quickly find a contact using Outlook's Find feature. In this chapter, you'll learn how to:

- Find a contact
- Use folders, categories, and views to organize contacts

Finding a Contact

What if you have several thousand contacts and you need to quickly find one? Outlook has a Find feature that leads you straight to what you're looking for. You can even search all the text of the contact if you don't know the exact name or company.

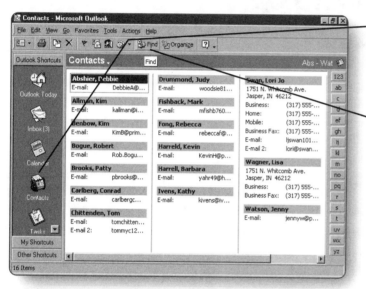

1. Click on the **Contacts icon** on the Outlook bar. Your contacts will appear in the Information viewer.

2. Click on **Find**. The Find messages in Contacts pane will appear.

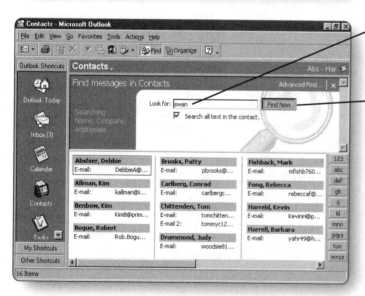

3. Type your **search criteria** in the Look for: text box. The text will appear.

4. Click on the **Find Now button**. Outlook will begin the search.

If Outlook finds a contact record that matches the search criteria, it will be displayed at the bottom of the screen. Click twice on the contact record to display the contact.

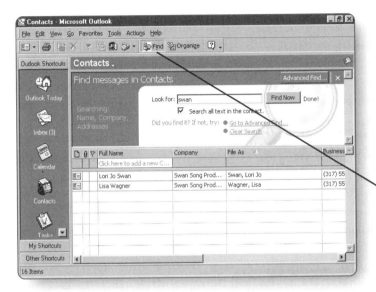

TIP

If Outlook does not find a record matching the search criteria, click on Advanced Find to further refine the search criteria.

5. Click on **Find**. The Find messages in Contacts pane will close.

Using Folders to Organize Contacts

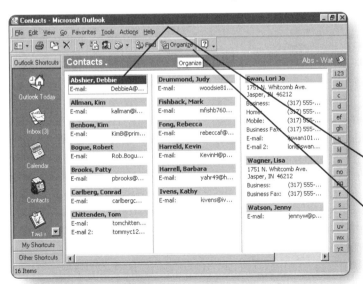

Folders are a great way to organize contacts. For example, you can create a client folder and place the client's contact record in the folder, along with e-mail messages, notes, or tasks related to the client.

1. Click on a **contact**. The contact will be selected.

2. Click on **Organize**. The Ways to Organize Contacts pane will appear.

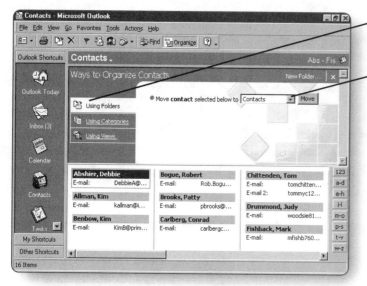

3. Click on **Using Folders**. The tab will come to the front.

4. Click on the **down arrow** next to the Move contact selected below to list box. The list of available folders will appear.

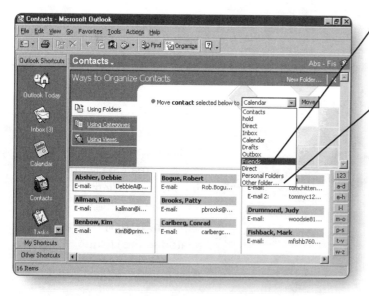

5a. Click on an **existing folder**. It will be highlighted.

OR

5b. Click on **Other folder** to create a new folder. It will be created.

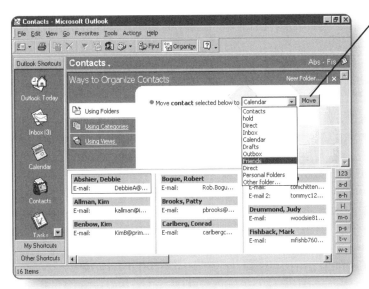

6. Click on the **Move button**. The contact will be moved to the new folder.

Using Categories to Organize Contacts

If you've already entered contact information without categories, you might think it's too late or too much bother to add them now. Not true! Outlook makes it easy to select multiple records and add them to a category. Using this method, you can quickly get your category list up to date and organized.

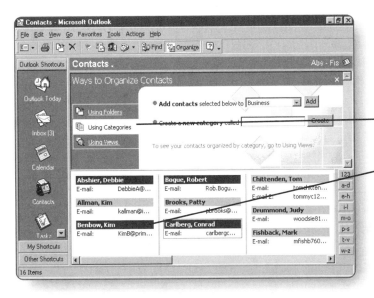

1. Click on **Using Categories**. The tab will come to the front.

2. Click on the **contact(s)** you want to add to a particular category. Those contacts will be selected.

NOTE

To select a range of contacts, click on the first contact, press the Shift key, and click on the last contact. To select non-contiguous contacts, hold down the Ctrl key and click on each contact that you want to select.

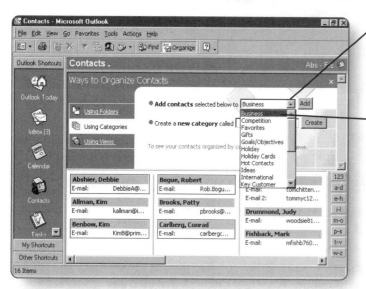

3. Click on the **down arrow** next to the Add contacts selected below to list box. The list of categories will appear.

4. Click on a **category**. Your selection will appear in the list box.

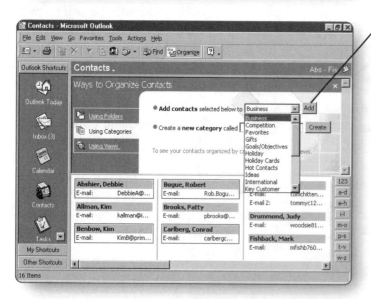

5. Click on the **Add button**. The contact(s) you've selected will be added to the selected category.

Using Views to Organize Contacts

Once you have a large contact list, you may find yourself changing views frequently. Some of the available views are Categories, Company, and Location. You can edit any of the existing views or create your own.

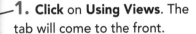

1. Click on **Using Views**. The tab will come to the front.

2. Click on the **up or down arrows.** You can scroll through the available views.

3. Click on **any view**. The view will change.

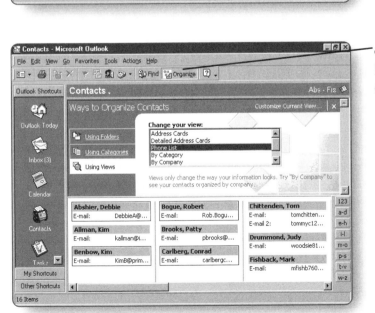

4. Click on the **Organize button**. The Ways to Organize Contacts pane will close.

Using Personal Distribution Lists

If you frequently send messages to the same group of people, you can save time by creating a personal distribution list. When sending a message, you can simply enter the list name rather than choose all the contacts individually.

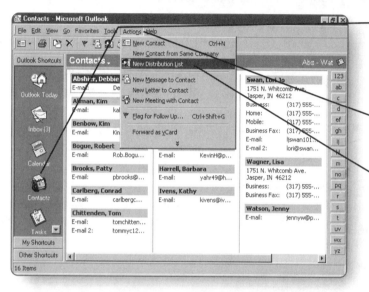

1. Click on the **Contacts icon** on the Outlook bar. Your contacts will appear in the Information viewer.

2. Click on **Actions**. The Actions menu will appear.

3. Click on **New Distribution List**. The Distribution List dialog box will open.

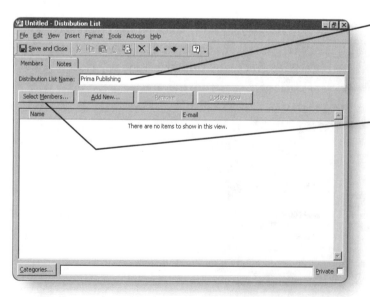

4. Click in the **edit box** next to the Distribution List Name: text box and **type** a **name** for the list.

5. Click on the **Select Members button**. The Select Contacts to add to Distribution List dialog box will open.

6. Select the **names** on the left that you want to add to the personal distribution list. The contacts will be highlighted.

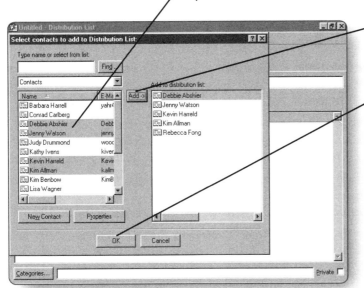

7. Click on the **Add button**. The names will appear on the right.

8. Click on **OK**. The dialog box will close and the Distribution List dialog box will reopen.

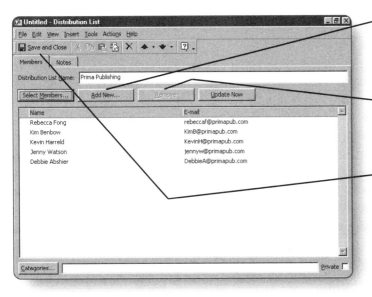

9. Click on the **Add New button** to create a new contact for the distribution list.

10. Click on **Remove** to delete a specific contact from the list. It will be deleted.

11. Click on **Save and Close**. The dialog box will close and your new distribution list will appear in the Information viewer.

Part IV Review Questions

1. Name the three types of addresses that can be stored in a contact. *See "Creating a New Contact" in Chapter 15*

2. How can you locate an address for a contact? *See "Viewing the Address Map" in Chapter 15*

3. How can you turn an e-mail address into a contact record? *See "Adding a New Contact from an E-mail Address" in Chapter 15*

4. Do you have to retype company information when creating a new contact from the same company? *See "Creating a New Contact from the Same Company" in Chapter 15*

5. How do you print a single contact? *See "Printing a Contact" in Chapter 16*

6. How do you send a letter to a contact? *See "Writing a Letter to a Contact" in Chapter 16*

7. How would you locate a single contact if you know the person's first name, but not their last name? *See "Finding a Contact" in Chapter 17*

8. Why would you want to use folders to organize contacts? *See "Using Folders to Organize Contacts" in Chapter 17*

9. How do you add multiple contacts to a category all at once? *See "Using Categories to Organize Contacts" in Chapter 17*

10. Why would you want to create personal distribution lists? *See "Using Personal Distribution Lists" in Chapter 17*

PART V

Staying on Top of Things with Tasks

18

Creating Tasks

With so much work to do, it helps to keep a list of the most important items that need to be completed. The Task List in Outlook will help you keep all of these items under control, and give you a record of which tasks have been completed. In this chapter, you'll learn how to:

- Add a new task
- Set a reminder
- Update task status
- Mark a task complete
- Delete a task

Adding a New Task

It's easy to add tasks to your task list. You can type directly into the list of tasks, or you can open a Task window and fill in more detail.

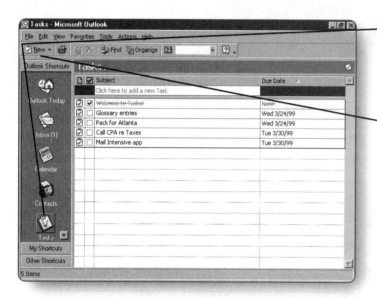

1. Click on the **Tasks icon** on the Outlook bar. Your tasks will appear in the Information viewer.

2. Click on the **New Task button**. A new Task window will appear.

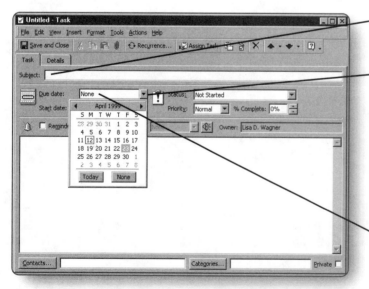

3. Type the **subject** of the task in the Subject: text box.

4. Click on the **down arrow** next to the Due date: list box. A drop-down list will appear.

5a. Click on a **due date.** The date will appear in the list box.

OR

5b. Click on **None.**

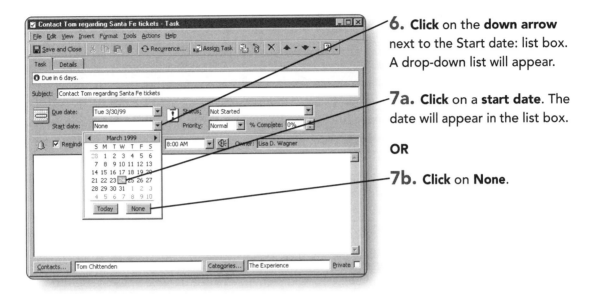

6. Click on the **down arrow** next to the Start date: list box. A drop-down list will appear.

7a. Click on a **start date**. The date will appear in the list box.

OR

7b. Click on **None**.

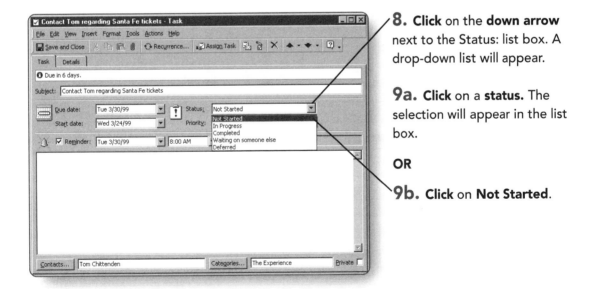

8. Click on the **down arrow** next to the Status: list box. A drop-down list will appear.

9a. Click on a **status.** The selection will appear in the list box.

OR

9b. Click on **Not Started**.

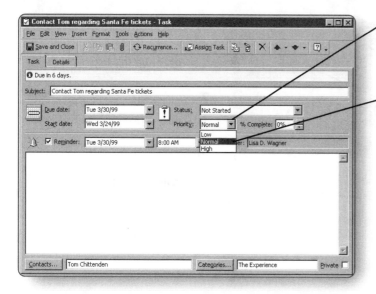

10. **Click** on the **down arrow** next to the Priority: list box. A drop-down list will appear.

11. **Click** on a **Priority.** The selection will be highlighted.

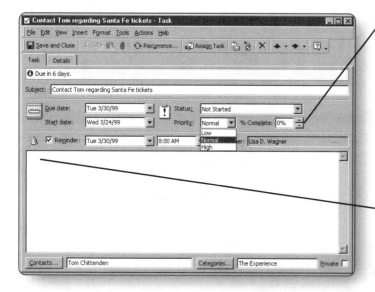

12. **Click** on the **up or down arrow** next to the % Complete: list box. A drop-down list will appear.

13. **Click** on a **percentage complete**. The amount of increase or decrease will appear in the list box.

14. **Click** in the **message box.** The insertion point will be in the message box.

15. **Type** any **notes** regarding the task. The text will be inserted into the message box.

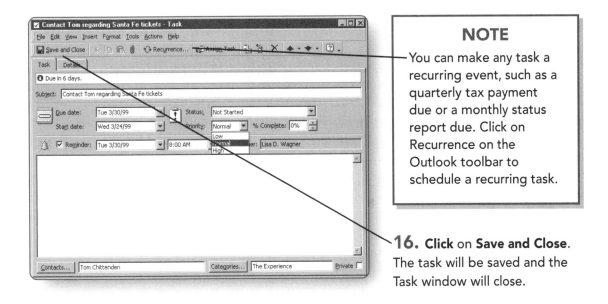

NOTE

You can make any task a recurring event, such as a quarterly tax payment due or a monthly status report due. Click on Recurrence on the Outlook toolbar to schedule a recurring task.

16. Click on **Save and Close**. The task will be saved and the Task window will close.

Setting a Reminder

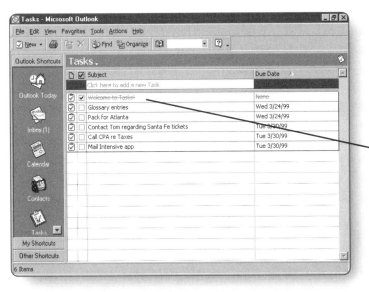

If a task is important, you may want to set a reminder. A reminder will pop up and let you know that the task is due. You can postpone or dismiss the task when you are reminded.

1. Double-click on the **task**. The details of the task will appear.

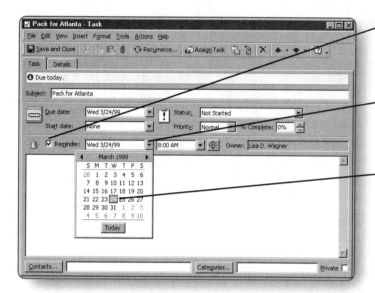

2. Click on the **Reminder check box**. A check mark will be placed in the box.

3. Click on the **down arrow** next to the Reminder: list box. A drop-down list will appear.

4. Click on a **date** to be reminded. The date will show in the list box.

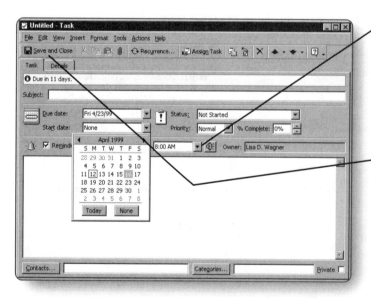

5. Click on the **down arrow** next to the time text box. A drop-down list will appear.

6. Click on a **time**. The time will show in the list box.

7. Click on **Save and Close**. The task window will close and any changes you've made will be saved.

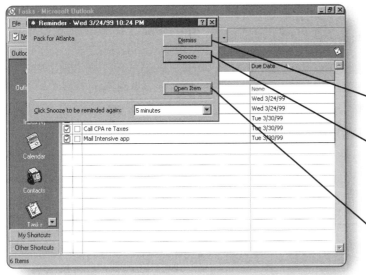

Reminders will only pop up while Outlook is running. There are three options when you have a reminder:

- **Dismiss**. Click on Dismiss to close the reminder.

- **Snooze**. Click on Snooze to delay the reminder. Select a time in the Click Snooze to be reminded again: list box.

- **Open Item**. Click on Open Item to open the task.

Updating Tasks with Status Information

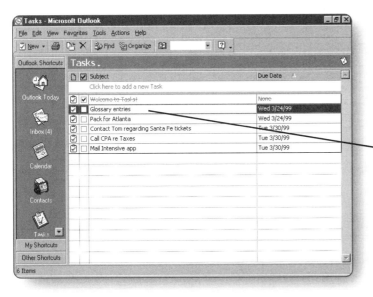

When a task is on your task list, you can update the task by changing the percentage complete detail. This will help you keep your task list up to date.

1. Double-click on the **task**. The details of the task will appear.

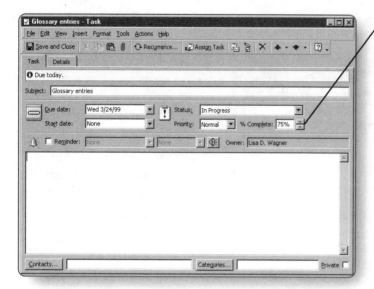

2. Click up or down on the **spin button** next to the % Complete: list box to increase or decrease the percentage complete. The change will appear.

NOTE

When the percentage complete is more than zero, the status automatically changes to In Progress. When the task is 100 percent complete, the status changes to Completed.

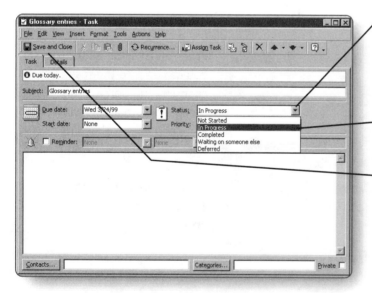

3a. Click on the **down arrow** next to the Status: list box. A list of status options will appear.

OR

3b. Click on a **status option**. The status will be updated.

4. Click on the **Save and Close button.** The changes will be saved and the task will close.

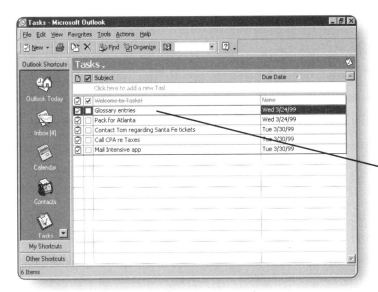

Sending Status Reports

You can send a status report to inform parties of the status of the task.

1. Double-click on a **task** in the task list. The task will open.

2. Click on **Actions**. The Actions menu will appear.

3. Click on **Send Status Report**. A new Task Status Report window will appear.

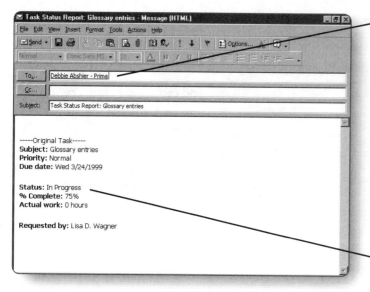

4. Type the **e-mail address** in the To: text box of the person to whom you want to send a status report. The address will appear.

> ### NOTE
> Like other messages, you can send a status report to an e-mail address or a fax number.

5. Type any **message** in the message text box.

6. Click on **Send**. A status report will be sent.

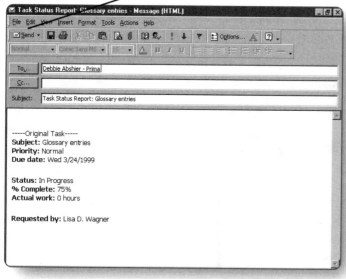

Marking a Task as Complete

When you are finished with a task, you can mark it as complete. A completed task does not disappear completely. It remains on your task list, and you can choose to display the task or not.

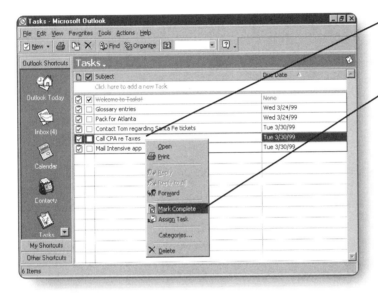

1. Right-click on a **task** in the task list. A shortcut menu will appear.

2. Click on **Mark Complete**. A check mark will appear next to the task in the task list.

TIP

Another quick way to mark a task as complete is to click on the Complete check box on the task list.

Deleting a Task

Occasionally a task may need to be deleted. If the task is no longer necessary, you can delete the task to clean up your task list.

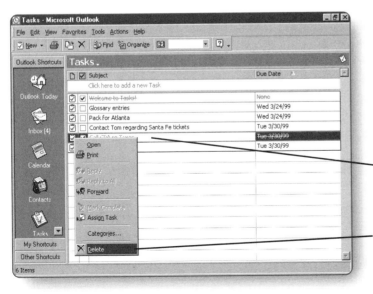

1. Right-click on a **task** in the task list. A shortcut menu will appear.

2. Click on **Delete**. The task will be deleted.

19

Assigning Tasks

If you are lucky, you will not have to handle all your tasks alone. Outlook has a feature called Task Request that lets you assign tasks to other people. They can accept, reject, or assign the task to someone else. In this chapter, you'll learn how to:

- Create a task request
- Respond to a task

Creating a Task Request

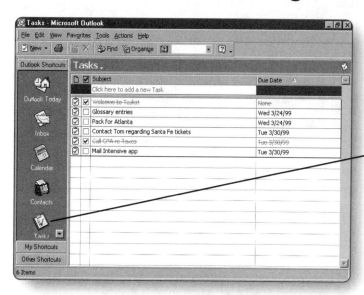

A *Task Request* is a task that you create and then assign to someone else. You can receive status reports so that you know the status of the task and when it has been marked complete.

1. Click on the **Tasks icon** on the Outlook bar. Your tasks will appear in the Information viewer.

2. Click on **Actions**. The Actions menu will appear.

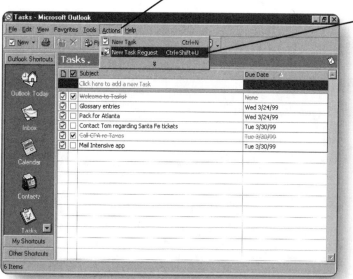

3. Click on **New Task Request**. A new Task window will appear.

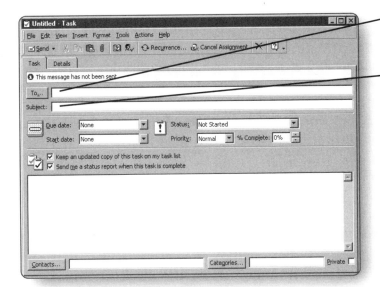

4. **Type** the **recipient's name** in the To: text box.

5. **Type** the **subject** in the Subject: text box.

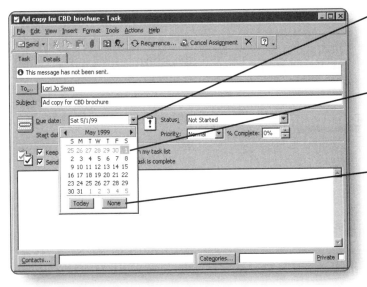

6. **Click** on the **down arrow** next to the Due date: list box. A drop-down list will appear.

7a. **Click** on a **due date.** The date will appear in the list box.

OR

7b. **Click** on **None**.

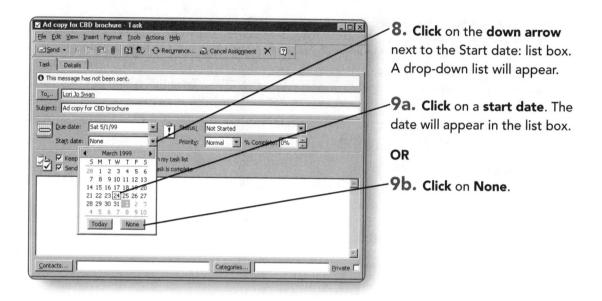

8. Click on the **down arrow** next to the Start date: list box. A drop-down list will appear.

9a. Click on a **start date**. The date will appear in the list box.

OR

9b. Click on **None**.

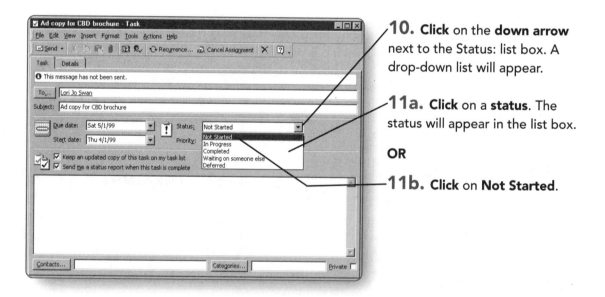

10. Click on the **down arrow** next to the Status: list box. A drop-down list will appear.

11a. Click on a **status**. The status will appear in the list box.

OR

11b. Click on **Not Started**.

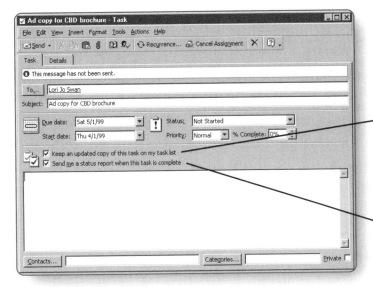

You have some tracking options available when assigning a task, which allow you to receive notification or automatic updates as progress is made:

- **Keep an updated copy of this Task on my Task List**. A copy of the task will stay on your task list and will be updated automatically.

- **Send me a status report when this Task is complete**. You will receive a message when the task is marked complete.

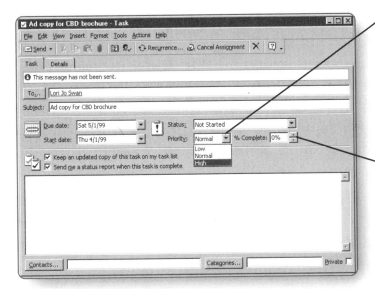

12. **Click** on the **down arrow** next to the Priority: list box. A drop-down list will appear.

13. **Click** on a **priority**. The selection will appear in the list box.

14. **Click** on the **up or down arrow** next to the % Complete: list box. The percent complete will increase or decrease.

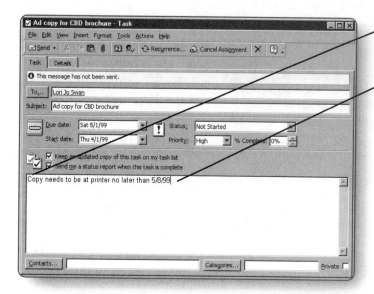

15. **Click** in the **message text box.**

16. **Type** any **notes** regarding the task. The note will appear in the message area.

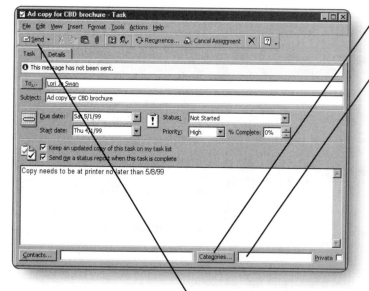

17. **Click** on the **Categories button.**

18. **Type** any **categories** you want to add. The categories will be added.

NOTE

You may need to maximize the Task Request to see the Categories text box.

19. **Click** on **Send**. The task will be sent to the recipient.

Task Requests will remain on your task list if you have selected the option to keep an updated copy on your task list.

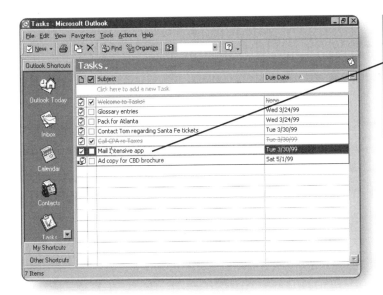

TIP

In the task list, you can distinguish a task from a Task Request by looking at the icon.

Responding to a Task

If you receive a Task Request, you have several choices. You can accept the task, reject the task, or assign the task to someone else. Outlook makes any of these options easy to choose.

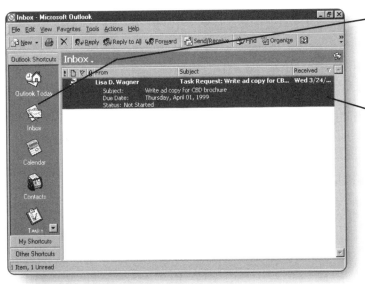

1. **Click** on the **Inbox icon** on the Outlook bar. The contents of your Inbox will appear in the Information viewer.

2. **Double-click** on the **Task Request**. The Task Request window will appear.

3a. **Click** on **Accept** to accept the task. The task will be added to your task list.

OR

3b. **Click** on **Decline** to decline the task. The task won't be added to your task list.

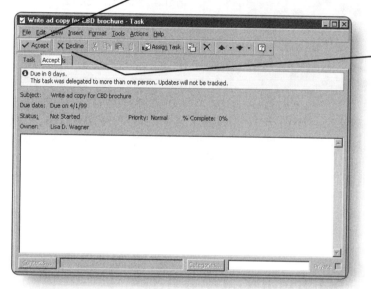

4a. **Click** on the **Edit the response before sending option button** to send a response.

OR

4b. **Click** on the **Send the response now option button** to accept or decline the task without sending a response.

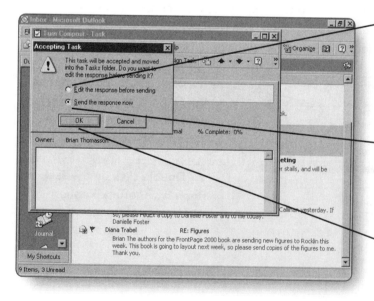

5. **Click** on **OK**. Outlook will either send your response, or allow you to edit it, depending on the option you chose in step 4.

Delegating Tasks

If you are unable to complete the task but can delegate the task to someone else, you can *reassign the task*. When you reassign the task, you give up ownership of the task; however, you can still keep an updated copy of the task on your task list.

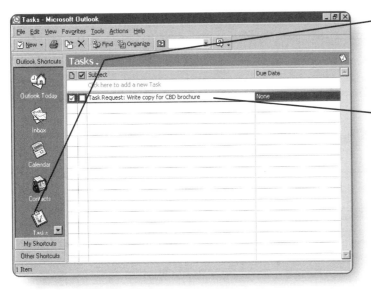

1. Click on the **Tasks icon** on the Outlook bar. Your tasks will appear in the Information viewer.

2. Double-click on the **Task Request** in the task list. The Task Request window will appear.

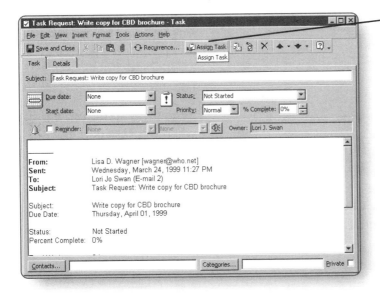

3. Click on the **Assign Task button**. A new Task window will open.

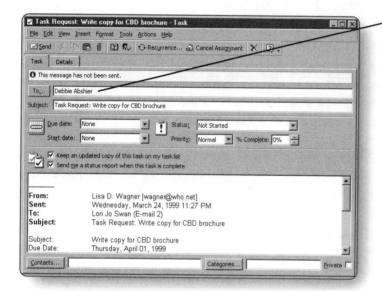

4. Type the **name** of the person in the To: text box to whom you are sending the task.

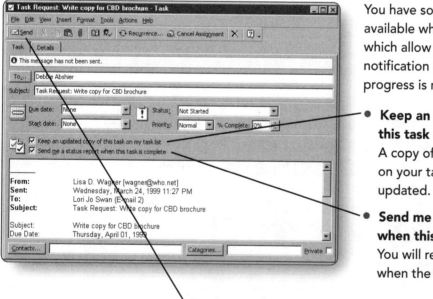

You have some tracking options available when assigning a task, which allow you to receive notification or updates as progress is made:

- **Keep an updated copy of this task on my task list**. A copy of the task will stay on your task list and get updated.

- **Send me a status report when this task is complete**. You will receive a message when the task is complete.

5. Click on **Send**. The task will be delegated to the person indicated in step 4.

Declining a Task After You Have Accepted It

Have you ever bitten off more than you can chew with pending projects? Outlook can help you out of a sticky situation by allowing you to decline a task you had previously accepted.

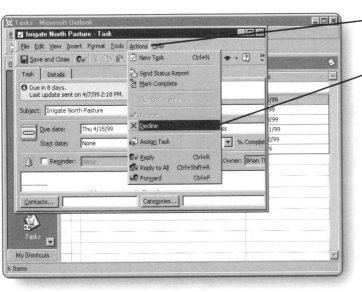

1. **Click** on the **Tasks icon** on the Outlook bar. Your tasks will appear in the Information viewer.

2. **Double-click** on the **task** in the task list. The task will appear.

3. **Click** on **Actions**. The Actions menu will appear.

4. **Click** on **Decline**. The Declining Task dialog box will open.

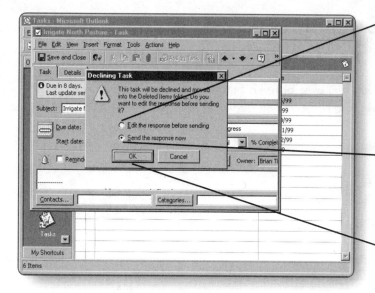

5a. **Click** on the **Edit the response before sending option button** to decline the task and add a response.

OR

5b. **Click** on the **Send the response now option button** to decline the task without sending a response.

6. **Click** on **OK**. Outlook will allow you to edit the task before you send it, or send it immediately, depending on the option you selected in step 5.

20

Organizing Tasks

If you have a long list of tasks, you will need a few tricks so you can see the most important tasks, or the tasks that are due today. Changing views and sorting the task list are fast and easy ways to get tasks under control. In this chapter, you'll learn how to:

- Use folders and categories to organize tasks
- Change the task list view
- Sort and print the task list

Using Folders to Organize Tasks

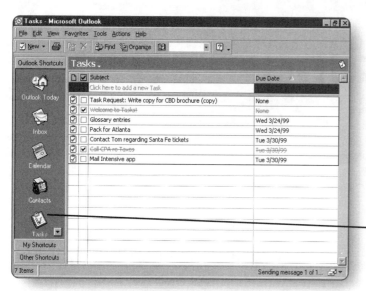

Outlook automatically stores tasks in the Tasks folder. After you have used Outlook for a while, the Tasks folder may grow to contain an enormous amount of tasks. Instead of scrolling through a long list of tasks, you can create subfolders under the Task folder, and view tasks by folder.

1. Click on the **Tasks icon** in the Outlook bar. Your tasks will appear in the Information viewer.

2. Click on **Organize**. The Ways to Organize Tasks pane will open.

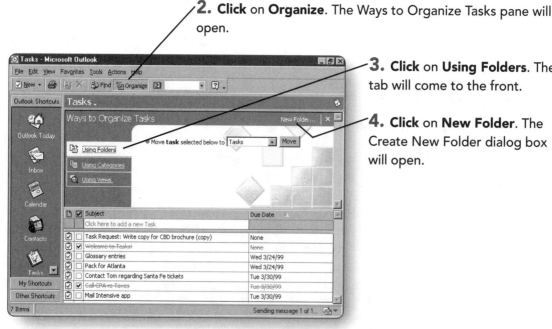

3. Click on **Using Folders**. The tab will come to the front.

4. Click on **New Folder**. The Create New Folder dialog box will open.

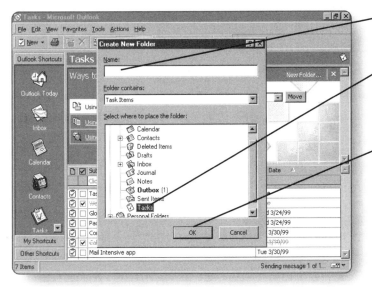

5. Type the **folder name** in the Name: text box.

6. Click on the **Tasks folder**. The new folder will be a subfolder of the Tasks folder.

7. Click on **OK**. The new folder will be created.

NOTE

You may receive a message asking if you want a shortcut to the new folder placed on the Outlook toolbar. If you do, click on Yes; otherwise, click on No.

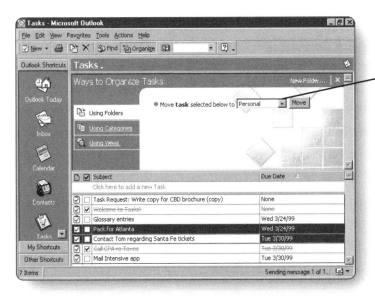

8. Click on **any task** in the Task list. The task will be selected.

9. Click on the **down arrow** next to Move task selected below to list box. A drop-down list will appear.

10. Click on a **folder**. The folder will be selected.

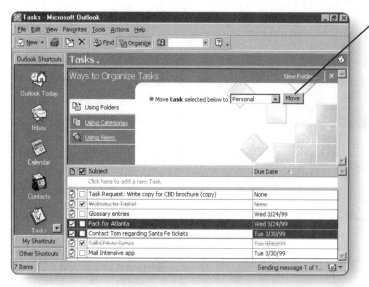

11. Click on the **Move button**. The task will be moved to the folder you selected in step 10.

Using Categories to Organize Tasks

Categories are words or phrases that can be applied to any Outlook item, such as an e-mail message, a note, or a task. Outlook comes with numerous categories, and you can add more categories to customize the category list. Using categories will keep all the tasks for a particular client or project tied together, and make sorting and viewing much easier.

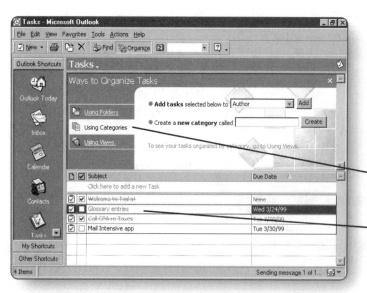

1. Click on **Using Categories**. The tab will come to the front.

2. Click on a **task(s)** in the task list. The task(s) will be selected.

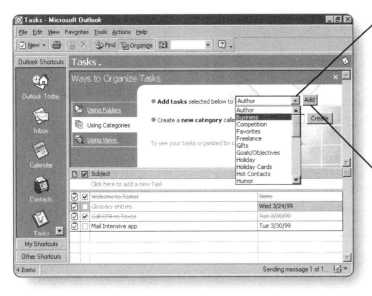

3. Click on the **down arrow** next to Add tasks selected below to list box. A drop-down list will appear.

4. Click on a **category**. It will be selected.

5. Click on **Add**. The category will be added to the selected tasks.

Using Views to Organize Tasks

Now that you have explored categories, you may be wondering how they will be used to organize the task list. It's easy! Changing the task list view is one quick way to organize the task list.

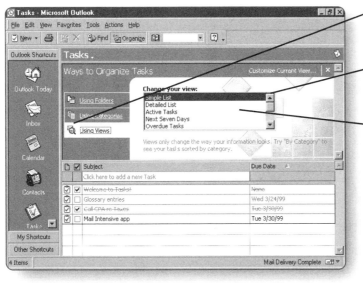

1. Click on **Using Views**. The tab will come to the front.

2. Scroll through the **list of views** to find your selection.

3. Click on **any view**. The task list view will change.

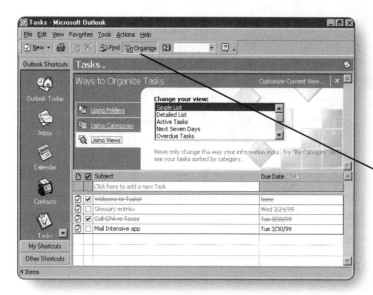

TIP

To view the tasks organized by categories, choose the By Category view.

4. **Click** on **Organize**. The Ways to Organize Tasks pane will close.

Remember that changing the task view does not delete any existing tasks, it simply removes them from view. To see all tasks, choose the Simple List view.

Sorting the Task List

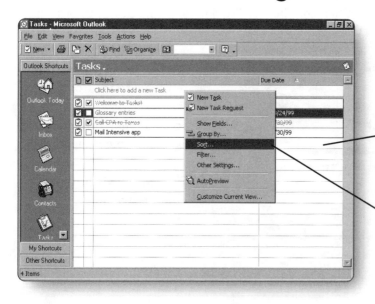

Some people prefer to sort their task lists instead of using views. You can sort by any field in a task, such as priority, due date, or subject.

1. **Right-click** on a **blank area** of the task list. A shortcut menu will appear.

2. **Click** on **Sort**. The Sort dialog box will open.

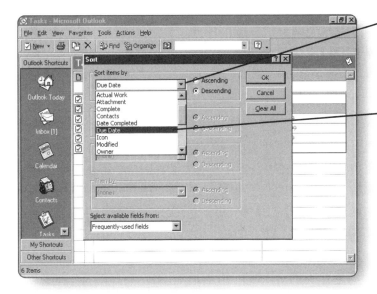

3. Click on the **down arrow** to the right of the Sort items by list box. A drop-down list will appear.

4. Click on a **field selection**. The selection will be highlighted.

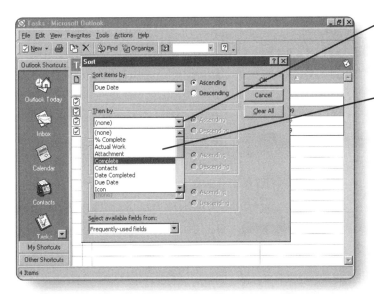

5. Optionally, **click** on the **down arrow** under Then by. A drop-down list will appear.

6. Click on a **field selection** to sort by multiple criteria.

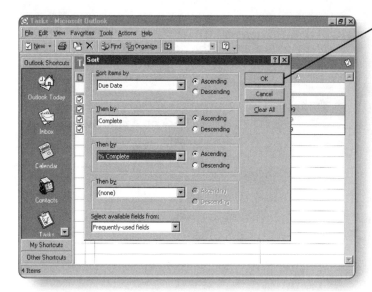

7. Click on **OK**. Your tasks will be sorted according to the criteria you've chosen in steps 4 and 6.

> ### NOTE
>
> If you select a sort field that is not currently displayed on the task list view, a message will open. To add the sort field to the view, click on OK; otherwise, click on No.

Printing the Task List

Before attending a meeting or going out of town, you may need to print a list of tasks. Outlook has several options for printing tasks that can give you exactly what you need.

1. Click on **File**. The File menu will appear.

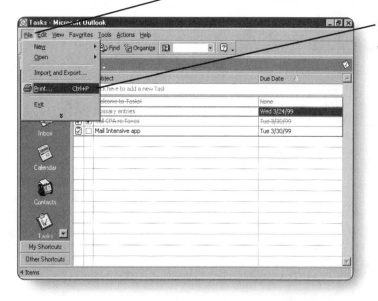

2. Click on **Print**. The Print dialog box will open.

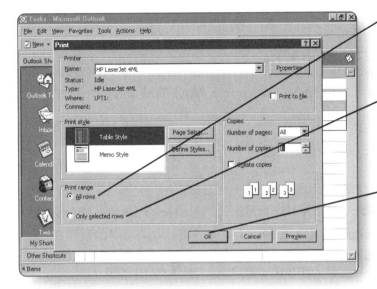

3a. Click on **All rows** to print all tasks. All tasks will print.

OR

3b. Click on **Only selected rows** to print only the selected tasks. Only selected tasks will print.

4. Click on **OK**. Outlook will print all your tasks, or just the ones you've selected, depending on which option you chose in step 3.

Part V Review Questions

1. How do you add a new task? *See "Adding a New Task" in Chapter 18*

2. What should you do if you are afraid of forgetting a task? *See "Setting a Reminder" in Chapter 18*

3. How do you let someone know the status of the task? *See "Sending Status Reports" in Chapter 18*

4. How can you send a task to someone else? *See "Creating a Task Request" in Chapter 19*

5. What are the two ways to reply to a task request? *See "Responding to a Task Request" in Chapter 19*

6. What can you do if you have accepted a task and can't complete it? *See "Declining a Task After You Have Accepted It" in Chapter 19*

7. How can you organize your tasks into folders? *See "Using Folders to Organize Tasks" in Chapter 20*

8. Can you view your task list by category? *See "Using Views to Organize Tasks" in Chapter 20*

9. How do you display sorted tasks? *See "Sorting the Task List" in Chapter 20*

10. Can you print one task or do you have to print the entire Task List? *See "Printing the Task List" in Chapter 20*

PART VI

Tracking Your Time with the Journal

21

Working with Journal Entries

The Journal is a feature that allows you to keep track of all the activities that you perform in the course of a day — whether it's responding to a meeting request, sending an e-mail, or opening a document. This feature is essential when billing time to clients or maintaining an accurate record of your daily activities. In this chapter, you'll learn how to:

- Automatically track Journal activities
- Create a new journal entry
- Modify a journal entry
- Delete a journal entry

Automatically Tracking Journal Activities

The easiest way to get started with the Journal is to have Outlook automatically record certain types of activities. Some examples of the types of activities that you can record are e-mail messages, meeting responses, and task requests.

1. **Click** on the **Journal icon** on the Outlook bar. The Journal will appear in the Information viewer.

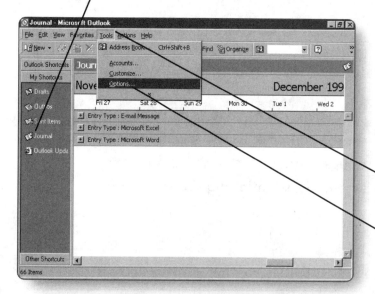

NOTE
You may need to click on the scroll arrows on the Outlook bar to see the Journal icon.

2. **Click** on **Tools**. The Tools menu will appear.

3. **Click** on **Options**. The Options dialog box will open.

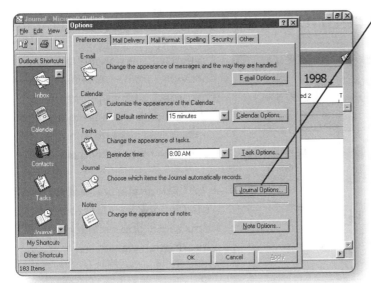

4. Click on the **Journal Options button**. The Journal Options dialog box will open.

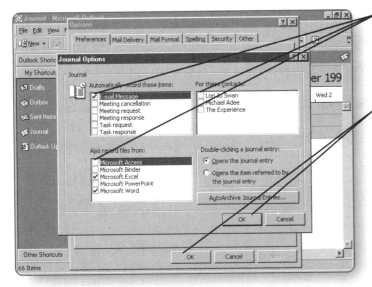

5. Click on the **check box** next to the type of items you want to record automatically. A check mark will be placed in the box.

6. Click on **OK** until all open dialog boxes are closed.

Creating a New Journal Entry

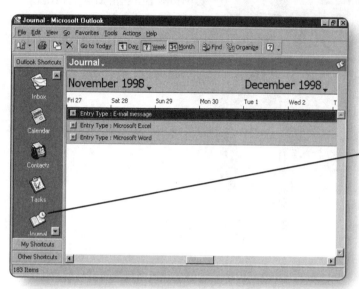

You may have noticed that some activities are not automatically recorded, such as phone calls. Don't worry, there are quick and easy ways to create a journal entry for these activities.

1. Click on the **Journal icon** on the Outlook bar. Your journal entries will appear in the Information viewer.

2. Click on **New**. The Journal Entry dialog box will open.

3. Click in the **Subject: text box** and **type** the **subject** of the journal entry. The subject will appear in the text box.

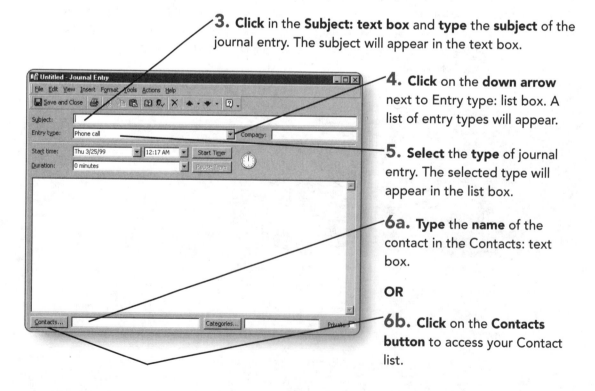

4. Click on the **down arrow** next to Entry type: list box. A list of entry types will appear.

5. Select the **type** of journal entry. The selected type will appear in the list box.

6a. Type the **name** of the contact in the Contacts: text box.

OR

6b. Click on the **Contacts button** to access your Contact list.

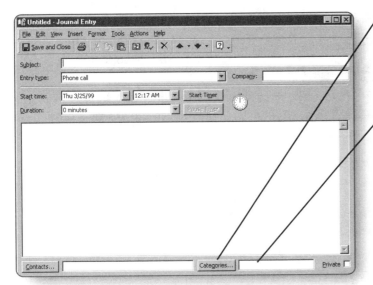

7a. Optionally, **click** on the **Categories** button to access the Categories list.

OR

7b. Optionally, **type** the **name** of the category or categories in the Categories text box.

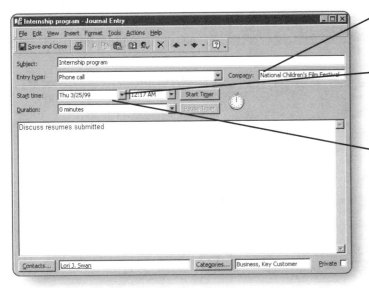

8. Type the **company name** in the Company: text box.

9. Click on the **down arrow** next to the Start time: list box. A calendar will appear.

10. Click on a **date** to **establish** the **starting date**.

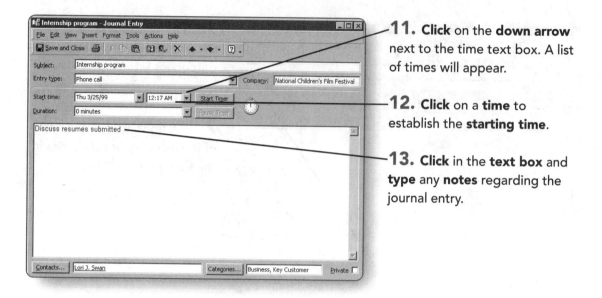

11. **Click** on the **down arrow** next to the time text box. A list of times will appear.

12. **Click** on a **time** to establish the **starting time**.

13. **Click** in the **text box** and **type** any **notes** regarding the journal entry.

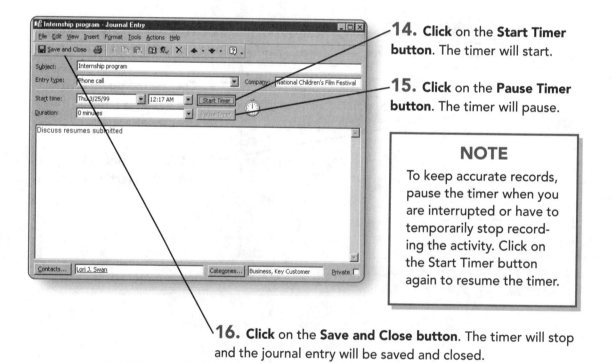

14. **Click** on the **Start Timer button**. The timer will start.

15. **Click** on the **Pause Timer button**. The timer will pause.

NOTE

To keep accurate records, pause the timer when you are interrupted or have to temporarily stop recording the activity. Click on the Start Timer button again to resume the timer.

16. **Click** on the **Save and Close button**. The timer will stop and the journal entry will be saved and closed.

Modifying a Journal Entry

What happens if you start recording a journal entry and forget to stop the timer when the activity is finished? Don't worry, it's easy to modify journal entries to change inaccurate information, or to add additional information to the entry.

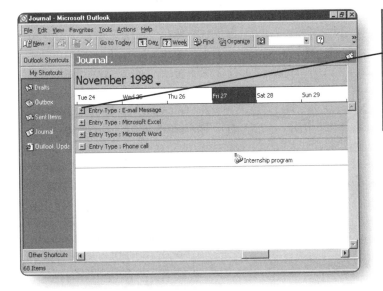

1. **Click** on the **Journal icon** on the Outlook bar. Your journal entries will appear in the Information viewer.

2. **Click twice** on any **entry**. The entry will appear.

NOTE

To view a particular entry, you may need to click on the plus (+) sign to expand the list of entries.

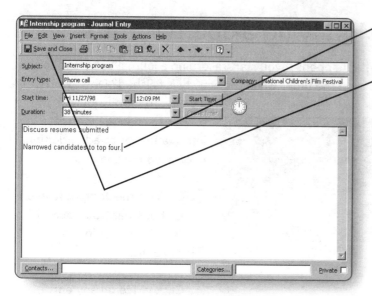

3. **Type** any **changes** to the entry. The changes will appear.

4. **Click** on the **Save and Close button**. The journal entry will close and any changes you've made will be saved.

Deleting a Journal Entry

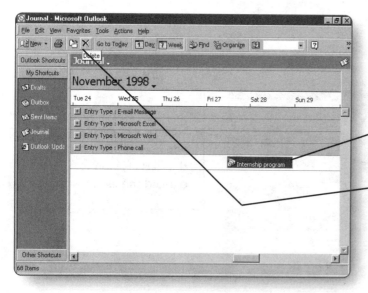

When journal entries are automatically recorded, you may end up with some unneeded entries. Deleting a journal entry is very easy with Outlook.

1. **Click** on any **journal entry**. The entry will be selected.

2. **Click** on the **Delete button**. The entry will be deleted.

NOTE

Journal entries are shortcuts that point to the actual item. Deleting the journal entry does not delete the actual item.

22

Changing the Journal View

In the previous chapter, you learned how to create, modify, delete, and automatically track journal entries. Now you can customize your Journal view to make it easier to find and change entries. Also, you'll learn how to tie journal entries to your contacts and organize journal entries by changing category assignments and view settings. In this chapter, you'll learn how to:

- View the Journal
- View the Journal entries for a contact
- Use categories and views to organize the Journal
- Customize Journal views
- Customize Journal entry actions

Viewing the Journal

There are several ways to view the Journal. You can display the entries by type, contact, category, or by looking at the last seven days. In some views, the Journal appears as a time line—you can scroll through the days to see the recorded activities.

1. **Click** on the **Journal icon** on the Outlook toolbar. The Journal will appear in the Information viewer.

2. **Click** on **View**. The View menu will appear.

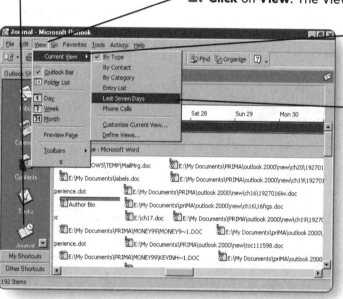

3. **Click** on **Current View**. The Current View submenu will appear.

4. **Click** on **any view**. The view will be selected.

If you select the By Type, By Contact, or By Category view, a time line will appear at the top of the Information viewer.

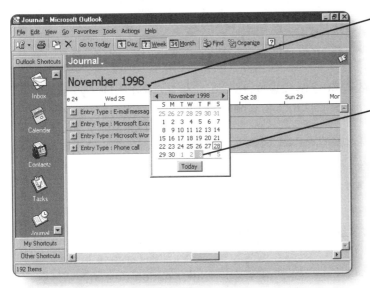

5. Click on the **down arrow** next to the month name in the banner. A Date Navigator will appear.

6. Click on **any date**. The Journal view will change to focus on the date you've chosen.

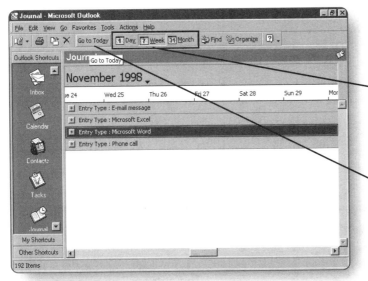

You can also change views with any of the buttons on the Standard toolbar.

7. Click on any of the **View buttons** to switch to day, week, or month view. You will be switched to that view.

8. Click on the **Go to Today button** to return to today's date. You will go back to today's date.

Using Categories to Organize the Journal

One of the best ways to organize the Journal is by using categories. Once you have added several items to the Key Customer category, you can view all related activities for Key Customer by viewing journal entries by category.

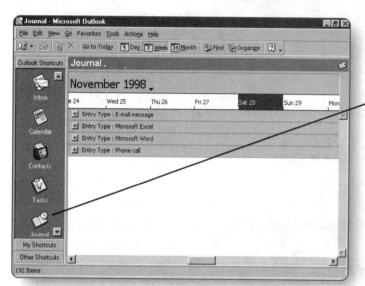

1. Click on the **Journal icon** on the Outlook bar. Your journal entries will appear in the Information viewer.

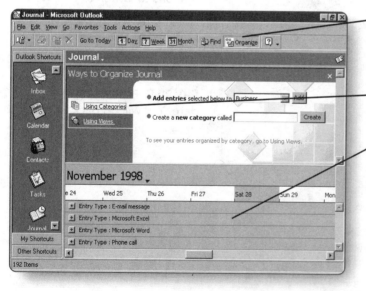

2. Click on the **Organize button**. The Ways to Organize Journal pane will appear.

3. Click on **Using Categories**. The tab will come to the front.

4. Click on **any journal entry**. The entry will be selected.

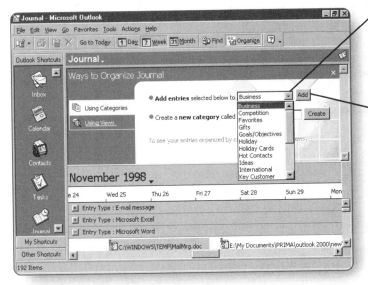

5. Click on the **down arrow** next to the Add entries selected below to list box and **select** a **category**.

6. Click on the **Add button**. The journal entry will be added to the category selected in step 5.

Displaying Journal Entries by Category

Once the selected items have been added to a category, you can use views to display journal entries by category.

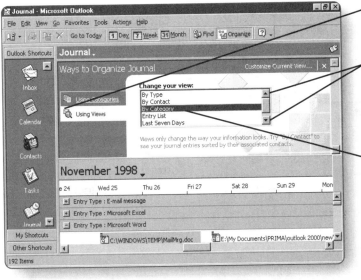

1. Click on **Using Views**. The tab will come to the front.

2. Click on the **scroll arrows** of the Change your view: scroll box. The available views will appear.

3. Click on **one of the views**. The Journal entries will appear in the selected view format.

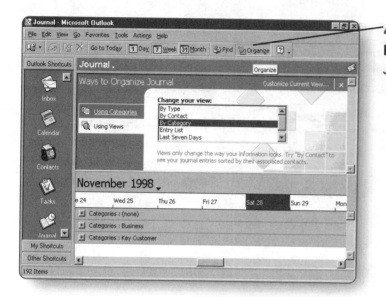

4. Click on the **Organize button**. The Ways to Organize Journal pane will close.

Customizing Views

Each of the views in the Journal have pre-defined settings that can easily be changed. Some of the items you can change are including or excluding labels on the journal icons, showing week numbers, or changing the font of the view.

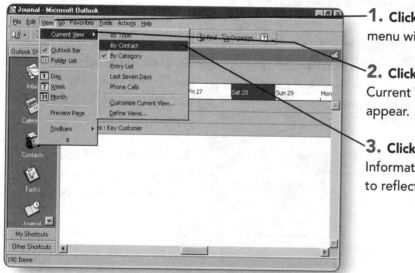

1. Click on **View**. The View menu will appear.

2. Click on **Current View**. The Current View submenu will appear.

3. Click on a **selection**. The Information viewer will change to reflect your selection.

4. Click on **View**. The View menu will appear.

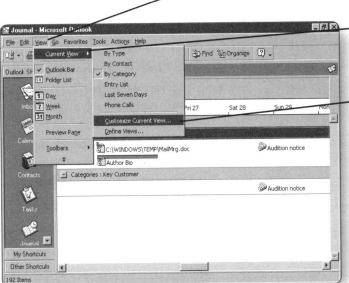

5. Click on **Current View**. The Current View submenu will appear.

6. Click on **Customize Current View**. The View Summary dialog box will open.

NOTE

Some options are available only for particular view formats. Depending on the current view you've selected, the options discussed in this section might not be available.

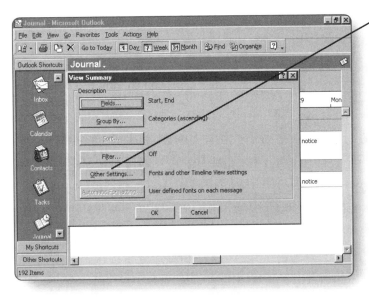

7. Click on the **Other Settings button**. The Format Timeline View dialog box will open.

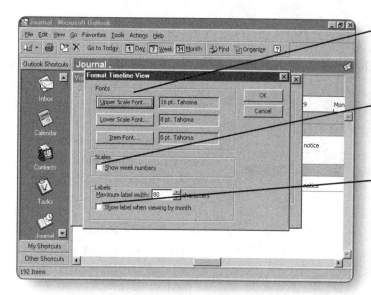

8. Click on any of the **buttons** in the Fonts area. The font will change accordingly.

9. Click on the **check box** next to Show week numbers. The week numbers will display.

10. Click on the **check box** next to Show label when viewing by month. The labels will display.

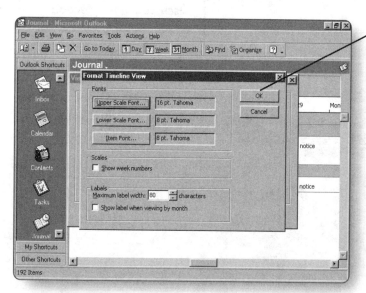

11. Click on **OK** until all open dialog boxes are closed. The Journal will reappear in the Information viewer.

TIP

You can change the default behavior of Outlook and journal entries. Click on Tools, Options, and then click on Journal Options. In the Double-clicking a Journal Entry section, click on Opens the Journal Entry or Opens the Item Referred to by the Journal Entry.

Part VI Review Questions

1. Name six types of activities that can be automatically recorded in the Journal. *See "Automatically Tracking Journal Activities" in Chapter 21*

2. How can you manually create a Journal entry? *See "Creating a New Journal Entry" in Chapter 21*

3. How can you temporarily stop the timer? *See "Creating a New Journal Entry" in Chapter 21*

4. How do you expand a list of Journal entries to see individual entries? *See "Modifying a Journal Entry" in Chapter 21*

5. Does deleting a Journal entry delete the item to which the entry refers? *See "Deleting a Journal Entry" in Chapter 21*

6. Name three Journal views that display a time line. *See "Viewing the Journal" in Chapter 22*

7. How would you view all the phone call entries for a single contact? *See "Viewing the Journal Entries for a Contact" in Chapter 22*

8. How would you add a category to a contact? *See "Using Categories to Organize the Journal" in Chapter 22*

9. How can you view all Journal entries by category? *See "Displaying Journal Entries by Category" in Chapter 22*

10. How can you display a label next to the Journal entry icons? *See "Customizing Views" in Chapter 22*

Capturing Your Thoughts with Notes

23

Working with Notes

The Notes feature in Outlook lets you quickly jot down any important thoughts, reminders, or other information. Use notes in Outlook instead of grabbing the closest scrap of paper around you. In this chapter, you'll learn how to:

- Create, edit, and delete a note
- Add a category to notes
- Turn a note into an e-mail or task

Creating a Note

Creating an electronic note in Outlook is easier than reaching for a pen and paper. Creating notes electronically guarantees that you won't have to transfer them to your computer later on.

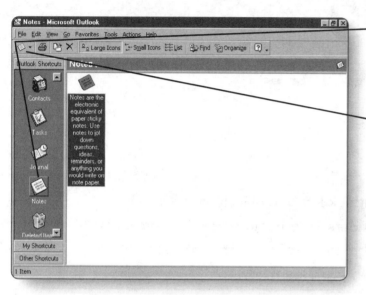

1. Click on the **Notes icon** on the Outlook bar. Your notes will appear in the Information viewer.

2. Click on the **New Note button**. A new note window will appear.

> ## NOTE
> If you don't see the date and time at the bottom of the note window, go to the Tools menu and select Options. Select the Other tab and click on the Advanced Options button. From the window that opens, click in the check box labeled When viewing Notes, show time and date in the Appearance options section.

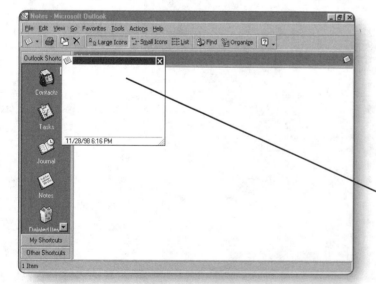

3. Type the **note**.

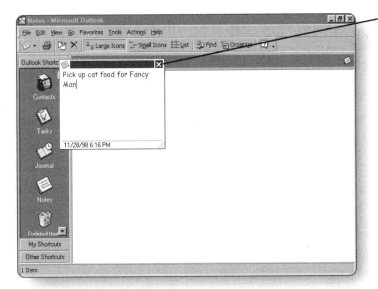

4. Click on the **Close button**. The note will be saved automatically.

TIP
You can press the Esc key to close a note.

NOTE
Only the first paragraph of the note will appear in the note preview in the Information viewer.

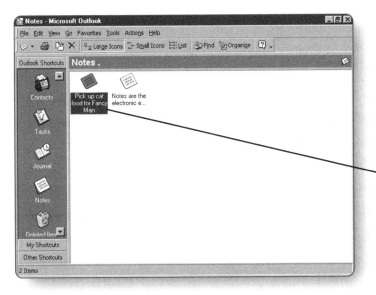

Editing a Note

If you gather more information after creating a note, don't worry — you can update the note even after you have closed it.

1. Double-click on any **note icon**. The note will open.

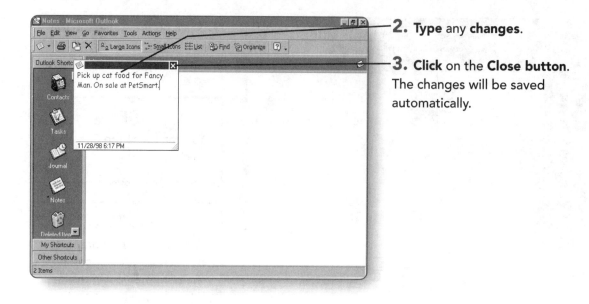

2. Type any **changes**.

3. Click on the **Close button**. The changes will be saved automatically.

Categorizing a Note

It's far easier to organize electronic notes than a stack of phone messages on your desk. You can use Categories in Outlook to group notes into subjects for easy identification and organization.

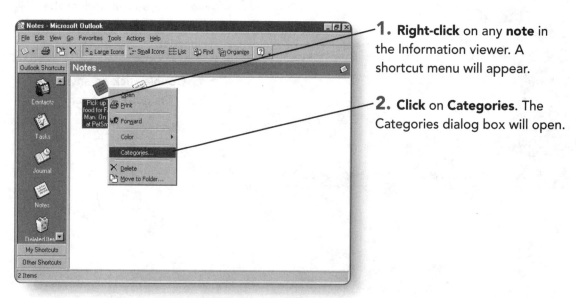

1. Right-click on any **note** in the Information viewer. A shortcut menu will appear.

2. Click on **Categories**. The Categories dialog box will open.

3. Click in any **check box** in the Available categories: scroll box. A check mark will be placed in the box.

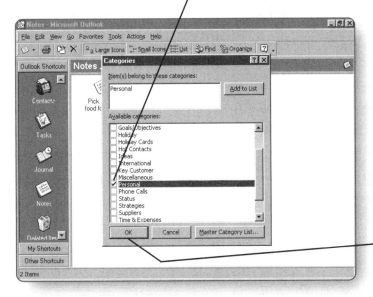

4. Click on **OK**. Your note will be added to the categories you've selected.

Turning a Note into Another Outlook Item

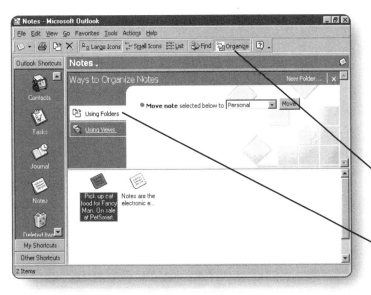

Do you want more from your notes? You can send the note content to another person, create a task from the note, or add an item to the calendar by dragging the note into another Outlook folder.

1. Click on **Organize**. The Ways to Organize Notes pane will open.

2. Click on **Using Folders**. The tab will come to the front.

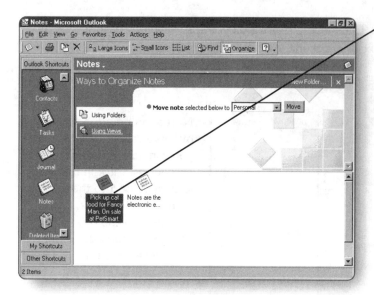

3. Click on any **note** in the note pane. The note will be selected.

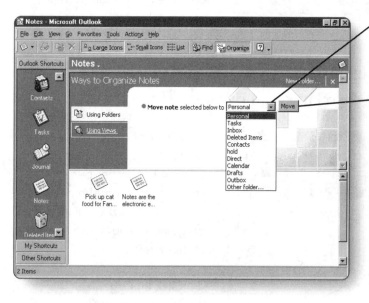

4. Click on the **down arrow** next to Move note selected below to and **select** a **folder**.

5. Click on the **Move button**. The selected note(s) will be moved to a new folder.

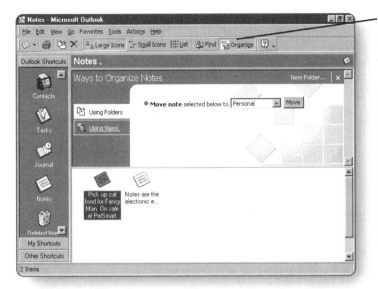

6. Click on **Organize**. The Ways to Organize Notes pane will close.

Deleting a Note

No longer need your note? Outlook makes it easy to delete notes and keep your desktop clean.

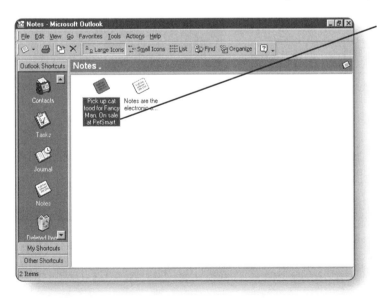

1. Right-click on a **note** in the Information viewer. A shortcut menu will appear.

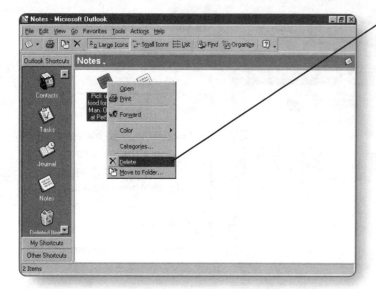

2. Click on **Delete**. The note will be deleted.

NOTE

Deleted notes move to the Deleted Items folder. If you later realize you need a deleted note, you can open the Deleted Items folder and drag the note back to the Notes folder.

24

Changing the Look of Notes

The Notes feature in Outlook lets you quickly jot down any important thoughts, reminders, or other information. You can change the appearance of notes to quickly find and identify which note you are looking for. In this chapter, you'll learn how to:

- Change note color and displays
- Use views to organize notes
- Sort or filter views

Changing Note Colors

If you are visually oriented, Outlook has a great feature that will allow you to organize your notes by color.

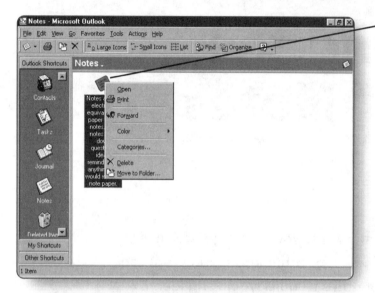

1. **Right-click** on any **note icon**. A shortcut menu will appear.

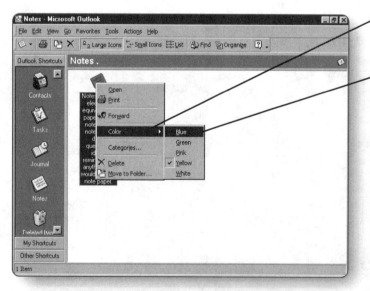

2. **Click** on **Color**. The Color submenu will appear.

3. **Click** on any **color**. The color will be applied to the note.

TIP

Colors can be used to organize notes into visual categories. For example, make personal items blue and important items pink.

Changing Note Defaults

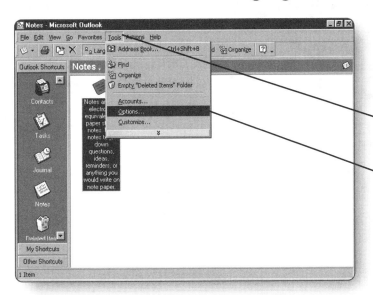

By default, notes are yellow and medium in size. You can change these defaults for any new notes added to the Notes folder.

1. Click on **Tools**. The Tools menu will appear.

2. Click on **Options**. The Options dialog box will open.

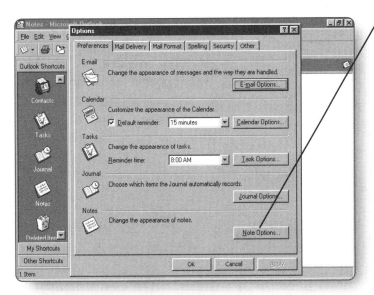

3. Click on the **Note Options button**. The Note Options dialog box will open.

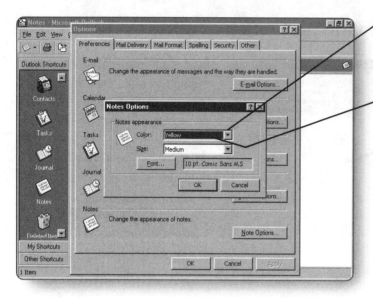

4. **Click** on the **down arrow** next to the Color: list box. A list of available colors will appear.

5. **Click** on a **color**. Your choice will appear in the list box.

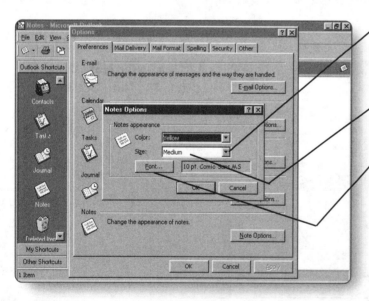

6. **Click** on the **down arrow** next to the Size: list box. A list of available sizes will appear.

7. **Click** on a **size**. Your choice will appear in the list box.

8. **Click** on the **Font button**. The Font dialog box will open.

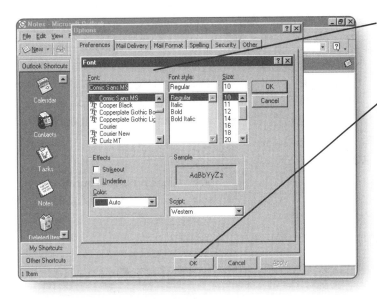

9. **Click** on a **font, font style, and size**. Your selections will be highlighted.

10. **Click** on **OK** until all open dialog boxes are closed. Your notes will reappear in the Information viewer.

Changing the Notes Display

Notes are displayed in the Information viewer as icons. You can change the size of the icon or display a simple list of notes instead.

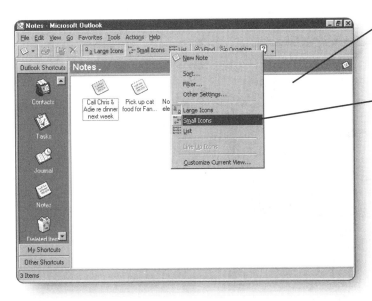

1. **Right-click** on a **blank area** in the Information viewer. A shortcut menu will appear.

2a. **Click** on **Small Icons**. Your notes will be displayed as smaller icons. You will be able to see more notes in the Information viewer, but you won't be able to see as much detail on each one.

OR

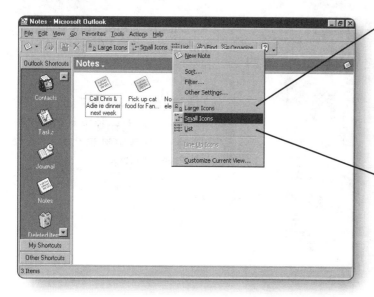

2b. **Click** on **Large Icons**. Your notes will be displayed as larger icons. You won't be able to see as many notes in your Information viewer, but you'll be able to see more details about each one.

OR

2c. **Click** on **List**. Your notes will be visible in a list format.

Changing the Notes View

Views let you change which notes appear on the screen. Using views is a great way to organize notes or to find the notes you need.

1. **Click** on **Organize**. The Ways to Organize Notes pane will open.

TIP
Use the Large Icons, Small Icons, and List buttons on the Standard toolbar to quickly change the list type.

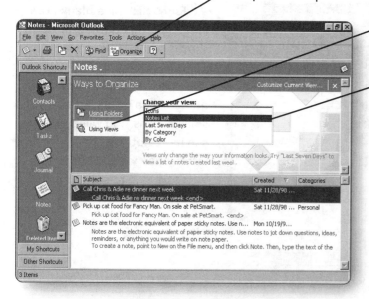

2. **Click** on **Using Views**. The tab will come to the front.

3. **Click** on any **view**. The view will change.

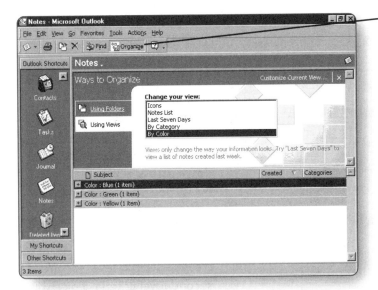

4. Click on **Organize**. The Ways to Organize Notes pane will close.

Sorting and Filtering Notes

Sorting notes will group together similar notes. Once notes have been sorted, you can scroll through all the notes to find the ones you want. Filtering notes allows you to show only the notes you need. The other notes are not deleted; they simply do not display onscreen.

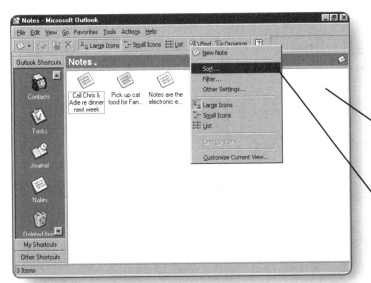

Sorting Notes

1. Right-click on any **blank area** of the Information viewer. A shortcut menu will appear.

2. Click on **Sort**. The Sort dialog box will open.

3. Click on the **down arrow** next to the Sort items by list box. A list of available sorting criteria will appear.

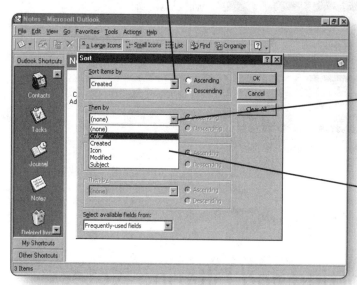

4. Click on a **sorting criteria**. Your choice will appear in the list box.

5. Optionally, **click** on the **down arrow** next to the Then by list box. A list of available sorting criteria will appear.

6. Click on a **sorting criteria** to create a second-level sort. Your second-level criteria choice will appear in the list box.

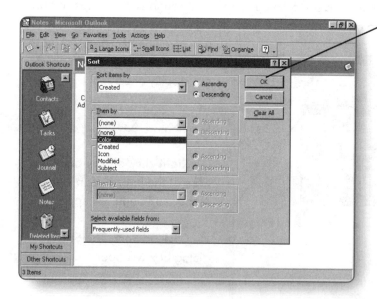

7. Click on **OK**. Your notes will be sorted according to the options you've selected.

Filtering Notes

Maybe you only want to see a particular type of note. For example, all personal notes, or all notes created on a certain date. Filtering will get to the notes you want without having to see all of the others.

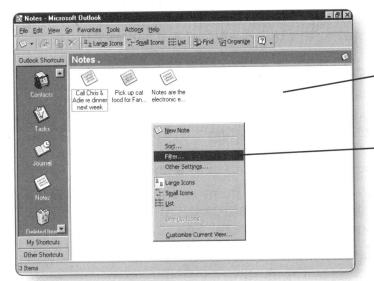

1. Right-click on any **blank area** of the Information viewer. A shortcut menu will appear.

2. Click on **Filter**. The Filter dialog box will open.

3. Click on any **tab** and select the desired filter criteria. Your choices will be selected.

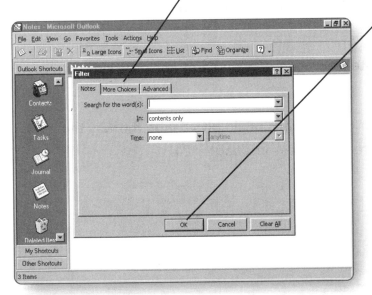

4. Click on **OK**. Your notes will be filtered according to the criteria you've selected.

NOTE

To remove filter criteria and display all notes, click on the Clear All button on the Filter dialog box.

Part VII Review Questions

1. How do you add a note? *See "Creating a Note" in Chapter 23*

2. How do you edit a note? *See "Editing a Note" in Chapter 23*

3. How do you add a category to a note? *See "Categorizing a Note" in Chapter 23*

4. Where do deleted notes go? *See "Deleting a Note" in Chapter 23*

5. How do you place the contents of a note in an e-mail message? *See "Turning a Note into Another Outlook Item" in Chapter 23*

6. Why would you change the color of a note? *See "Changing Note Colors" in Chapter 24*

7. How can you get notes to appear in a different color, size, or font? *See "Changing Note Defaults" in Chapter 24*

8. Name three display settings for notes. *See "Changing the Notes Display" in Chapter 24*

9. What are the five note views? *See "Changing the Notes View" in Chapter 24*

10. Does applying a filter delete notes or simply change the way the notes look? *See "Filtering Notes" in Chapter 24*

PART VIII

Customizing Outlook

25

Accessing Frequently Used Commands

Most common Outlook commands appear on the toolbars at the top edge of the screen. If there is a command you use that does not appear on the screen as a toolbar button, don't worry! Outlook allows you to completely customize the toolbars and the Outlook bar, providing you with one-click access to the tasks or folders you need. In this chapter, you'll learn how to:

- Add commands to toolbars
- Delete commands from toolbars
- Reset toolbars
- Add groups and shortcuts to the Outlook bar
- Add shortcuts to the Outlook bar

Adding Commands to Toolbars

Do you want to click on a button and have an often-performed task occur? You can add any Outlook command to the toolbars.

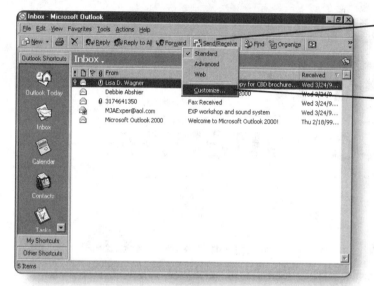

1. Right-click on any **toolbar button**. A shortcut menu will appear.

2. Click on **Customize**. The Customize dialog box will open.

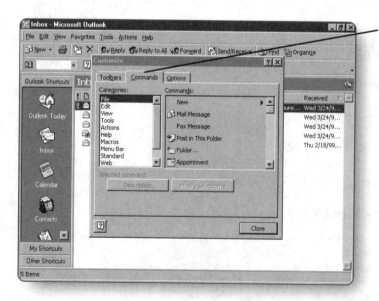

3. Click on the **Commands tab**. The tab will come to the front.

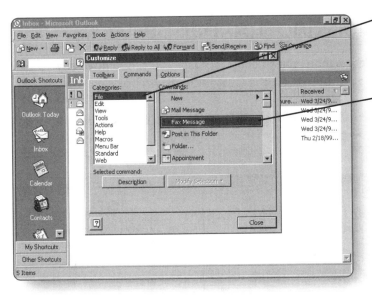

4. **Click** on any **category**. You will see the commands associated with the category.

5. **Click** on any **command**. The command will be selected.

6. **Click** and **drag** the **command** to an existing toolbar. The command will be added.

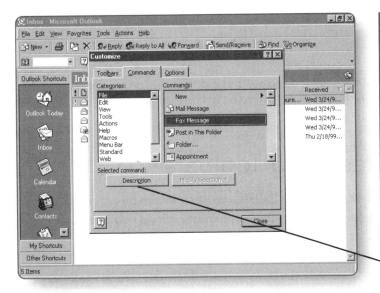

NOTE

As you drag the command, there will be a small X attached to the mouse pointer. When the pointer changes to a plus (+) sign, release the mouse button to place the command on the toolbar.

TIP

Click on a command in the Customize dialog box, and then click on the Description button to see a description of how the command works.

Deleting Toolbar Buttons

Want a more streamlined toolbar? You can remove any toolbar button via the Customize dialog box.

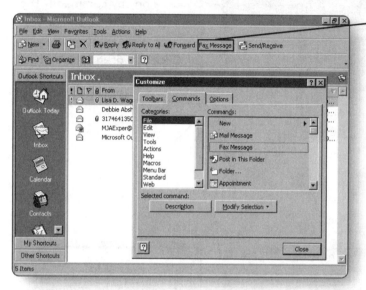

1. **Click** on the **toolbar button** that you want to remove. It will be selected.

NOTE

The Customize dialog box must be open to add or delete buttons from the toolbars.

---

2. **Click** and **drag** the **button** away from the toolbar. A small X will appear below the button.

3. **Release** the **mouse button**. The button will be removed from the toolbar.

Resetting Toolbars

Whoops! Did you delete a toolbar button by accident? If you've changed a toolbar, Outlook allows you to quickly restore toolbar buttons to their original settings.

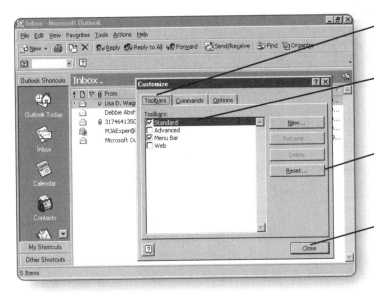

1. **Click** on the **Toolbars tab**. The tab will come to the front.

2. **Click** on the **toolbar** that you want to reset. It will be selected.

3. **Click** on **Reset**. The toolbar will be restored to its original settings.

4. **Click** on the **Close button**. The Customize dialog box will close.

Adding Groups to the Outlook Bar

A quick way to access the folders you need is by clicking on the Outlook bar. Folders on the Outlook bar are arranged into groups, and you can add or delete any group on the Outlook bar.

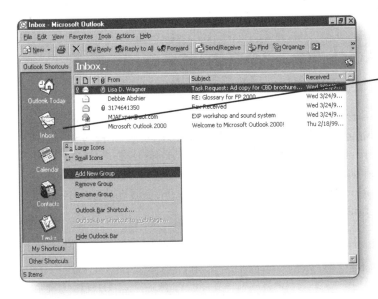

1. **Right-click** on any **blank area** of the Outlook bar. A shortcut menu will appear.

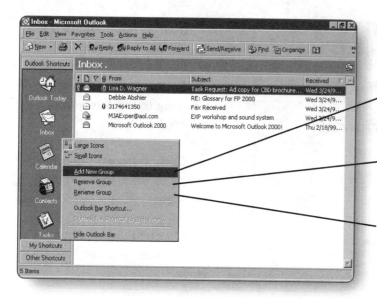

2. Click on a **Group command** on the shortcut menu. The available commands include:

- **Add New Group**. Click on this option to add a new group to the Outlook bar.

- **Remove Group**. Click on this option to remove a group from the Outlook bar.

- **Rename Group**. Click on this option to rename any group on the Outlook bar with a new name.

NOTE

Deleting a group from the Outlook bar will not remove the folders or their contents from Outlook. The icons on the Outlook bar are merely shortcuts that point to the actual items.

Adding Shortcuts to the Outlook Bar

Shortcuts are pointers to frequently used folders. For example, if there is a client folder on the network, you may want to create a shortcut pointing to the folder so that you can access its files quickly. Once you have a shortcut on the Outlook bar, all you have to do is point and click to navigate to a new location.

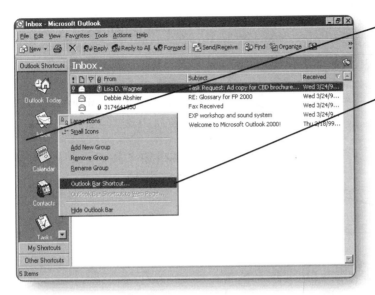

1. **Right-click** on a **blank area** of the Outlook bar. A shortcut menu will appear.

2. **Click** on **Outlook Bar Shortcut**. The Add to Outlook Bar dialog box will open.

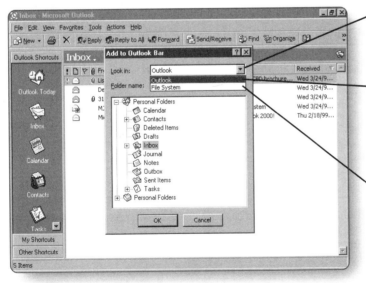

3. **Click** on the **down arrow** next to the Look in: list box. Two choices will appear.

4a. Click on **Outlook**. Shortcuts to all Outlook folders will appear.

OR

4b. Click on **File System**. Shortcuts to any folders on your computer or network will appear.

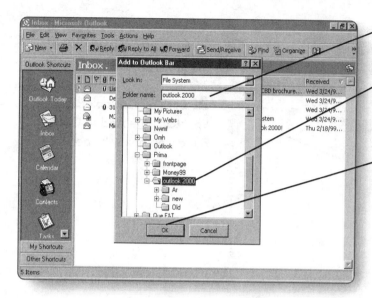

5. Type the **name** of the group in the Folder name: text box.

6. Click on the **folder** to which you want to add a shortcut. It will be highlighted.

7. Click on **OK**. The shortcut will be added.

26

Customizing Your Messages

Are you tired of plain e-mail messages? The white background, the gray headers—maybe it's a little too dull. Don't spend hours trying to spruce up your e-mail messages— let Outlook do it for you! In this chapter, you'll learn how to:

- Send mail messages with stationery
- Use Microsoft Word as your e-mail editor

Sending Mail Messages Using Stationery

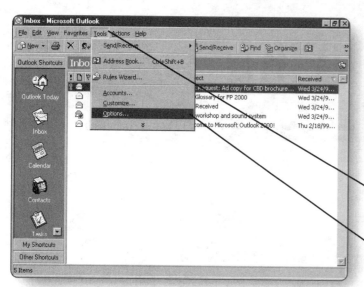

If you want a new look for your electronic correspondence, you can use stationery to brighten up your messages. But before you can use stationery, Outlook needs to change the format of the e-mail messages to HTML. This is a one-time procedure.

1. **Click** on **Tools**. The Tools menu will appear.

2. **Click** on **Options**. The Options dialog box will open.

3. **Click** on the **Mail Format tab**. The tab will come to the front.

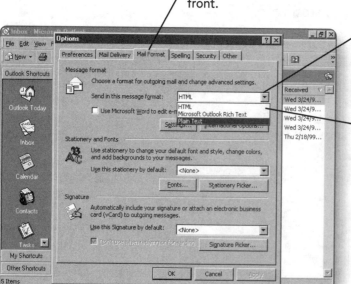

4. **Click** on the **down arrow** next to the Send in this message format: list box. A drop-down list will appear.

5. **Click** on **HTML**. It will be selected.

Now that Outlook knows that you want to use HTML, you can set a default stationery, change the font, or edit the stationery.

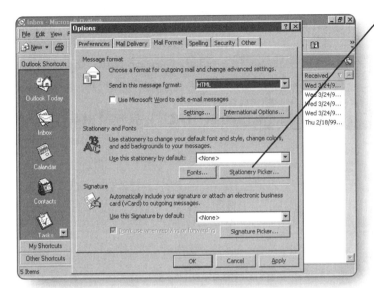

6. **Click** on **Stationery Picker**. The Stationery Picker dialog box will open.

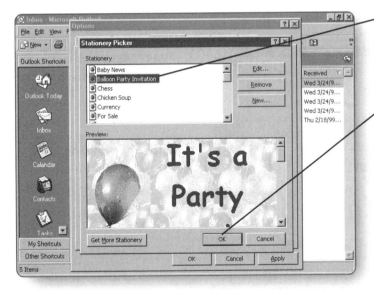

7. **Click** on any **stationery type** in the Stationery: list box. You will see a preview of the stationery.

8. **Click** on **OK**. The stationery you chose will be the default for all new messages.

9. Click on **File**. The File menu will appear.

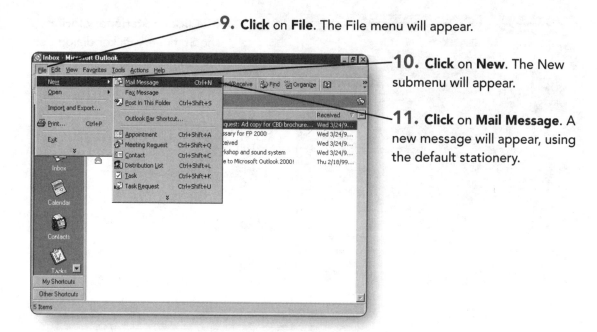

10. Click on **New**. The New submenu will appear.

11. Click on **Mail Message**. A new message will appear, using the default stationery.

12. Type the required **information** for the message in the Subject: text box. The text will appear.

13. Click on **Send**. The message will be sent on the stationery that you've selected.

NOTE

Some e-mail users cannot properly view messages in HTML format. For those recipients, the message text can be read, but it may contain miscellaneous codes or characters, and the stationery you select may instead be received as an attached file. To avoid this problem, select Send Using Plain Text in that contact's settings.

Using Other Stationery Patterns

Once you've selected your default stationery, you can still use other stationery patterns or send a plain e-mail message.

1. **Click** on the **Inbox icon** on the Outlook bar. Your e-mail messages will appear in the Information viewer.

2. **Click** on **Actions**. The Actions menu will appear.

3. **Click** on **New Mail Message Using**. A submenu will appear.

4a. **Click** on **More Stationery**. You will be able to access all of the stationery.

OR

4b. **Click** on **HTML (No Stationery)**. Your original, default message background will be used.

OR

4c. **Click** on **Plain Text**. Your message will be sent with no formatting features.

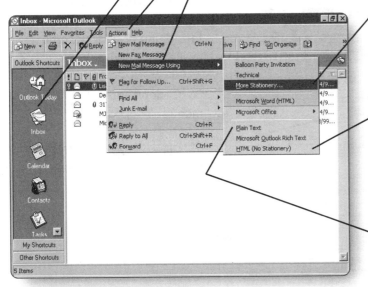

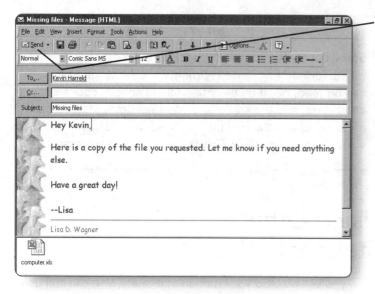

5. Click on **Send** when you're finished addressing and composing the message. The message will be sent with the stationery setting you've chosen.

Using Microsoft Word as Your E-mail Editor

If you have used Microsoft Word, you know how many formatting options are available in the application. By using Microsoft Word as your e-mail editor, its full range of formatting options become available to you.

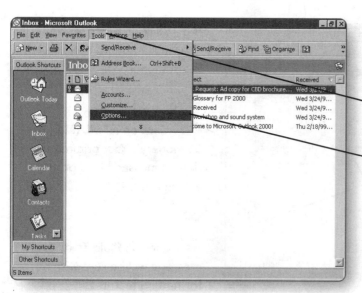

1. Click on **Tools**. The Tools menu will appear.

2. Click on **Options**. The Options dialog box will open.

3. Click on the **Mail Format tab**. The tab will come to the front.

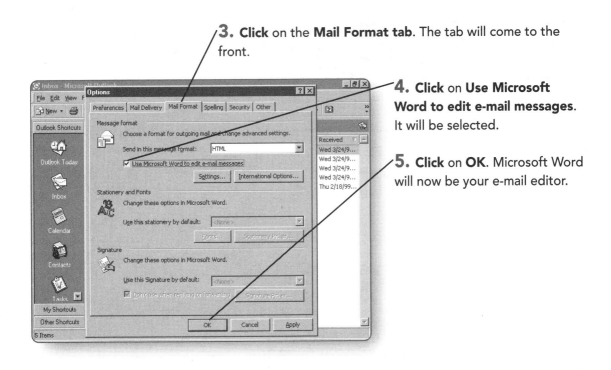

4. Click on **Use Microsoft Word to edit e-mail messages**. It will be selected.

5. Click on **OK**. Microsoft Word will now be your e-mail editor.

6. Click on **File**. The File menu will appear.

7. Click on **New**. The New submenu will appear.

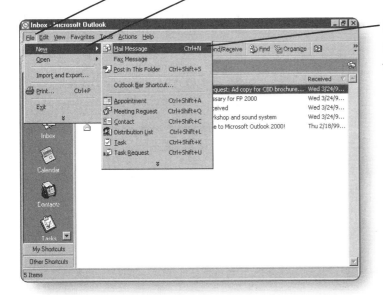

8. Click on **Mail Message**. A new message will appear, using the default WordMail template.

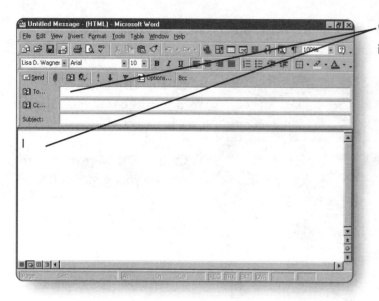

9. Type the required **information** for the message.

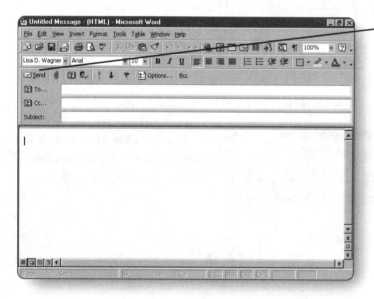

10. Click on **Send**. The message will be sent.

> ### NOTE
> When you send e-mail using WordMail or stationery, the e-mail recipient must have Outlook in order to see the special formatting.

> **TIP**
> To change WordMail's default template, open Word, then click on Tools and choose Options. In the Options dialog box, click on E-mail Options and choose the theme or stationery that you want to use as the standard template.

Sending Messages Directly from Word

If you have a document in Word that you want to use as an e-mail message, you don't have to create a message in Outlook first and then attach the document. Instead, Outlook can help you send your Word document directly from Microsoft Word in a few simple steps.

1. **Open** or create the **Word document**.

2. **Click** on the **E-mail button** on Word's toolbar. The WordMail tools will appear.

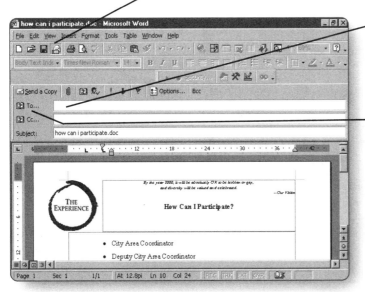

3a. **Type** the recipient's **name(s)** in the To text box.

OR

3b. **Click** on the **To button** to select recipients from your Contacts list.

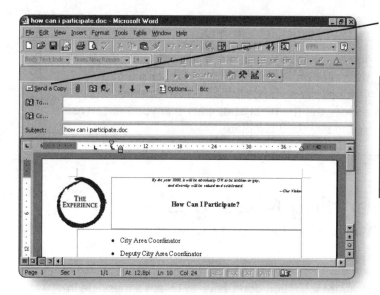

4. **Click** on **Send a Copy**.
Outlook will send the message.

NOTE

If the recipient does not use Microsoft Office, the Word document will be received as an attachment.

27

Changing Preferences and Options

One of the most powerful features of Outlook is its ability to adapt to your preferences. If you don't like the way your mail, calendar, or other folders operate, you can easily change your environment. In this chapter, you'll learn how to:

- Customize e-mail options
- Customize preferences

Customizing E-mail Options

You may have noticed that there are numerous default e-mail settings in Outlook. If you don't like the way Outlook e-mail works, you can change it! For example, you can specify what occurs when you close an e-mail message or receive a new e-mail message, and what to do with items in the Deleted Items folder when you exit Outlook.

1. Click on **Tools**. The Tools menu will appear.

2. Click on **Options**. The Options dialog box will open.

3. Click on the **Preferences tab**. The tab will come to the front.

4. Click on the **E-mail Options button**. The E-mail Options dialog box will open.

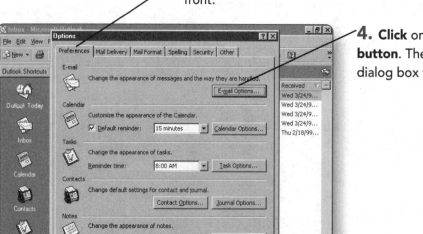

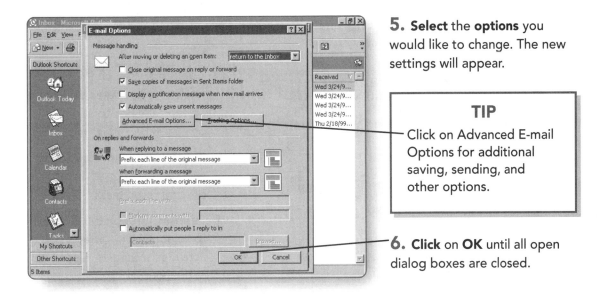

5. Select the **options** you would like to change. The new settings will appear.

TIP

Click on Advanced E-mail Options for additional saving, sending, and other options.

6. Click on **OK** until all open dialog boxes are closed.

Customizing Preferences

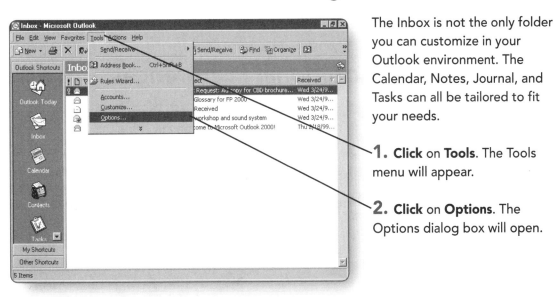

The Inbox is not the only folder you can customize in your Outlook environment. The Calendar, Notes, Journal, and Tasks can all be tailored to fit your needs.

1. Click on **Tools**. The Tools menu will appear.

2. Click on **Options**. The Options dialog box will open.

3. Click on the **Preferences tab**. The tab will come to the front.

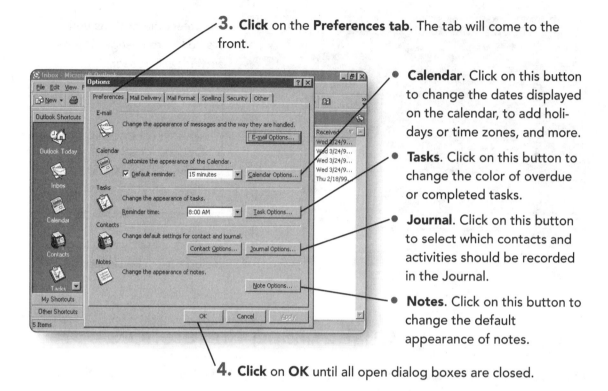

- **Calendar.** Click on this button to change the dates displayed on the calendar, to add holidays or time zones, and more.

- **Tasks.** Click on this button to change the color of overdue or completed tasks.

- **Journal.** Click on this button to select which contacts and activities should be recorded in the Journal.

- **Notes.** Click on this button to change the default appearance of notes.

4. Click on **OK** until all open dialog boxes are closed.

Additional Preferences

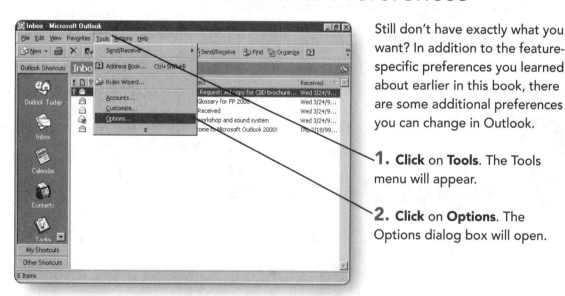

Still don't have exactly what you want? In addition to the feature-specific preferences you learned about earlier in this book, there are some additional preferences you can change in Outlook.

1. Click on **Tools**. The Tools menu will appear.

2. Click on **Options**. The Options dialog box will open.

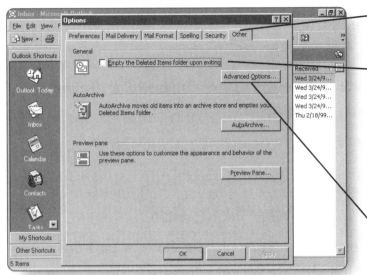

3. **Click** on the **Other tab**. The tab will come to the front.

4. **Click** on the **check box** next to Empty the Deleted Items folder upon exiting. A check mark will appear in the box and the deleted items will be emptied every time you exit the program.

5. **Click** on the **Advanced Options button**. The Advanced Options dialog box will open.

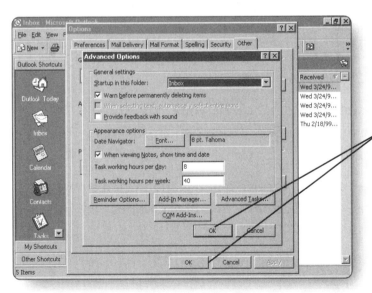

6. **Click** on the **check box** next to the options you want to select. A check mark will appear next to those options that you select.

7. **Click** on **OK** until all open dialog boxes are closed.

Part VIII Review Questions

1. How do you add a command button to your toolbar? *See "Adding Commands to Toolbars" in Chapter 25*

2. How do you reset your toolbar? *See "Resetting Toolbars" in Chapter 25*

3. How do you add a new group of folders to your Outlook bar? *See "Adding Groups to the Outlook Bar" in Chapter 25*

4. How do you add a shortcut to a group on your Outlook bar? *See "Adding Shortcuts to the Outlook Bar" in Chapter 25*

5. In order to use stationery for messages, what format must your e-mail messages be in? *See "Sending Mail Messages Using Stationery" in Chapter 26*

6. How do you set a default stationery? *See "Sending Mail Messages Using Stationery" in Chapter 26*

7. If you have a default stationery set, how do you choose no stationery for a single message? *See "Using Other Stationery Patterns" in Chapter 26*

8. Where do you set the option to receive a notification when a new e-mail message arrives? *See "Customizing E-mail Options" in Chapter 27*

9. How do you add holidays to your calendar? *See "Customizing Preferences" in Chapter 27*

10. How do you make Outlook empty your Deleted Items folder upon exiting? *See "Customizing Preferences" in Chapter 27*

P A R T   I X

Appendixes

A

Office 2000 Installation

Installing Office 2000 is typically very quick and easy. In this appendix, you'll learn how to:

- Install Office 2000 on your computer
- Choose which Office components you want to install
- Detect and repair problems
- Reinstall Office
- Add and remove components
- Uninstall Office 2000 completely
- Install content from other Office CDs

Installing the Software

The installation program for the Office 2000 programs is automatic. In most cases, you can simply follow the instructions onscreen.

> ### NOTE
> When you insert the Office 2000 CD for the first time, you may see a message that the installer has been updated, prompting you to restart your system. Do so, and when you return to Windows after restarting, remove the CD and reinsert it so that the Setup program starts up automatically again.

1. **Insert** the **Office 2000 CD-ROM** into your computer's CD-ROM drive. The Windows Installer will start and the Customer Information dialog box will open.

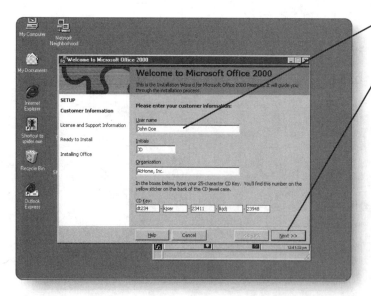

2. **Type** all of the **information** requested.

3. **Click** on **Next**. The End User License Agreement will appear.

> ### NOTE
> You'll find the CD Key number on a sticker on the back of the Office CD jewel case.

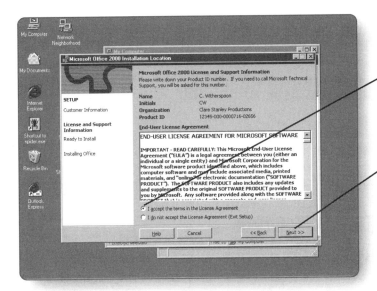

4. **Read** the **License Agreement**.

5. **Click** on the **I accept the terms in the License Agreement option button**. The option will be selected.

6. **Click** on **Next**. The Ready To Install dialog box will open.

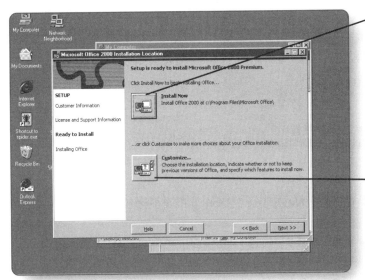

7a. **Click** on the **Install Now button.** Use this option to install Office on your computer with the default settings. This is the recommended installation for most users.

OR

7b. **Click** on the **Customize button**, if you want to choose which components to install or where to install them. The Installation Location dialog box will open. Then see the next section, "Choosing Components," for guidance.

8. **Wait** while the **Office software** installs on your computer. When the setup has completed, the Installer Information box will open.

9. Click on **Yes**. The Setup Wizard will restart your computer. After your computer has restarted, Windows will update your system settings and then finish the Office installation and configuration process.

Choosing Components

If you selected option 7b in the previous section, you have the choice of installing many different programs and components.

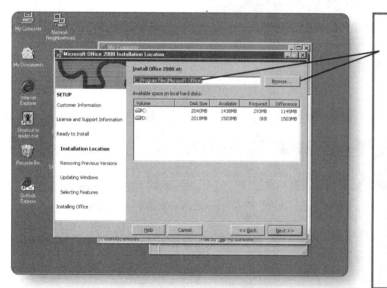

NOTE

For a custom installation, you have the option of placing Office in a different location on your computer. It is recommended that you use the default installation location. If you want to install Office in a different directory, type the directory path in the text box or click on the Browse button to select a directory.

1. Click on **Next**. The Selecting Features dialog box will open.

2. Click on a **plus sign (+)** to expand a list of features. The features listed under the category will appear.

3. Click on the **down arrow (▼)** to the right of the hard drive icon. A menu of available installation options for the feature will appear.

4. Click on the **button** next to the individual option, and choose a setting for that option:

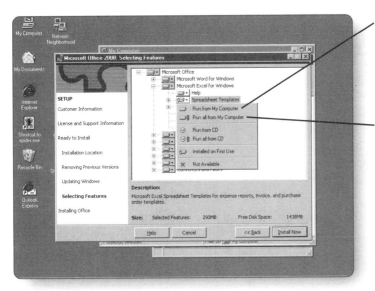

- **Run from My Computer**. The component will be fully installed, so that you will not need the Office CD in the CD-ROM drive to use it.

- **Run all from My Computer**. The selected component and all the components subordinate to it will be fully installed.

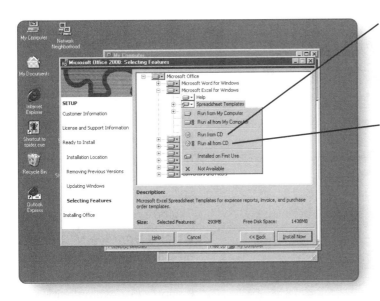

- **Run from CD**. The component will be installed, but you will need to have the Office CD in the CD-ROM drive to use it.

- **Run all from CD**. The selected component and all the components subordinate to it will need to have the Office CD in the CD-ROM drive to use it.

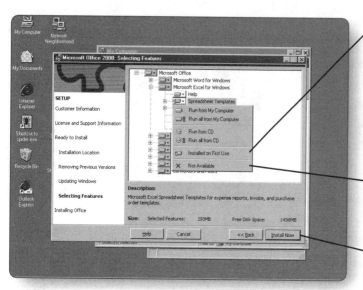

- **Installed on First Use**. The first time you try to activate the component, you will be prompted to insert the Office CD to fully install it. This is good for components that you are not sure whether you will need or not.

- **Not Available**. The component will not be installed at all.

5. Click on **Install Now**. The Installing dialog box will open.

In a Custom installation, you'll be asked whether you want to update Internet Explorer to version 5.0. Your choices are:

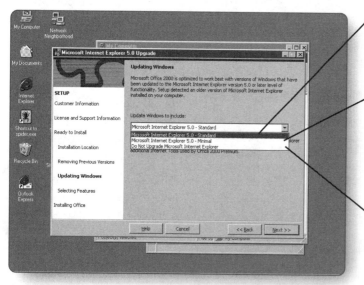

- **Microsoft Internet Explorer 5.0—Standard**. This is the default, and the right choice for most people.

- **Microsoft Internet Explorer 5.0—Minimal**. This is the right choice if you are running out of hard disk space but still would like to use Internet Explorer 5.0.

- **Do Not Upgrade Microsoft Internet Explorer**. Use this if you don't want Internet Explorer (for example, if you always use another browser such as Netscape Navigator, or if you have been directed by your system administrator not to install Internet Explorer 5).

Working with Maintenance Mode

Maintenance Mode is a feature of the Setup program. Whenever you run the Setup program again, after the initial installation, Maintenance Mode starts automatically. It enables you to add or remove features, repair your Office installation (for example, if files have become corrupted), and remove Office completely. There are several ways to rerun the Setup program (and thus enter Maintenance Mode):

- Reinsert the Office 2000 CD. The Setup program may start automatically.

- If the Setup program does not start automatically, double-click on the CD icon in the My Computer window.

- If double-clicking on the CD icon doesn't work, right-click on the CD icon and click on Open from the shortcut menu. Then double-click on the Setup.exe file in the list of files that appears.

- From the Control Panel in Windows, click on the Add/Remove Programs button. Then on the Install/Uninstall tab, click on Microsoft Office 2000 in the list, and finally, click on the Add/Remove button.

After entering Maintenance Mode, choose the button for the activity you want. Each option is briefly described in the following sections.

Repairing or Reinstalling Office

If an Office program is behaving strangely, or refuses to work, chances are good that a needed file has become corrupted. But which file? You have no way of knowing, so you can't fix the problem yourself.

If this happens, you can either repair Office or completely reinstall it. Both options are accessed from the Repair Office button in Maintenance Mode.

1. **Click** on the **Repair Office button** in Maintenance Mode.

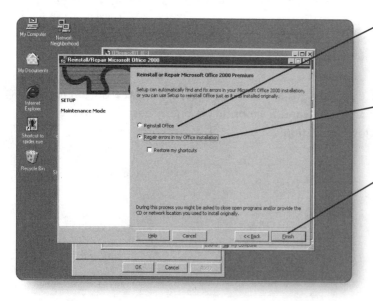

2a. **Click** on **Reinstall Office** to repeat the last installation.

OR

2b. **Click on Repair errors in my Office installation** to simply fix what's already in place.

3. **Click** on **Finish**. The process will start.

TIP

You can also repair individual Office programs by opening the Help menu in each program and clicking on Detect and Repair. This works well if you are sure that one certain program is causing the problem, and it's quicker than asking the Setup program to check all of the installed programs.

Adding and Removing Components

Adding and removing components works just like selecting the components initially.

1. **Click** on the **Add or Remove Features button** in Maintenance Mode. The Update Features window will appear. This window works exactly the same as the window you saw in the "Choosing Components" section earlier in this appendix.

NOTE

Some features will attempt to automatically install themselves as you are working. If you have set a feature to be installed on first use, attempt to access that feature. You will be prompted to insert your Office 2000 CD, and the feature will be installed without further prompting.

Removing Office from Your PC

In the unlikely event that you should need to remove Office from your PC completely, click on Remove Office from the Maintenance Mode screen. Then follow the prompts to remove it from your system.

After removing Office, you will probably have a few remnants left behind that the Uninstall routine didn't catch. For example, there will probably still be a Microsoft Office folder in your Program Files folder or wherever you installed the program. You can delete that folder yourself.

CAUTION

If you plan to reinstall Office later, and you have created any custom templates, toolbars, or other items, you may want to leave the Microsoft Office folder alone, so that those items will be available to you after you reinstall.

Installing Content from Other Office CDs

Depending on the version of Office you bought, you may have more than one CD in your package. CD 1 contains all the basic Office components, such as Word, Outlook, PowerPoint, Excel, Access, and Internet Explorer. It may be the only CD you need to use.

The other CDs contain extra applications that come with the specific version of Office you purchased. They may include Publisher, FrontPage, a language pack, or a programmer and developer resource kit. Each of these discs has its own separate installation program.

The additional CDs should start their Setup programs automatically when you insert the disc in your drive. If not, browse the CD's content in My Computer or Windows Explorer and double-click on the Setup.exe file that you find on it.

B
Using Keyboard Shortcuts

You may have noticed the keyboard shortcuts listed on the right side of several of the menus. You can use these shortcuts to execute commands without using the mouse to activate menus. You may want to memorize these keyboard shortcuts. Not only will they speed your productivity, but they will also help decrease wrist strain caused by excessive mouse usage. In this appendix, you'll learn how to:

 Get up to speed with frequently used keyboard shortcuts

 Use keyboard combinations to work with e-mail messages

 Use keyboard combinations to work with the calendar, contacts, and other Outlook features

Top Ten Keyboard Shortcuts in Microsoft Outlook 2000

1. Use Outlook Help   Press F1

2. Send/receive mail on default accounts   Press F5

3. Go to the Inbox   Press Ctrl+Shift+I

4. Create a new message   Press Ctrl+Shift+M

5. Create a new contact   Press Ctrl+Shift+C

6. Create a new appointment   Press Ctrl+Shift+A

7. Print the selected item(s)   Press Ctrl+P
                                             (open the Print dialog box)

8. Reply to message   Press Ctrl+R

9. Forward message   Press Ctrl+F

10. Send the message   Press Ctrl+S

Learning the Basic Shortcuts

Trying to memorize all these keyboard shortcuts isn't as hard as you may think. Windows applications all share the same keyboard combinations to execute common commands. Once you get accustomed to using some of these keyboard shortcuts in Outlook, try them out on some of the other Microsoft Office programs.

Using Menu Item Hot Keys

You can execute any menu command in a Windows application by pressing Alt, then pressing the command's *hot key*, the key underlined in the menu command's name (such as File or Format). In Outlook, for example, you can send items in your Outbox from your default mail account(s) using only the keyboard. Go to the Inbox and follow these steps:

1. Press the **Alt** key. The first menu name on the menu bar, **File**, will be highlighted.

2. Press **T** for **Tools**. The Tools menu opens.

3. Press **E** for **Send/Receive**. The Send/Receive submenu opens.

You can also use the arrow keys to navigate menus, open submenus, and highlight menu items. If the menu item does not have a hot key, press the Up or Down arrow until the item is highlighted, then press Enter to execute. (To complete the above example, highlight which account to use and press Enter to send the messages waiting in that account.)

NOTE

Remember that Outlook 2000's menus expand and reveal additional commands after they are open for a moment. If you have a command's hot key memorized, you don't have to wait for the menu item to appear before you can execute the command. Just press the shortcut key combination—Outlook will know what to do.

Hot key shortcuts are notated in this appendix as **Alt+x+y**, where *x* and *y* are the underlined key on a menu name or command. For example, the previous steps would be shown as **Alt+T+E**.

You might want to use some commands no matter where you are in Outlook, such as composing mail or getting help. The following table includes some keyboard shortcuts that you can use anywhere in Outlook.

To execute this command	Do this
Use Outlook Help	Press the F1 key
Use the What's This? Button	Press the Shift and F1 keys simultaneously (Shift+F1)
Select all items or text	Press Ctrl+A
Copy selected text or item	Press Ctrl+C
Cut selected text or item	Press Ctrl+X
Paste selected text or item	Press Ctrl+V
Delete selected text or item	Press Ctrl+D
Undo last edit or action	Press Ctrl+Z
Move selected items to a different folder	Press Ctrl+Shift+V
View the contents of another folder (open the Go to Folder dialog box)	Press Ctrl+Y
Work Offline	Press Alt+F+K
Close Outlook	Press Alt+F+X

Working with Messages

You probably use Outlook's e-mail features more than anything else. The following table shows you a few of the more common keyboard shortcuts that can save you time when working with your messages.

Receiving and Reading Messages

You can download, open, and read your mail without ever touching the mouse. The following table shows you some of the keyboard shortcuts you can use when reading and replying to your e-mail.

> **NOTE**
> You must be in Inbox view to use these shortcuts.

To execute this command	Do this
Switch to the Inbox	Press Ctrl+Shift+I
Send and receive mail from all default accounts	Press F5
Open or close the Preview Pane	Press Alt+V+N
Open the selected message(s)	Press Ctrl+O
Mark the selected message(s) as Read	Press Ctrl+Q
Switch to next open message	Press Ctrl+>
Switch to previous open message	Press Ctrl+<
Find text in current message	Press Ctrl+F
Save a message's attachments	Press Alt+F+N
Flag a message for follow-up	Press Ctrl+Shift+G
Reply to the current message	Press Ctrl+R
Reply to all recipients of the current message	Press Ctrl+Shift+R
Forward the current message	Press Ctrl+F
Print a message	Press Ctrl+P
Move current message to another folder	Press Ctrl+Shift+V
Close the current message	Press Alt+F4

Composing and Sending Messages

When you're composing new messages, it's often more convenient to use a keyboard shortcut than to dig through the Outlook menu structure. The following table lists a few of the common keyboard shortcuts for creating and sending messages.

> **NOTE**
> You must be in Inbox view to use these shortcuts.

To execute this command	Do this
Create a new message	Press Ctrl+Shift+M
Address the message (open the Address Book)	Press Ctrl+Shift+B
Display the Bcc field in the message header	Press Alt+V+B
Format the selected text (open the Text dialog box)	Press Alt+O+F
Format the selected paragraph (open the Paragraph dialog box)	Press Alt+O+P
Insert an attachment or file	Press Alt+I+F
Insert a hyperlink	Press Alt+I+H
Check the spelling of a message	Press F7
Save the message to the Drafts folder	Press Ctrl+S
Send the message using the default account	Press Alt+S
Close the current message without saving	Press Alt+F4

Working with Other Outlook Features

Outlook's Calendar, Contacts, and other features also support keyboard shortcuts. The shortcuts in this section will help you work with those features more efficiently and effectively.

Calendar

You can use keyboard shortcuts to navigate the Calendar and create and edit appointments, meetings, and events. The following table lists some shortcuts for the commands you're most likely to use with the Calendar:

> **NOTE**
>
> You must be in Calendar view to use these shortcuts.

To execute this command	Do this
Switch to the Calendar folder	Press Alt+G+F+C
View the 5-day work week calendar	Press Alt+R
Go to Today	Press Alt+D
Find text in appointments	Press Alt+I
Plan a meeting	Press Alt+A+P
Create a new appointment	Press Ctrl+N
Create a new meeting request	Press Ctrl+Shift+Q
Create a new recurring appointment	Press Alt+A+A
Create a new recurring meeting	Press Alt+A+C

Contacts

Once you have selected the text to which you want to make the editing changes, apply one of the combinations in the following table.

> **NOTE**
>
> You must be in Contacts view to use these shortcuts.

To execute this command	Do this
Switch to the Contacts folder	Press Alt+G+F+O
Create a new contact	Press Ctrl+Shift+N
Create a new distribution list	Press Ctrl+Shift+L
Create a new message to the selected contact	Press Alt+A+M
Start a mail merge	Press Alt+T+G
Start a new call	Press Ctrl+Shift+D

Notes and Tasks

How many times have you been working diligently along on something when another thought pops into your head that you need to write down? Using Outlook's keyboard shortcuts, you can pop up a new note or task instantly, capture the thought, and go right back to what you were working on without skipping a beat. The following table lists a few common keyboard shortcuts for working with notes and tasks. You can use these commands from anywhere in Outlook.

To execute this command	Do this
Create a new task	Press Ctrl+Shift+K
Create a new task request	Press Ctrl+Shift+U
Create a new note	Press Ctrl+Shift+N
Save and close a task	Press Alt+S
Save and close a note	Press Alt+Spacebar+C
Forward the selected note(s) or task(s)	Press Ctrl+F

Glossary

A

Address Book. An electronic file that allows the storage of e-mail addresses and other information. An address book may be global or personal.

Address Map. A way to view the location of an address on a map via the Internet.

Adult Content Mail. Mail that would not be suitable for individuals under the age of 18.

Appointment. A scheduled block of time on the calendar. Appointments can contain information about the purpose, location, and duration of the engagement.

Archive. A process of retrieving dated information and placing it into another location. Archived information is still available; it is simply located in another folder.

Attachment. A document or file that is a part of an e-mail message.

AutoPreview. An Inbox view that allows the display of the first three lines of text in an e-mail message.

AutoArchive. A process of automatically retrieving dated information and placing it into another folder. AutoArchiving will reduce the size of the folders and keep Outlook operating optimally. By default, Outlook will prompt to AutoArchive items older than 14 days.

Automatic Signature. A way to include a signature and other information automatically at the bottom of every e-mail message.

AutoPick. AutoPick allows Outlook to search for a mutually available meeting time for all meeting attendees.

B

Bullets. Symbols that precede an item in a list.

C

Calendar. An Outlook folder that displays meetings, appointments, and events.

Categories. Words or phrases used to group together similar Outlook items.

Certificates. Companion files that contain digital identification codes (also known as Digital IDs).

Contacts. An electronic Rolodex. May include information such as addresses, phone numbers, e-mail addresses, and Web pages.

Current View. An option on the View menu that allows the control of the display of items on the screen. Outlook offers standard views or one can be designed.

D

Date Navigator. A thumbnail picture of a month. The Date Navigator is a quick way to change the day, week, or month displayed on the screen.

Desktop. When the computer starts, the large area on the screen is called the desktop.

Dialog Box. A box that appears onscreen and presents settings that can be selected and activated.

Directory Server. The server that hosts an online meeting. An example is uls.microsoft.com.

Draft Message. A message that has not yet been sent. Saving the message will place it in the Drafts folder for later retrieval.

E

E-mail Address. A unique identifier that allows others to deliver electronic messages. An individual may have more than one e-mail address. An example is elvis@graceland.com.

E-mail Editor. The interface used to compose e-mail messages.

Event. Any appointment that lasts longer than 24 hours.

Exchange Server. A computer that processes messages and other Outlook items. Think of it as an electronic post office.

Extended Menus. A menu command that has a right-pointing arrow. When an extended menu is clicked, another menu appears next to it.

F

Field. A space in which information is entered. Some examples of fields in e-mail messages are Subject and Date Received.

Filter. A filter excludes certain types of items. For example, it is possible to filter e-mail to include only those received in the last seven days.

Flag. Use a flag to mark an item for special attention. For example, a flag can indicate that an item needs further review.

Folder. In Outlook, folders store items. Folders include the Inbox, Calendar, Tasks, Contacts, Journal, and Notes.

Form. An Outlook window designed to create or edit a specific type or group of information. Messages, contacts, journal entries, and calendar items are all examples of forms.

Forward. An e-mail message can be sent to a person who was not on the original distribution list.

G

Global Address List. A place to keep addresses that can be accessed by many people.

Groups. A set of items (messages, tasks, and so on) with a common element, such as messages of high priority or contacts from the same company. Groups can be sorted, expanded, and collapsed.

H

HTML. HyperText Markup Language. Used for composing e-mail messages with stationery.

I

Icon. A picture that represents a command or folder.

Inbox. The Inbox stores all incoming e-mail messages.

Information viewer. The display area for e-mail messages, calendar items, contacts, tasks, journal items, or notes.

J

Journal. The Journal is an Outlook folder that stores records of phone calls, meetings, meeting responses, and other activities.

Journal Entry. An individual record of a single activity, such as a phone call.

Junk Mail. Unsolicited e-mail.

M

Menu Commands. Options that appear on the menu bar that will perform a function.

Message Recall. A method for retrieving an e-mail message from the recipient's Inbox before it is read.

Microsoft NetMeeting. Free, downloadable software from Microsoft that allows an online meeting.

Microsoft Office. A suite of software applications from Microsoft Corporation. It includes Word, Outlook, Excel, PowerPoint, and Access.

N

Navigate. A way to locate and select a computer directory or date.

Notes. An Outlook folder that allows the posting of ideas, thoughts, or quick bits of information on electronic sticky notes.

O

Office Assistant. A Help system from Microsoft that answers questions regarding Outlook.

Online Meeting. A method of communicating with others simultaneously across the Internet. Online meetings can contain typed discussions, real-time video, and spoken conversation.

Online Meeting Request. The command used to invite other individuals to an online meeting and to give them the information they need to join the meeting.

Organize. An Outlook feature that presents different ways of arranging items in the Information viewer.

Outbox. An Outlook folder in which outgoing e-mail messages are stored. This is a temporary holding bin; once the items are sent, they are moved from the Outbox to the Sent Items folder.

Outlook Bar. The gray column on the left of the screen that contains shortcuts to the Outlook folders.

Outlook Today. A snapshot preview of the day's activities, e-mail messages, and tasks.

P

PDL. Personal Distribution List. A PDL is a maintained list of created e-mail addresses. The name of the PDL can be entered on the To line of a message, instead of typing each individual address.

Personal Address Book. A storage location for personal e-mail addresses— sometimes referred to as a PAB file.

Personal Distribution List. See PDL.

Plan a Meeting. An option that allows the review of the meeting attendees' schedules before requesting a meeting time.

Preview Pane. A preview of each item in the folder. The preview shows most of the items without opening it.

Print Style. The print style consists of the pre-defined font, page setup, and header and footer settings for a print job. The user can create new print styles or modify existing ones.

Profile. Outlook identifies the user by this setting. Profiles allow more than one person to access Outlook at each computer.

Properties. Settings assigned to each folder that determine permissions, synchronization, and more. Properties are accessed by right-clicking on a folder in the Outlook bar.

R

Recurring Appointment. An appointment that occurs more than once, such as a daily, weekly, or monthly meeting.

Reminder. An electronic update that notifies a certain time before an appointment, meeting, or task due date.

Reply. An electronic response to the sender of an e-mail message.

Reply to All. An electronic response to the sender and all other recipients of an e-mail message.

Resource. A resource can be a conference room or a piece of audiovisual equipment. Resources appear in the Location box in the Meeting Request.

Right Mouse Click. Moving the mouse pointer over an item and clicking the button located on the right side of the mouse to display a shortcut menu. Sometimes referred to as an *alternate click*.

Rules Wizard. A step-by-step guide for creating rules that manage incoming messages.

S

ScreenTip. A box that pops up on the screen when the mouse pointer is held over a toolbar button.

Scroll. The action of clicking on scroll arrows on a list box to display more of the item on the screen.

Scroll bar. The horizontal or vertical bar used to navigate through numerous items. Clicking on the scroll arrows, or clicking and dragging the box on the scroll bar, will change the items displayed.

Sensitivity. A level of privacy attached to a mail item. Items can be set to Normal, Personal, Private, or Confidential sensitivity.

Sent Items Folder. An Outlook folder that contains all sent items, such as e-mail messages, meeting requests, and task requests.

Shortcut. A pointer to an item or folder that provides one-click access. Deleting a shortcut does not delete the actual item or folder.

Snooze. Temporarily suspending a reminder. Similar to a snooze button on an alarm clock.

Sort. A method of displaying items in a certain order in the Information viewer.

Start Page. The default display of Outlook when the application is started. Any Outlook folder, including Outlook Today, can be set as a start page.

Stationery. A background for e-mail messages.

Stationery Picker. A method for choosing or designing stationery.

Status Report. An update on the progress of a task.

T

Task Request. A task sent to another person. An individual receiving a task request can accept, tentatively accept, or decline the task.

Tasks. An Outlook folder that contains items in a task list. Tasks are useful for recording a to-do list and prioritizing assignments.

Toolbar. A bar at the top of the screen that contains Outlook commands. Toolbars can display toolbar buttons or drop-down menus. Outlook toolbars can be customized.

Toolbar Button. A button on a toolbar allows one-click access to perform a command.

Tracking Options. A method for tracing the progress of an item as it is sent and read by the recipient.

V

View. The display for the Information viewer. The view can be changed to any of several other Outlook views, or new views can be created.

W

Web Page Address. The location of a Web page, usually starting with http://www.

Index

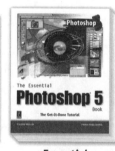

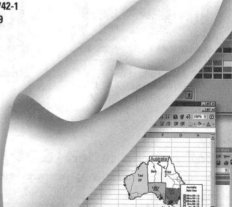